No Fear Finance
An introduction to finance and investment for the non-finance professional

No Fear Finance

An introduction to finance and investment for the non-finance professional

Guy Fraser-Sampson

LONDON PHILADELPHIA NEW DELHI

Publisher's note

Every possible effort has been made to ensure that the information contained in this book is accurate at the time of going to press, and the publishers and authors cannot accept responsibility for any errors or omissions, however caused. No responsibility for loss or damage occasioned to any person acting, or refraining from action, as a result of the material in this publication can be accepted by the editor, the publisher or the author.

First published in Great Britain and the United States in 2011 by Kogan Page Limited

120 Pentonville Road	1518 Walnut Street, Suite 1100	4737/23 Ansari Road
London N1 9JN	Philadelphia PA 19102	Daryaganj
United Kingdom	USA	New Delhi 110002
www.koganpage.com		India

© Guy Fraser-Sampson, 2011

The right of Guy Fraser-Sampson to be identified as the author of this work has been asserted by him in accordance with the Copyright, Designs and Patents Act 1988.

ISBN   978 0 7494 6387 8
E-ISBN 978 0 7494 6388 5

British Library Cataloguing-in-Publication Data

A CIP record for this book is available from the British Library.

Library of Congress Cataloging-in-Publication Data

Fraser-Sampson, Guy.
  No fear finance : an introduction to finance and investment for the non-finance professional / Guy Fraser-Sampson.
    p. cm.
  ISBN 978-0-7494-6387-8 – ISBN 978-0-7494-6388-5 (ebk.)
  1. Finance. 2. Business enterprises–Finance. 3. Investments. I. Title.
  HG173.F725 2011
  332–dc22
                             2011010665

Typeset by Saxon Graphics Ltd, Derby
Printed and bound in India by Replika Press Pvt Ltd

CONTENTS

The figures contained in this book are also available on the Kogan Page website. To access, go to http://www.koganpage.com/editions/no-fear-finance/ 9780749463878

DON'T PANIC

Douglas Adams, *The Hitchhiker's Guide to the Galaxy*

01
Learning about finance

Introduction

It could be argued that the only absolutely essential things that people really need to learn about, the most important life skills, are sex and finance. However, whereas sex education now forms part of most school curricula, finance does not. This seems difficult to justify given that people enter into financial transactions every day of the week, be it as mundane as withdrawing cash from an ATM terminal, or as potentially life-changing as borrowing money to buy a property or choosing which type of pension provision you should have, and how much of it.

These are decisions that we should be able to make on an informed basis, but mostly cannot. This is knowledge that we should possess but do not, and are therefore disadvantaged. This seems neither fair nor socially desirable. Surely we have a right to expect, given a reasonable amount of application on our part, that our education should leave us financially literate, able to discuss and enter into financial transactions with a good level of understanding, particularly where other people's money may be at stake as well as our own?

Who will find this book useful?

The writer has come across five broad groups of people who come to feel this lack of understanding very keenly. First, there are people who sign up for a business course, perhaps an MBA, but do not have a quantitative background and find themselves both alienated and baffled by finance classes. Incidentally, it is partly at the insistent urging of many of these people that this book has been written.

Second, there are people who find themselves thrust into a position of financial responsibility, perhaps as a pension fund trustee, or who would like to put themselves forward for such a position but feel held back by their lack of knowledge.

Third, there are those who get promoted at work and suddenly find that for the first time they are required to attend meetings where finance is discussed, and who feel excluded from that debate.

Fourth, there are entrepreneurs who have set up their own business but are frustrated to find that the whole process of business plans and dealing with banks seems somehow to require the use of special language and techniques, neither of which they comprehend.

Fifth, and perhaps most numerous of all, there are the general readers out there who, though well educated in other areas, feel that they really ought to understand finance, but recognize that they do not.

What is 'difficult' about learning finance?

In a sense a book like this really should not be necessary. The fact that it is bears testament to a widespread belief that finance is somehow difficult or complicated, and that in order to understand it one requires a deep level of mathematical expertise. In fact, none of these things are really true. It is not difficult, just often badly taught. It is not complicated, though it is quite complex (ironically, much more complex than those who teach it would like to believe). Nor do we need involved mathematics, just simple arithmetic. We will return to this point a little later.

People who seek to learn about finance fall into two broad categories: those who have some sort of quantitative background (whom we will call 'mathematicians' for the sake of simplicity, since they will typically have some sort of mathematically based qualification), and those who do not. Those who do not, the non-mathematicians, make up the five groups described above. If we ignore very specialist courses such as a Masters in Finance (usually an MSc qualification), then the first category are a tiny minority of the whole – certainly no more than about 10 per cent. Yet finance classes are taught in such a way that they will make sense to the 10 per cent, but probably not to the 90 per cent. This seems crazy, so why does it happen?

It has to do partly with the sort of people who typically teach finance, and partly with how they perceive the subject. These factors are separate, but closely linked. Those who come to teach finance are invariably mathematicians, perhaps not strictly speaking but certainly as we have defined them above. Like any specialist group of knowledge workers, they have a techno-babble all of their own, and find it difficult to break away from this; the writer knows one finance lecturer who uses phrases like 't superscript n' in everyday conversation. Let us concede at once that they are hardly alone in this; the worlds of IT, law and medicine all come instantly to mind as areas where specialist jargon reigns supreme.

Yet where this jargon gets in the way of communication, and thus understanding, we have a problem. To communicate is the first and most important duty of any teacher; if your audience (all of them) cannot understand what you are saying, then you have failed totally. This tends to be quite well done in the law, where a lecturer will usually explain the term when they first introduce it, and give the conceptual background before diving into case names, statutes and section numbers. In finance, things just do not seem to happen like this.

A good mathematician, a natural mathematician, is a rare animal. We can all think back to maths classes at school and remember the one or two truly gifted individuals who not only had a natural grasp of mathematics, thinking of an equation instinctively as a curve, but could reach out to what they perceived as the real beauty of numbers and be inspired by its seductive claims to offer a basis for universal understanding of the world around us.

What happens later is that these one or two people come together in undergraduate maths classes, which are populated by the one or two people like them from schools all over the country. There thus rapidly opens up a huge gulf, as their knowledge base rapidly expands to match their abilities, while at the other end of the scale we find people who struggle all their lives with decimals and percentages. Interestingly, this does not happen with a subject like law. Since it is rarely taught in schools, then most students come to it from a study of some other academic area such as history, or languages, or chemistry.

Finance and mathematics

This is one prong of the problem. These mathematicians go out into the world to teach finance, and though they appreciate that they have to assume a lower level of mathematical understanding in their students, they do not properly appreciate just how much lower it is. It is not just a question of knowing what the accounting equation is, for example, but about being comfortable with everything that implies, such as being able to see instantly the different ways in which any equation can be arranged, and how and why. It is not so much the numbers, but all the implicit assumptions that underlie being able to work with them. It would be like teaching law to first-year undergraduates and expecting them already to have a thorough grasp of causation, subjectivity and linguistic philosophy. They don't, and it is these peripheral skills that make the difference between understanding the law, and merely knowing the law.

With finance, however, we encounter an additional problem, which is perhaps unique to quantitative areas of study – panic (hence the advice you will already have seen from *The Hitchhiker's Guide to the Galaxy*). With the possible exceptions only of a tarantula, a hooded cobra and an enraged Italian mother-in-law, nothing in the world has the same capacity for striking intense, irrational, downright hysterical fear into a grown man or woman as does a mathematical formula. Being confronted with it on a board and being expected to work with it is rather like being asked to pick up the cobra and pet it. Brave, certainly. Scientific, possibly. But as a practical proposition it has all the appeal of jumping out of an aeroplane knowing that said mother-in-law has personally packed your parachute.

This is a very real and very crucial point. It is emotion, in this case panic, which is the biggest thing to get in the way of learning about finance. If you can manage to hold it in check, then you will discover that, no matter how terrifying they may seem, most finance calculations can either be made simple, or even actually started off that way in the first place. We will return to this point because it is so important, but let us first complete our analysis of the second prong of the problem. How do finance teachers perceive finance?

Here we run into another major problem area. As far as finance teachers are concerned, finance is a science, and almost certainly a branch of applied mathematics. In fact, it can be argued that both these assumptions are highly questionable, but such a debate lies beyond the scope of this book. We are concerned not with challenging finance theory (though we will touch on some of its current limitations in the last chapter), but with understanding it. To note that it is perceived as mathematical is nonetheless very important, since it leads to the one aspect of the way in which it is commonly taught that many non-mathematicians find most off-putting.

Finance is concerned with what can be mathematically calculated, and not with what cannot. Therefore you are not allowed to ask open questions, to which you have to preface your answer with 'Well, it all depends what you mean by...', for finance tells you what it means by something and expects you to accept it. If it cannot tell you what it means by something then it expects you to ignore it. It is very important though, that you should understand that as far as finance is concerned, nothing actually 'means' anything unless it can be calculated.

An illustration may serve to make this clear. In *The Hitchhiker's Guide to the Galaxy*, which should surely be recommended reading for any finance student, a race of super-intelligent beings build a super-computer, Deep Thought, to answer the ultimate question: Life, the Universe and Everything.[1] After thinking about it for several million years, Deep Thought gravely announces that the answer is 42. Why? Well, being a computer, it is incapable of conceptual thought, and thus has substituted a question to which it can calculate an answer for one to which it cannot. It may not be the question that needed answering, but it is at least a valid question, whereas the other was not. To Deep Thought, and to the world of finance, this seems a logical approach.

Open and closed questions – concepts and calculations

This way of thinking is actually based upon a revolution in philosophy brought about by a group of thinkers called the Logical Positivists.[2] Searching for a new basis of thought, they sought to apply pure logic in the form of logic propositions expressed in algebraic or other symbolic form. Anything that could not be so expressed should be disregarded. As Bertrand Russell put it, you may not ask a question unless you know in advance that you can answer it. Thus 'What is the radius of a circle?' would be a valid subject of philosophical enquiry, while 'What is truth?' would not.

Though clearly silly, this idea went largely unchallenged, perhaps because few people really understood what the Logical Positivists were saying (a common problem with philosophers). Indeed, it seems to be a central feature of modern philosophy that the sillier an idea is, the more likely it is to go unchallenged. Which is a shame, because it formed the way of thinking for 20th-century scientists, amongst whom finance academics are eager to number themselves. As the novelist Aldous Huxley, who himself came from a distinguished family of scientists, said, science disregards anything which it cannot calculate.

All of which may be great as an approach to a body of mathematical knowledge, but causes we non-mathematicians a lot of problems. Many of us come from disciplines where quantitative methods play at best a peripheral role, and subjective and qualitative assessment may be all there is upon which to base decision-taking. Others, for example lawyers, are accustomed to using linguistic and conceptual analysis as the starting point of any intellectual enquiry, and can experience intense disorientation when this is taken away from them. To be asked 'What is the risk of this investment?' only to discover to your horror that nobody has the slightest interest in enquiring what is meant by 'risk' in this or indeed in any context can feel like suddenly realizing that you live in the mental equivalent of a police state.

In short, what finance teachers are usually concerned with giving you is the means to arrive at a numerical solution. It is important that you understand two important implications of this. First, what finance will give you will be a piece of arithmetic, not an explanation of the conceptual background of what you are doing, or why. Second, finance believes that there is always one right answer to every question, and *only* one right answer; that you can reduce any practical situation to a mathematical expression, making such assumptions as may be necessary along the way, and that, being a mathematical expression, you can now solve this to find the one right answer.

This is not necessarily desirable, but it is just the way it is, and you need to be able to think yourself into the finance lecturer's mind-set if you are to understand properly what they are telling you. Before we move on to actually start looking at finance, however, there are two more possible stumbling blocks that we must dismantle.

Finance and reality

The phrase 'making such assumptions as may be necessary along the way' masks a particularly acute problem, namely the relationship between financial theory and financial (or one might say investment) reality. Again, it is not the function of this book to question the validity of financial theory, but this is an important point that you need to understand, and certainly one that has puzzled successive cohorts of MBA students around the world.

The philosopher Karl Popper pointed out that in order to qualify as a 'science', an area of study must be prepared to 'falsify' its rules. In other words, if a rule can be proved false by experimentation, even once, then it must be discarded and a new hypothesis adopted. As the physicist Dick Feynman, surely the only man ever to have been both declared mentally unfit to serve in the US military and to win a Nobel Prize, said: 'Even if a rule is proved a little bit wrong, it makes a big difference.'

Finance, however, does not do this. Rather than altering its rules to fit reality, it alters reality to fit the rules. We can illustrate this principle with yet another example from the *Hitchhiker's Guide to the Galaxy* series. The inhabitants of a planet called Kriket believe as a matter of religious dogma that they are the only intelligent life-form in the galaxy. One day they are given incontrovertible proof that this cannot be true, when an alien spaceship crash-lands on their world. Does this cause them to change their beliefs? No. Instead, they build a race of killer robots to go out into space and systematically destroy any intelligent life-form that they may encounter, thus bringing reality into line with their beliefs. This is exactly how it is in finance; look out for the killer robots.

Finance does this by making assumptions. Every time that a financial proposition is found to be false, an assumption is drawn up that explains away this apparent anomaly, thus getting around the inconvenient necessity to come up with a new rule instead, one that might actually work in the real world. Again, you are required to accept these assumptions, no matter how illogical or unrealistic they may appear. A particularly memorable one occurs in the case of something called the Capital Asset Pricing Model, which you will learn all about in a later chapter. This requires you to assume that all investors are rational, and goes on to define a 'rational investor' as 'one who will always accept the outcome of the Capital Asset Pricing Model'. This is surely akin to a politician saying 'I am only going to allow you to vote in the next election if you can prove that you are sane, and the only way in which you can prove that you are sane is to vote for me, since I am the only rational choice.'

The reference to dogma is also appropriate. Financial theory is not really theory at all; it is dogma, and again you will find your voyage of discovery much easier if you learn to accept this from the beginning. As we all know, dogma is what gets laid down by a religion as something that we are required to believe; we do not have a choice. So, Galileo might have worked out by observation and calculation that the Sun did not go round the Earth, but that was just tough, since the Catholic Church had already decided as a matter of dogma that it did, and he was thus faced with the choice of accepting their point of view or being burnt at the stake. As Dorothy Parker sympathetically observed, 'You can't teach an old dogma new tricks.' Remember her words as you journey through Finance World; they will serve you well.

Problems with language

Finally, we have the problem of language. This is actually a double problem. First, some words are used in finance in a different sense than their ordinary, everyday meaning. 'Risk' would be a good example of this. In part, this is a follow-on from the prohibition of conceptual discussion. Finance has decided what it wants this word to mean, and that is that. Which would be fine, except that nobody ever bothers to explain this to you, thus leading to much scope for confusion.

The other problem is that finance sometimes uses, or appears to use, the same word with different meanings at different times. Don't worry, this will be fully pointed out and explained in this book, but again, usually it isn't.

The approach this book will take

Hopefully by now it will be pretty obvious what line this book is going to take on all of this. We are not here to question finance theory but to learn it. Yet the writer believes firmly that in order to learn any facet of finance *and understand it*, it is necessary first to explain the underlying concept, complete with any unusual language, and only then to turn to the numbers. It is remarkable how much easier the whole business of 'how' becomes when you already understand the 'what' and the 'why'.

'Unusual language' takes two forms. First, financial jargon. This will be explained as we go along and you will find a glossary at the end of the book as a ready reference guide. Second, where a word is used in a potentially misleading or ambiguous sense. Again, this will be pointed out and explained the first time we come across it.

The numbers

Yes, finance is about numbers, and normally your first finance class will only be a few minutes old before the board is covered in formulae and letters from the Greek alphabet. At this stage at least half the class starts either glancing around panic-stricken, or staring straight ahead with a glassy and unblinking expression.

Note the word 'normally', however, because that is where this book is different. Once an aspect of finance has been described in conceptual terms, and we finally do get around to dealing with a formula, you will first be told exactly what we are trying to achieve and why, and only then will you be taken slowly and gently through the arithmetic. In addition, you will see that there are break-out sections that may give more explanation of straightforward arithmetic, or a practical example, or even offer a more advanced description for those who would like to take things a little further. Thus, one way or another, you can proceed comfortably at your own pace. You might even decide to read the book straight through at a fairly simple level, and then come back to it again for more of the details.

To suggest that we can study and understand finance without dealing with numbers would be an attractive idea, but quite unworkable. Like it or not, finance regards itself as a branch of applied mathematics, and, as we have already seen, the idea that you can calculate the one right answer to any question is one of its central beliefs. We need to be able to understand how all of this gets done and, indeed, be able to do it ourselves.

However, the word 'mathematics' is perhaps unnecessary, and certainly rather misleading. It conjures up visions of hugely complicated numerical processes that can only be understood properly by maths geeks, yet this is neither a fair nor an accurate description of finance.

For one thing, most financial formulae are either very simple to start with (provided you don't panic – see below), or can be made simple. For another thing, rather than calculation, what is usually required more than anything is simply substitution; substituting values (which you are either given or can calculate simply) for symbols. Finally, when calculation *is* required, it is arithmetic rather than mathematics – the sort of simple arithmetic that we all learnt at school when we were about 12 years old.

So, bearing this in mind by way of reassurance, let us take a quick look at some tips that can help us cope with all this.

Coping with formulae and calculations

DON'T PANIC! You will have seen this exhortation, again from *Hitchhiker's Guide to the Galaxy*, at the very front of this book. It represents the best piece of advice that anybody could ever give to someone from a non-quantitative background who is embarking on the study of finance. It is very easy to allow yourself to become phobic about numbers, and lapse into a cold sweat whenever you see any mathematical symbols. In this state you will not be able to think clearly about anything, except perhaps 'What am I doing here?'

As we have seen, this is something of which the mathematicians should be aware, but aren't, and is one of the reasons why finance is often not well taught. Looking at it from their point of view, one can appreciate how and why it happens. They have a background in mathematics, and what they regard as 'just a few simple calculations' is not the same thing as what we understand by that phrase. Consequently, they tend to over-estimate their students' base quantitative skills, and under-estimate the power of numbers to throw people into a blind panic. It also does not help that they find it difficult to explain a piece of maths except by the use of other pieces of maths; witness some of the 'simple' explanations of things by mathematicians that you may have seen on the internet.

So, don't panic. This is easy advice to give but more difficult to follow, yet it is absolutely vital. Unless you can bring yourself to take a deep breath, calm down, and say to yourself: 'OK, this really can't be so terrible. Let's just take a long, hard look at it,' then you will be lost before you start.

Perhaps you are already wondering whether you have made a dreadful mistake in wanting to know more about finance, but don't put the book down just yet. How about learning a few things that may just make you feel a whole lot less troubled about the whole exercise?

For a start, one of the most numerous symbols with which we are going to be dealing is the number 1. Believe it or not, it is one of the most common components in the formulae that we are going to be looking at. Now, it really doesn't matter just how nervous you are about maths; since the age of about six you have never had any trouble doing calculations using the number 1, have you?

Another thing is that, as has already been mentioned, most of the time the challenge is about substitution, rather than complicated calculation – and even here, the word 'challenge' would be appropriate only to a young child. It is simply a matter of taking values (which we are given – so how difficult is that?) and putting them in place of the symbols that represent them. Let's take a look at a quick example just to prove the point.

An example of using substitution

$$A = \frac{B}{C}$$

Where A = the value that we wish to find,
B = 10, and
C = 2

We can substitute 10 for B and 2 for C thus:

$$A = \frac{10}{2}$$

and we all remember our two times table, so there is no need even to reach for the calculator. We know that 5 times 2 is 10, so

$$A = 5$$

Yes, it really is as simple as that. Of course, the formula may look a little more forbidding. For example, it may have some brackets within it. Again, don't panic. These are there to help you. They are a big signpost saying 'deal with me first'. In other words, you perform the substitution and/or calculation that is within the brackets first, make a note of the answer, and then move on. Should there be more than one set of brackets nestling within each other, then you work from the inside outwards.

Let's illustrate this with a slightly more complicated formula, this time introducing that terrifying character the number 1, and an even more terrifying set of brackets.

A more complex example

This time let's solve the formula:

$$A = 2\left(\left|\frac{B}{C}\right| - 1\right)$$

Where A = the value we wish to find,
B = 10, and
C = 2

There, that looks a lot more frightening, doesn't it? Well, actually it's not, as long as you keep your head and remember the couple of rules we just learnt:

(1)   substitute values for symbols where necessary, and

(2)   solve what is in the brackets first (and where there are brackets within each other, work from the inside outwards).

First, let's do the substitution:

$$A = 2\left(\left|\frac{10}{2}\right| - 1\right)$$

Now we start our calculations with the inner brackets, and solve 10 / 2, which we know is 5. So:

$$A = 2(5 - 1)$$

Now we solve what is inside the outer set of brackets. 5 minus 1 is 4, so now we have:

$$A = 2 \times 4$$

Note that in algebra such as this, the multiplication sign is usually dropped, so ab is the same thing as a × b and 2(5 – 1) is the same thing as 2 × (5 – 1). The multiplication sign is implied.

And, of course:

$$2 \times 4 = 8, \text{ so}$$

$$A = 8$$

There, you see, that really wasn't so difficult, was it? Believe it or not, there is probably only one formula in this whole book that is any more difficult than that, and most readers will probably be able to pass straight over that one anyway, because they will never need to use it. So, just like the one we have just dealt with, they are only difficult if you treat them that way. In reality, the apparent complexity is produced by our own fear, and as long as we stay calm and take them step by step then they are simple arithmetic, not complex mathematics.

The rest of the book

First we will look at what a business is and how it finances itself through the use of both equity (which is a fancy name for stocks or shares) and debt. Then we will walk around to the other side of the table and look at things from the direction of the people who provide that finance. How can they decide whether they should do so or not? And, if they decide they should, at what price? Similarly, what happens when they want to sell those financing instruments to other people? Or buy more?

In the process we will be covering all the theory that is normally taught in a finance course, but assuming no prior experience at all of finance or investments, and no knowledge of even vaguely complicated arithmetic. In consequence, some readers may from time to time feel that things are being dealt with too simplistically (although it may be that this is the greatest compliment that can be paid to a teacher of complex material!). Hopefully the book has been designed in such a way that, if so, they will simply be able to skip a few pages and find that they are back in their target learning zone.

At the end of each chapter you will find a summary. This is useful as a tool for ensuring that you really have understood everything you have just read, and also as a study aid for those exam candidates who believe in a truly last-minute approach to revision.

A full set of key financial formulae appear as an Appendix. Most finance exams are now 'open book', at least to the extent of allowing you a list of formulae, but this will in any event be a good quick reference guide. Should you suddenly be seized one day with a burning desire to work out an annuity calculation, then this is the place to look.

Finally, from time to time you will see terms that are in bold print. These are the ones you will find in the glossary of financial terms when you turn to the back of the book. If you do not turn to the back of the book, then you will not find the glossary, in which case the sum total of your human experience will be sadly diminished.

Summary

- This book is aimed at people who have two things in common: a non-quantitative background and a need or desire to learn about finance.
- Finance is commonly regarded as a very complicated area, which can be understood only by a privileged few. In fact, this is not true, although this often seems to be the way in which it is taught!
- In fact, the main stumbling block is a psychological one. Many people understandably 'freak out' when confronted with numbers, and even more so when faced with formulae and mathematical symbols. Unfortunately, this is usually the way in which finance theory is presented.

- The second main stumbling block lies in the financial mind-set. People used to studying other subjects come to finance expecting the sort of open-ended discussions and conceptual analysis with which they are familiar. In fact, finance is not interested in this approach, and largely ignores it, which means that many basic questions never get asked (or answered!).
- Third, there is a problem of language. In finance, a word may well be used with a different meaning from its everyday sense, and sometimes also with a different meaning in a different situation. This problem is exacerbated by the tendency of finance teachers and practitioners to use jargon that is often incomprehensible to their audience.
- In the failure of traditional teaching to recognize and overcome these problems lies the need for this book.
- Because the problem is, at least in part, psychological, then so does its solution need to be. 'Don't panic!' is the best advice that can ever be given to anyone embarking upon the study of finance.
- If you remain calm, then you will find that most financial formulae are in fact deceptively straightforward, and can be solved by simple substitution and basic arithmetic.
- The topics covered by this book fall into three broad areas. First, the nature of a business and how it finances its activities. Second, the position of people who provide that finance in what is called the primary market. Third, the position of investors who buy and sell those financial instruments in what is called the secondary market. These two markets can be thought of as analogous to the markets for new and second-hand cars respectively.
- At the end of the book you will find both an Appendix of the key financial formulae and a glossary of financial terms.

Notes

1 Which is of course not really a question at all.
2 Chiefly G E Moore, Bertrand Russell and Ludwig Wittgenstien.

02
Types of business

Let us think about what happens when either one person or a group of people decide to set up a business. Of course, their most pressing concern will be how they are going to find the money to finance it, but we will leave this issue to the next chapter. The reason for this is that in order to be able to understand fully the different forms that business finance can take, we first need to appreciate the different forms that a 'business' itself can take.

Once upon a time there were only three possibilities: (1) a sole trader, (2) a partnership, or (3) a **company** (corporation). While the picture is now more complicated, it might be useful to describe these three basic categories before we go on to discuss their more exotic variants.

Trading as a sole trader

This is the most straightforward option of all. An individual will simply trade under their own name. Suppose, for example, that somebody called Sid Smith wants to set up in business as an electrician. He can simply have business cards and stationery printed headed 'Sid Smith, Electrical Services' or some such description and start looking for customers. There is one slight legal issue here, which we will consider later in this chapter, but broadly speaking there are no real complications about setting up in business in this way. Subject to the one small exception that we will come to later, no particular legal documentation is necessary, and nor is any registration required.

The most important point to grasp here is that there is no separation between Sid Smith and his business; they are one and the same. This has some important consequences, both legal and practical.

Unlimited liability

As we will discuss in more detail when we turn our attention to accounting, a business can be viewed in many ways, but one important point is that it will always have liabilities of one sort or another. A few examples will suffice for our present purposes.

Example 1

Sid Smith decides that he would like an overdraft facility (overdraft protection) from his bank to give him some flexibility in paying his suppliers should he experience difficulty or delay in receiving money from his customers. As soon as his account becomes even the smallest amount overdrawn, this will represent a liability, since the bank has effectively lent him money (by allowing the account to become overdrawn) in order to pay a third party, and this loan, like all loans, will need to be repaid.

Example 2

Sid Smith needs to buy some cabling to use on a job. His neighbourhood electrical supplier sells him the cabling on credit, ie on the basis that Sid Smith need not pay for it straight away, as he would if he were buying a packet of chewing gum from a shop, but may pay for it some time later (customarily something like 30 days later). Unless and until he does actually pay for it, this unpaid amount will represent a liability. It is as if the supplier has extended him a loan, which he must repay.

Incidentally, the giving of credit is central to business around the world. The vast majority of transactions that take place do so on credit. That is why when credit ceases to be available, either generally in the case of a banking crisis or singly in respect of a particular business, it can have very serious effects. When a general 'credit crunch' occurs it usually results in a contraction of trade generally, particularly international trade. When credit is withdrawn from a single business, the rapid failure of that business is almost assured.

Under what circumstances would credit be withdrawn from a business? There are two possible answers to this question, one of which relates to the management of the business, while the other depends on independent, external factors.

The first answer is that the person or people in charge of the management of the business build up a bad record of not paying their debts on time, and perhaps also breaching the limit or terms of their agreed overdraft. If, for example, Sid Smith does not pay his supplier within 30 days as agreed, then that supplier is most unlikely to be prepared to sell him further goods on credit in the future. On the contrary, he is likely to insist on settlement in cash before he delivers the goods. Similarly, if Sid Smith breaches the terms of his overdraft (for example, by writing a cheque that would take the overdraft beyond its agreed limit), then not only is the bank likely to consider terminating the facility, but they may well also insist on its full amount being repaid before any further credit arrangement is considered.

The second situation arises as a result of external factors. During a general credit crunch, each bank manager may be instructed to reduce their overdraft exposure by, say, 10%. They may choose to do this by unilaterally reducing all overdraft facilities by 10%, or by cancelling altogether and 'calling in' those that they consider the most high-risk (which will generally be perceived as the smallest and/or newest businesses). In either case, a reduction in the credit available to Sid Smith is a probable outcome.

Another possibility is that a large customer may use its relative bargaining power to insist that a business that supplies it should extend the days of credit available to the customer, perhaps from 30 days to 45 days. Equally, large businesses may use their bargaining power to insist on reducing the number of days within which their customers must pay them, perhaps from 30 days to 21 days. This is known as 'stretching your creditors' and 'squeezing your debtors' respectively. Obviously those most at risk are businesses that have one very large customer, or a large sole supplier. Some supermarket businesses, for example, have gained a particular reputation with regard to this sort of working capital management.

Obviously these two circumstances can be connected. When a general credit squeeze is in operation, not only is much less bank credit available but, as the effects of the squeeze begin to bite, large companies redouble their efforts to squeeze their own customers and stretch their own debtors. This is why banking crises and related credit squeezes are a matter of such concern for governments and economists. They risk descending into an ever-tightening downward spiral with small businesses being forced into bankruptcy, which in turn frightens the banks into tightening their credit control processes still further, and so on.

In the case of a business failing, what happens is that it becomes unable to settle all its liabilities. This can be as a result of cash-flow difficulties. In other words, its customers keep it waiting so long for its money that it is unable to pay its suppliers within their agreed credit period, or is forced to breach the terms of its overdraft facility. It can also be more fundamental. In this scenario then even if it could collect in all amounts outstanding from its customers it would *still* be unable to settle all its outstanding liabilities. In the former case then sooner or later either the bank or one or more suppliers will lose patience with the situation and force Sid Smith out of business. In the latter case then even if they do not, Sid Smith himself comes under a legal obligation to do something about it, since trading while insolvent (bankrupt) is regarded as a serious offence in most countries. At the very least, he would have to close down his business and summon a meeting of his creditors to discuss what to do next.

It is here that the concept of unlimited liability comes into play. Because Sid Smith is trading as a sole trader, there is no legal distinction between him and the business. He and his business are effectively one and the same. This means that his business creditors can come against his personal assets when seeking payment of the amounts due to them. Suppose that Sid owns the house in which he lives, or has been saving up for his children's college fees. These will be available to the bank and the suppliers when they come looking for their money. Thus in the worst case scenario, Sid could end up both homeless and penniless. Should the value realized by his personal assets be less than the amount claimed by his creditors, then he will be made personally bankrupt.

Legal personality

The other thing that we need to be aware of, though it is probably implicit in what we have just been discussing, is the concept of legal personality. In the eyes of the law, we are only considering one legal 'person' here, and that is Sid Smith. The business that he runs is part of the same legal 'person' as he is himself. This may seem a rather strange point to be making, but all will become clear shortly when we examine ways in which the business can actually be made a 'person' in its own right.

This has various implications. First, we do not need to worry about who has authority to represent the business in its dealings with the outside world, such as banks, customers and suppliers. The business is Sid Smith, and clearly Sid is able legally to make his own decisions and enter into his own agreements, provided he is both adult and of sound mind (though not if he is currently an undischarged bankrupt as a result of some previous unsuccessful business venture).

Second, it means that, except to the extent that he may be required to do so for tax purposes, he is under no obligation to open a separate bank account for the business, or to keep separate books of account for it. Needless to say, both these steps would be very sensible ones to take from a practical point of view, but he is not obliged to do so if he does not wish to. Many sole traders happily run their business from their personal bank account, for example.

Trading as a partnership

A partnership can perhaps most conveniently be thought of as a collection of sole traders coming together to carry out business together. However, while a business can begin to operate as a sole trader simply by the sole trader deciding to do so, the creation of a partnership requires agreement. It has to be given birth to, and the act of childbirth is the partners agreeing together to establish the partnership. Before this act of childbirth, it does not exist.

It is quite possible for a partnership to be created by verbal agreement. It will then operate as what is known as a partnership at will. However, this is most inadvisable in practical terms. For one thing, a partnership at will can be brought to an end at any time by any partner serving notice on the others. For another, **profits** must be shared equally between the partners and this may well not be appropriate if the partnership's capital has not been subscribed equally, or if some partners are more senior than some others, or where some are full-time working partners and others are not.

Finally, there are all sorts of technical matters relating to tax and accounting that really should be laid out for everybody's benefit. These will provide, for example, for the keeping of separate books of account for the partnership's business, together with the opening of a separate bank account and agreement as to how this may be operated, and by whom.

A partnership can be of fixed duration. However, this is usually only the case where a partnership is used as an investment fund (in which case it is known as a closed-end fund). Where a partnership is used for business purposes then it is more usual for it to be open-ended, with provision for partners leaving and joining the partnership without necessitating its termination. Many professional firms around the world, for example, operate by way of some form of partnership structure.

The reason why it may be convenient to think of a partnership as a group of sole traders operating together is that the partners remain personally liable for all the liabilities of the partnership. In other words, their personal assets will be available to their business creditors in just the same way as if they were trading on their own. In fact, arguably, their situation may be thought of as even worse, for here they are liable not only for their own business liabilities, but for those of the entire partnership, of whose capital they may constitute only a small part. Furthermore, this liability is known as 'joint and several', which means that creditors can come against the assets of any one partner for all the liabilities of the partnership. Should this happen, it would then be a matter for this unfortunate individual to seek indemnification from the remaining partners.

The obvious question might be: if joint and several liability is so onerous, why should anybody ever seek to become a member of a partnership? The answer is that there may well be compensating advantages. It may be possible as a group of partners to carry on a business that is much larger than that which can conveniently be handled by a sole trader. Also, notwithstanding joint and several liability as regards the outside world, the capital risk of the business is at least theoretically being shared among the partners, rather than all being borne by one individual.

Legal personality

An ordinary partnership is not a 'person' in the eyes of the law (this is subject only to one small exception, which we will consider below). Thus the partners are still carrying on business as themselves. The only difference between them and a sole trader is that they are doing so collectively rather than individually. There are, however, two practical matters of which to be aware, one good and the other not so good.

The first is that in most countries a partnership can sue and be sued in its own name (the name of the firm) rather than having to list the names of all the individual partners. This can be of particular benefit to those partnerships that carry on business as professional practices. It is important to note that this concession is granted as a matter of legal convenience; it does not make the partnership a 'person' in its own right, but simply allows it to be treated as if it were one for certain very limited purposes.

The second point to be aware of is that in most countries a partnership will be treated as a separate entity for the purposes of tax collection. There is also a very important distinction here, which can easily be overlooked or misunderstood. It is a separate entity for tax *collection*, not a separate *taxable entity*. Let us explore this point a little further.

In any country that recognizes partnerships (the main exceptions are currently mostly in Asia), the profits of the partnership are divided up between the partners pro rata to their share in the partnership, and they are then taxed individually on their total personal income, of which their own share of the partnership profits will form a part. The same will be true of any capital gains that have been made by the partnership.

In other words, the partnership itself will not pay any tax. This is consistent with the partnership not being a 'person' for legal purposes.

For this reason, a partnership is often referred to by tax lawyers as either 'tax transparent' or (mostly in America) as a 'look-through' entity or vehicle. It is as if the partnership were a pane of glass in a window. You know that it is there, because you can reach out and touch it, but if you look at it you do not see it, only the partners themselves who are on the other side of the window. Partnerships can also be referred to as 'flow-through' vehicles in that incoming cash-flows flow through the partnership to the individual partners, just as if the partnership were some kind of water pipe. Incidentally, it is these 'look-through' and 'flow-through' qualities that make a partnership variant (which we will meet below) particularly attractive as an investment fund vehicle for a wide variety of asset types ranging from private equity, through real estate, to oil and gas royalties, and even forestry.

However, the tax authorities will at the very least require the partnership's accounts to be submitted to them for approval, so that they can be satisfied that the profits have been accurately assessed and divided. They may, however, seek to go further than this. For example, should there ever be occasion to launch an enquiry into the tax affairs of the partnership, then they may seek also to investigate *all* the tax affairs of each individual partner, even those that have nothing to do with the partnership or its business. They may also refuse to agree the tax affairs of any one partner until all the partners have properly submitted their own tax filings; thus one rogue partner can cause acute inconvenience to all.

Trading as a company (corporation)

Whereas trading as a sole trader requires nothing more than a decision to do so, and partnerships are formed by agreement, companies or corporations (different words for the same thing) are brought into existence by operation of law – which these days usually consists of nothing more than filing some documents with a government registry.

Companies may be either public (in which case their shares may be offered to the public and become eligible to be listed on a stock exchange) or private. Private companies are typically subject to less onerous regulation, especially reporting requirements (see below). In Russia, for example, private companies do not have to file accounts.

Trading as a company represents a quantum leap from everything we have so far discussed in this chapter in two important respects: limited liability and legal personality.

Limited liability

Should Sid Smith decide to pursue his business through the medium of a company, whether alone or with others, he will only be liable for any debts of the company up to the value of whatever share capital he chooses to subscribe.

Limited liability companies (corporations) were largely unknown even in the world's leading capitalist markets until after the middle of the 19th century, when statutory regimes were introduced at about the same time in various different countries. Previously in the UK a private Act of Parliament had been required in each case – obviously a cumbersome and time-consuming procedure that rapidly came to be seen as unworkable.

In the UK in particular, limited liability was seen as a great privilege bestowed upon businessmen and as potentially unfair, or at least disadvantageous, to creditors, and thus something that should be subject to strong safeguards. One of these we have already met; not only was it potentially a criminal offence to allow a company to trade while insolvent, but the directors who did so could be made personally liable for the company's debts.

Other safeguards revolved around the filing of accounts and other documents within fixed time limits. It was deemed essential as a matter of public policy that those dealing with a limited liability company should be able to glean as much information about it as possible before doing so, in order to be able to decide whether to extend credit to the company. This involved the filing of information about who the directors and shareholders of the company might be at any one time, and the location of a registered office where it could be served with legal documents.

More importantly, however, it also required the company to file up to date statements of its financial affairs, and indeed continues to do so. These take the form of a **balance sheet** and a **profit and loss account** (**earnings statement, income statement,** P&L), and we will be considering these in more detail in a later chapter.

The final requirement is that nobody should be in any doubt that they are dealing with an entity that has limited liability. Thus either 'limited' or 'limited liability' must appear prominently on all letters, orders, business cards, and so on. In most jurisdictions, failure to do this will render the limited liability ineffective.

In practice, limited liability may be severely limited. For example, it is commonplace for a bank to ask the directors and/or controlling shareholders of a private company to sign a personal guarantee before extending overdraft or loan facilities to the company, and similarly in the case of a landlord as a condition of granting a lease to the company.

Ironically, it seems that many people feel more comfortable dealing with a one-man company than with the same individual trading as a sole trader, though logically this should of course be the other way around, given that the latter does not enjoy limited liability. It is possible that this may be based on an instinct that a company must somehow be bigger and more permanent than any one person.

Attempts to get around the concept of limited liability are made from time to time, arguing that the 'veil of incorporation' should be 'lifted' or 'pierced'. In so-called Anglo-Saxon legal jurisdictions these are limited to very special circumstances, one of which we have already met: where the directors may be held liable for the debts of the company if they have allowed it to trade while insolvent. However, be aware that in other jurisdictions, such as France, things are less clear-cut. There have, for example, been legal arguments that some shareholders, such as banks, should be liable for the debts of the company where they have encouraged third parties to carry on doing business with it.

Legal personality

The second main difference between a company (corporation) and either a sole trader or a partnership is that a company is recognized by law as a distinct 'person', separate from its shareholders and directors. Various consequences flow from this:

- A company can bring legal proceedings against third parties, and can itself be sued just like any natural person.
- A company can enter into contracts just like any natural person.
- It is essential that separate banking and accounting arrangements are put in place in the name of the company.
- The question of who has authority to make legally binding decisions on behalf of the company will be a valid issue for third parties who deal with it, such as banks.
- A company is a separate taxable entity, and will pay corporate taxes on its profits.

Other possibilities

We have now met and examined the three broad categories of business vehicle. However, it is necessary to mention at least two others for the sake of completeness, not least because they are becoming increasingly common outside North America, where these concepts originated.

Limited partnerships

A **limited partnership** is still a true partnership, as the name suggests, but one in which some (but not all) of the partners may enjoy limited liability. The condition that must be satisfied in order to qualify as a limited partner is that you should take no active part in the management of whatever business the partnership is carrying on; effectively you must be nothing more than a passive investor, leaving all the decision making and key business processes to others. If you do indeed satisfy this condition then your liability for the debts of the partnership will be limited to the amount of partnership capital that you have agreed to invest ('commit'). The other partners, the ones who do take some part in the management of the business, have unlimited liability just as in the case of an ordinary partnership, and they are known as general partners, to distinguish them from the limited partners.

Incidentally this is why, together with tax transparency, limited partnerships are felt to be eminently suitable for use as investment funds for a wide variety of asset types, particularly where investors may be tax exempt in their own country, such as pension funds, endowments and sovereign wealth funds. This is because in many countries capital gains (as distinct from income) are not taxable in the hands of non-residents, and the use of a flow-through vehicle makes for tax efficiency, ensuring that investors do not have to pay tax in other jurisdictions from which they would have been exempt in their own.

Hybrid vehicles

In sophisticated legal jurisdictions such as the US and the UK, legislators have responded to the demands of the commercial marketplace by introducing vehicles that share some of the characteristics of both a company (in having limited liability) and a partnership (in having tax transparency). In some countries, this has also got around various previously existing practical problems, such as a limit on the number of partners in any individual partnership. These vehicles are known as LLCs (limited liability companies) in the United States and LLPs (limited liability partnerships) in the UK. The US title is sadly misleading, as of course a limited liability company in most other parts of the world, including the UK, is something very different. It is likely that this confusion stems from a company in its proper (ie non-US) sense commonly being referred to as a corporation in the United States. The British title is strictly descriptive.

Apart from their use in certain highly specialized financing structures, these vehicles will most commonly be encountered as professional firms, such as lawyers and accountants. For reasons that will become apparent in the next chapter, this book will not be dealing with them any further.

Business names

Our consideration of the methods of carrying on business would not be complete without mention of business names. Strictly speaking, these come into existence any time that a sole trader, partnership or company carries on business in anything other than their own name, or a recognizable variation of it. Thus Sid Smith could probably legitimately carry on business with no regulatory requirements at all as 'S. Smith', but probably not as 'Sid Smith Electrical Contractors' and certainly not as 'Wizard Electricians'.

Again, the common sense principle holds good that everybody has a right to know exactly with whom they are doing business. Thus in most jurisdictions a business name must be registered by the proprietor of the business. The legal form is to add 't/a' (trading as) followed by the business name on all bank accounts, stationery, etc.

Summary

- There are three basic ways of carrying on business: as a sole trader, as a partnership, or as a company.
- A sole trader is simply an individual who decides to set up in business, usually in their own name. There is no separation at all between the person and the business, which means a sole trader's personal assets will be at risk should the business get into difficulties.
- A partnership is where two or more people come together to carry on a business. A partnership is formed by agreement between the parties, and it is strongly recommended that this should be written rather than verbal. There is still no separation between the business and the partners. Each partner will be taxed on their individual share of the partnership's profits, and each individual partner will be personally liable for all the debts of the partnership; this is known as joint and several liability.

- A company is formed by operation of law, usually by filing certain documents at a central registry. A company is a separate person, distinct from its directors and shareholders. One consequence of this is that a company is a taxable entity in its own right, and will pay corporate tax on its profits; in other words, it is not a 'look-through' or 'flow-through' vehicle as a partnership is.
- A company has limited liability. The shareholders cannot be held liable for the debts of the company beyond the amount of the company's share capital, which they have subscribed. However, if it can be shown that the directors allowed the company to continue trading while it was insolvent, then they (the directors, not the shareholders) may be held liable for the company's debts.
- A variant of the partnership is the limited partnership, a concept that originated in the United States. Here any partner who takes no part in the management of the business can be a limited partner, with their liability for the debts of the partnership limited to the amount of the partnership's capital that they have 'committed' (contracted to provide). The others, the general partners, will have unlimited liability as before.
- Certain hybrid forms have come into existence in recent years, which share some of the features of both a partnership and a company. Examples are a limited liability company (LLC) in the United States and a limited liability partnership (LLP) in the UK.

03
How business is financed

We have already seen that if you decide to set up in business then you can choose between three basic ways of doing this. You can simply trade as an individual (a 'sole trader'), or you can enter into a partnership, or you can form a company. For the remainder of this book, we will be ignoring the first two possibilities and focusing on companies. This is because later in the book we will be covering some more advanced aspects of finance, such as how public investment markets work, and the instruments that we will need to consider at that time are really only appropriate to companies.

Incidentally, this is not quite as arbitrary as it seems. Many people who trade on their own account actually do so through a limited company rather than as a sole trader, while in most countries partnerships are rare, except in the case of professional practices.

Having seen how to differentiate between the different types of business entity and, where appropriate, how these may be established, it is necessary to move to the question of finance. After all, to start any sort of business requires money, whether to buy stock, to rent an office, to hire staff or even just to have business cards printed. Where does this money come from, and what form might it take?

Let us answer the second question first. The financing of a company can take only two basic forms, though there may be many subdivisions within each of these types. It may be equity or debt. These are very different in nature and, in answer to the first question we just asked, usually supplied from different sources. Let us take a look at each in turn.

Equity

'Equity' is simply a technical term for shares, or stocks. It represents, in the case of a private company, capital that is introduced into the business by its owners, who are often the same people as its directors. In the case of a public company it represents capital introduced into the company by investors who, while they are still technically the owners of the company, will normally take no part in its management.

Incidentally, this is a very important difference between public and private companies as far as financial theory is concerned. As long ago as 1776, in his great work *The Wealth of Nations*, Adam Smith examined what were then known as joint stock companies and criticized this separation of ownership (the shareholders) from control (the directors). Noting that the directors had the management 'rather of other people's money than of their own', he commented 'it cannot well be expected that they should watch over it with the same anxious vigilance with which the partners in a [partnership] frequently watch over their own'. Gloomily, he predicted that 'negligence and [extravagance]' will 'always prevail, more or less, in the management of the affairs of such a company'.

In fairness to Adam Smith, it is important to put his remarks in historical context. The 18th-century experience of joint stock companies (the forerunner of today's large corporations) had not been a happy one, having already witnessed both the South Sea bubble and the Mississippi bubble, the latter also bringing down the Banque Royale in France. However, his argument is still used today by the supporters of leveraged buyout (LBO) transactions, who argue that all they are doing is reconnecting ownership and control by allowing the directors of a business also to hold a significant number of its shares.

Let us develop this theme of ownership a little. Ownership of a share, evidenced by being entered on the company's Register of Members, does represent in a very real sense 'a share in the company', in other words being a part owner of the company, though obviously in the case of a retail investor buying a few shares in a public company, that share of ownership will be a very small one indeed. Shareholders are said to be 'members' of the company, but it is better for practical purposes to think of them collectively as its owners. This ownership carries four basic rights.

Reporting

Every member of a company is entitled to know what is going on within the company, but this right is effectively limited to the right to receive regular audited accounts, and to ask questions about them at the company's General Meeting. Incidentally, this right is a fairly nominal one, since in many countries, including the UK, these accounts will in any event become publicly available for all to see once they are lodged with the national Companies' Registry.

In practice, the board of a company will strive to answer any reasonable query from a shareholder at any time, but this is a matter of professional management and good investor relations, rather than the result of any legal obligation. Public companies have always made a point of holding regular update meetings with their largest shareholders, just as with professional analysts, but this practice is much less widespread than it used to be, since an understandable eagerness by governments to clamp down on insider dealing (buying or selling shares on the strength of confidential information that is not known to the market at large) now places very severe restrictions on what can be said on these occasions.

Voting

Shareholder consent is required on a number of key issues, namely the re-appointment of the company's auditors, the periodic re-election of directors and, in some cases, authorization of the directors' remuneration arrangements. In certain circumstances, shareholder approval may also be required for the issue of new shares and the authorization of some types of financial transactions.

All shareholders have equal voting rights, but in the case of most public companies there will usually be a small number of large institutional shareholders who between them hold so many shares in the company that their collective decision is likely to be decisive, particularly as many small shareholders do not bother to vote. Incidentally, many institutional investors, particularly those from the public sector, are now required to keep a register of how they have cast their votes in the case of each company, and will operate a policy of voting in accordance with certain specified ethical or socially responsible guidelines.

Dividends

Shareholders have the right to participate in any **profits** that the company makes. However, it is the directors, not the members, who decide whether to declare a dividend in respect of a particular year. They are under no obligation to do so, and even if they do they are under no obligation to distribute all the profits of that year by way of a dividend. Indeed, it would be extremely unusual to do so, since it will normally be desirable to keep some of the profits for use in future years; these are known as 'retained earnings'. So, the reality will be that some part of the company's profits made during the year will be distributed to the shareholders as a dividend; incidentally, a dividend payment is often referred to as a 'distribution' in legal rather than financial circles.

Dividends are paid *after* tax. In other words, the directors cannot treat the dividend payment to shareholders as a business expense of the company and set it off against tax in the same way that they could with something like office rent or lawyers' fees. They must settle the amount of their taxable earnings first, then pay tax on them, and only then can they pay the dividend.

In practice this is usually done by declaring the amount of the dividend 'gross' (before deduction of tax) but then paying the shareholder the amount 'net' (after deduction of tax). The part that the shareholder does not receive in cash is known as a withholding tax, since the company is required to withhold it from the shareholder and account for it to the tax authorities, which it does by setting it off against its overall corporate tax bill. So the shareholder will receive cash in respect of the net amount, and a certificate of tax deducted, which they can use for the purposes of their own tax affairs, in respect of the balance.

In order to measure the attractiveness of the dividend that is being paid, it is customary to calculate the 'dividend yield'. This is a very straightforward process, simply dividing the amount of the dividend into the market price of the share. Thus, if a share was currently trading at £5 and a net dividend was paid of 25 pence, the dividend yield would be 5%.

It is easier to see this if we think of £5 as 500 pence, and a percentage as being a number divided into 100. We know that we start with 25 pence as the dividend and 500 pence as the price of the share, and we know that we want to divide one into the other, thus:

$$\frac{25}{500}$$

If we divide both the top and the bottom by 5, then we do not affect the overall value (if this is not clear, please see 'A note on equations', Chapter 4, page 39) but we arrive at:

$$\frac{25}{500} = \frac{5}{100}$$

So:

$$\frac{25}{500} = 5\% \text{ (because } \frac{5}{100} \text{ is the same thing as 5\%)}$$

Please note that we have calculated the net dividend yield here. If we wanted to calculate the gross yield then we would need to use the figure in respect of the gross dividend declared, whatever that might be.

Liquidation

The last right of ownership enjoyed by a shareholder is the right to participate in a liquidation, or in other words the right to their share of the value of the company's assets should it be wound up. In practice, however, this right is largely nominal, since the shareholders are right at the end of the queue, and can only participate once all the company's creditors have been paid, plus the costs of the liquidation itself. Since the most usual cause of a winding-up is that the company is unable to pay its debts (insolvent or bankrupt), then in practice there is usually little or nothing left for the shareholders.

Note that we have here been talking about **ordinary shares**, or **common stock**. There is a special type of share known as a **preference share**, or preferred stock, that is allowed to participate in a liquidation ahead of the ordinary shareholders. Instead of a discretionary dividend they will usually be entitled to a fixed dividend, agreed in advance. They will usually also be 'cumulative', meaning that if the dividend is not paid in any one year then it will be carried forward as a continuing obligation on the part of the company. These shareholders may have restricted voting rights; they may, for example, only be allowed to vote if the preference dividend is in arrears (unpaid).

Incidentally, it is the fact that shareholders (even preferred ones) are most unlikely to get back anything like the full cost of their shares in a liquidation that gives rise to the assumption in financial theory that in normal circumstances it should always be more expensive for a company to issue new shares than to take on new debt. Because shareholders are at more risk in a liquidation, the argument goes, they should expect a higher return than a debt provider in order to compensate them for that extra risk. Thus the rate of dividend required as 'the cost of equity' (the cost to the company of issuing new shares) should logically be greater than the rate of interest demanded by a debt provider ('the cost of debt').

We will examine this argument further below, but before we can do so we need to take a look at debt.

Debt

Just as equity is the technical name for company shares, so debt is the name for a company's loan obligations, though as these may take various forms it is probably better to describe them as loan-type obligations.

Whereas a share may be thought of as value owned by the company, debt is value *owed* by the company; in accounting terms, it is a liability of the company. Once a shareholder has subscribed capital into the company they cannot take it back; it represents part of the company's permanent wealth. The shareholder has given up ownership of their money in return for part of the ownership of the company. A loan, however, represents value that is owned by a debt-provider, such as a bank, and simply lent to the company. Sooner or later the company is going to have to pay it back.

Thought of another way, a share confers a right on the company: a right to use the money that the shareholder has subscribed. Debt, on the other hand, confers an obligation: an obligation to pay back both the capital amount and the agreed interest payments on the due dates. The cash obtained from shareholders becomes a permanent asset of which the company has both the use and the ownership, whereas the cash obtained from debt-providers is only a temporary asset of which the company has the use for a limited time. It is for this reason, as we will see, that they are treated very differently for accounting purposes.

There are various types of debt and we shall look at the two most commonly encountered. These are loans and bonds.

Loans

Lending money to a company covers a huge range of different situations, and can take one of any number of forms. In order to simplify things as much as possible, however, we will assume that different types of lending are perhaps a little more similar to each other than they are in real life. No real harm is done, since anybody who finds this chapter firing in them an insatiable desire to know more about bank lending will find plenty of sources out there that will be only too happy to tell them all about it in exquisite detail. Incidentally, bank lending in general has become known as 'credit' in investment circles and there is talk of it increasingly being seen as an asset class to which investors might allocate some of their money just as much as, say, hedge funds or commodities.

Try as we might to simplify matters, however, it is probably necessary to identify at least three different types of lending.

Lending (1): trade finance

Many businesses buy and sell goods from each other, and in some cases across national borders. Where shipping is involved, then things become even more complicated, as shipping companies and those who use them traditionally require a certain very specialized type of financing instrument to underpin the process of despatching and taking delivery of cargos. This is typically provided by a bank in the form of a trade finance facility, an amount against which may be drawn bills of exchange, one of the special types of instrument to which we have just referred. We will not be referring to trade finance again, but we should at least note that it exists, since it can form an important part of a company's debt obligations.

While not strictly falling under the definition of 'trade finance', we should consider also trade creditors. There probably is not a company in the world that could continue to operate if it was required to pay for all its stock, raw materials or professional services up front in cash. Global trade depends on being able to buy things on credit, with the expectation of paying for them later. Just as your suppliers extend credit to you, so you extend credit to your own clients or customers.

These trade creditors, however, are just as much debt-providers to your company as is your bank. There is no distinction in either legal or accounting terms between the obligation to pay a trade creditor and the obligation to repay any other type of loan. We will explore this in more detail when we look at working capital.

Lending (2): overdraft or revolving facility

Just about every business will have an **overdraft** facility from its bank, although in financial language this will often be referred to as a 'revolving facility' or just a 'revolver'. This operates in exactly the same way as a personal overdraft facility. It is an agreed amount that the bank is prepared to make available to cover a company's day to day needs. For a private company, the bank overdraft can be its most valuable source of finance. Great hardship is thus caused, with many small businesses being pushed into liquidation, when the banks suddenly and unilaterally start withdrawing overdraft facilities at times of financial panic.

It is this very unpredictability that is the main Achilles heel of relying on an overdraft as your main source of finance. Success in business requires, among other things, good planning, and good planning requires as little uncertainty as possible if it is to prove effective. If your main funding stream can be cut off at any time, then clearly you are operating in an environment of very high uncertainty, in which it is difficult to plan anything other than a few days or weeks ahead.

Lending (3): term loans

This is a more formalized way for banks to supply credit to a company. As the name suggests, these will be specific amounts of money lent for a 'term', or number of years. Unlike a revolving facility they have the advantage of certainty since, provided the company does not fall into default under the loan agreement, the bank cannot ask for its money back until the term of the loan expires. It is this type of lending to which the investment community has given the title 'credit', the theory being that it might be possible to persuade a bank to assign (transfer) its interest in a loan to an investor, preferably at discount to its face value, and the investor then steps into that bank's shoes and receives repayment of the principal plus any agreed interest payments on the due dates.

Bank loans to companies are typically 'interest only', with the principal sum being repaid in one amount at the end of the term. Indeed, this is usually to the bank's advantage, since it enables it to enter into related transactions on financial markets, should it so wish. For example, it may have matched that loan to a customer with one that it has taken from a third party for the same term, thus locking in the interest rate differential, or it may have **syndicated** ('laid off') some of the loan to another bank.

In some types of loans, however, the interest too is deferred, and paid only at the end of the term at the same time as the principal is repaid. These are known as **balloon** loans, with the interest element of the final lump sum being the 'balloon payment'.

Interest

Interest rates may be fixed or variable. If fixed, then this will be stated as some percentage of the principal sum, say 5.85% (in which case the interest payable would be £5.85 a year for each £100 borrowed). If variable, it will be stated by reference to some publicly available benchmark, such as LIBOR (London Interbank Offer Rate), and state the required margin above this. This can be expressed in 'basis points' (bps) or 'bips', each basis point being 1 per cent of 1 per cent. Thus an interest rate of LIBOR plus 135 bps would be equivalent to LIBOR plus 1.35%.

Unlike dividend payments, loan interest is a tax-deductible business expense, which means that interest is paid before tax, representing a considerable advantage to a business over equity in terms of capital efficiency. This is sometimes referred to as 'the tax advantage'.

Security

Just as a mortgage lender will take security over the property in respect of which it is lending money, security by way of a legal charge (it is actually this legal charge that is the 'mortgage', not the loan), so lenders to a company will commonly take security over the company's assets. Again, a legal charge is involved, but there are two types, fixed and floating.

A **fixed charge** is put in place at the beginning of the loan, and remains in place until the debt is discharged. It can operate either over all of the company's assets or over one or more specified assets, such as an office building or a factory. In both cases there can be both first and second charges; the holder of the first charge is entitled to have their claim settled in full first, and only if there is anything left over after that has been done does the holder of the second charge get their chance to 'go against' the asset (which can also be known as 'distraint' or, less precisely, 'foreclosure').

A **floating charge** is a rather more complex animal. It too is put in place at the beginning of the loan but, unlike the fixed charge, it does not actually attach to any of the company assets. Instead, as its name suggests, it floats around in mid-air. Unless and until the company commits an act of default under the loan agreement, the charge has no effect at all; indeed, it might as well not exist. Once an act of default is committed, however, then the floating charges 'crystallizes' and comes down out of thin air to attach itself to the company's assets, effectively turning into the equivalent of a fixed charge.

A floating charge is attractive to the company since unless and until it crystallizes it retains complete freedom to deal with its assets in any way it wishes. Subject to what other charges may already be in existence, it can also be attractive to a lender since they know that when crystallization occurs it will attach to all the company's assets and is therefore more desirable than a fixed charge, which may be limited to one specific asset.

Seniority

It is entirely possible that there may be various different suppliers of various different types of debt to a company. Where the company is associated with a leveraged buyout, an infrastructure project or a major property development, this is almost a certainty. Broadly, such debt suppliers are divided into 'senior' and 'junior' debt. Senior debt is secured, and therefore senior in the sense that it ranks more highly in a liquidation process, while junior is not. Senior debt is normally granted (at least in normal times) at a fairly conservative valuation of the business, while junior debt is usually prepared to accept a higher valuation and/or less **interest cover** (a ratio showing the number of times the company's cash-flow matches the required interest payments under the loan). To compensate for these extra risks, junior debt providers charge a significantly higher interest rate, which means that junior debt represents a much higher cost of debt to the company than senior debt does.

In practice, the situation is more complicated than this. There will usually be different layers of both senior and junior debt, and there may also be something referred to as 'second lien' in between; this is debt that is secured by a second rather than a first charge. The different layers of both senior and junior debt are usually referred to as A, B, C, etc and thus the inter-creditor agreement that regulates relations between all the different debt-providers is usually referred to as an 'alphabet note'.

Bonds

Whereas term loans are a contractual arrangement between the borrower and the lender, bonds are instruments, like shares. However, unlike shares they are debt, not equity. There is a due date when the money is to be paid back (the **maturity date**) and a rate of interest (often called the coupon) in the meantime.

Because they are an instrument that can be freely transferred, bonds can trade on public markets, being sold from minute to minute at whatever price is currently being quoted. This means that the sort of people who buy bonds are usually institutional investors such as pension funds and insurance companies, as opposed to banks, which are the prime source of term loans. Incidentally, bonds are issued by governments as well as companies (corporations); UK government bonds are generally known as 'gilts'. Unlike bank lending, bonds are usually unsecured, though there will be provisions for what happens should the issuer default on either the interest payments or the final redemption.

One particular form of corporate bond, which is often found as part of the financing structure of a leveraged buyout ('LBO'), is a payment in kind or **PIK bond**.

This contains an arrangement whereby the issuer can elect to pay the interest not in cash but by a further issue of bonds.

We will look at bonds and shares in much more depth in a later chapter when we consider their characteristics as investments.

The Miller Modigliani Theory

As we have now seen, there is both a cost of debt (in the form of interest payments) and a cost of equity (in the form of dividend payments). There is a famous theory, dreamed up by two finance academics, that, given certain conditions, the capital structure of a company (how it chooses to finance itself with a mix of debt and equity) is irrelevant to the value of the company for any potential purchaser.

If you take two identical companies, they say, one of which is financed entirely by debt and the other of which is financed entirely by equity, they are actually worth the same. If an investor wants to buy the **leveraged** (financed by debt) company, then they can do so, but taking into account in their valuation the interest payments that the company is liable to pay. If the investor wishes to buy the unleveraged (financed by equity) company, then they can simply borrow the amount (the same amount borrowed by the leveraged company) with which to do so. The net result is the same in either case. The only difference is who makes the interest payments.

Not so, of course. For a start, the theory assumes that everybody can borrow money at the same rate. Second, it assumes that it would be equally desirable from a tax point of view to have the interest paid by the purchaser as by the company. Third, it assumes that any purchaser would be unconcerned by the much higher default risk and risk of bankruptcy within the leveraged firm. Fourth, it takes no account of when the debt might have to be repaid. In fact, this theory represents one of a long line of academic financial models that have little grounding in reality. The only constant that seems to emerge is that the further they are away from reality, the more likely their creators are to be awarded the Nobel Prize.

It is not necessary that you know the arithmetic that underlies all of this, but simply that you are aware of 'MM' as it is usually referred to, and what it says. Interestingly, some of its supporters have now started to say that what is important is that the theory does *not* work in practice because its assumptions are false, thus highlighting the sensitivities that operate upon the funding of companies in practice. This is an inventive approach, and perhaps those who adopt it should consider switching to a career in politics.

The Theory of the Efficient Firm

There is another theoretical approach that needs to be outlined. The **Theory of the Efficient Firm** imagines a company that is financed purely by equity. Suppose that it has a paid-up share capital of £100M and has earnings before tax of £10M. Let us suppose a tax rate of 30 per cent, so that the net earnings (the earning after paying tax) are £7M, giving a net return on equity[1] of 7 per cent.

Earnings   £10M
Tax @ 30%   £3M
Net earnings   £7M
Share capital   £100M
Net return on equity $\frac{7}{100}$ = 7%

Now suppose that we could obtain £50M of debt at an interest rate of 8 per cent, and use this money to buy back £50M of shares. Should we do it? The answer, says the Theory of the Efficient Firm, is yes. In looking at the following calculation, please remember that loan interest is paid before tax, in other words it is deductible as a business expense.

Earnings   £10M
Loan interest @ 8%   £4M
Earnings before tax   £6M
Tax @ 30%   £1.8M
Net earnings   £4.2M
Share capital   £50M
Net return on equity $\frac{4.2}{50}$ = 8.4%

All that the Theory of the Efficient Firm is saying is that whenever borrowing money will be 'return enhancing', taking into account the tax advantage of being able to offset interest against earnings, then it makes sense to borrow money and use it to pay back equity. Of course, the more debt there already is within the company the higher the interest rate that the bank will demand, as it will grow increasingly nervous about extending yet more credit to the business. So, logically, there will come a point at which to borrow more money becomes so expensive to the company that is no longer return enhancing, at which point we stop; it may even be the case that one needs to adjust slightly in the other direction by issuing new shares in order to pay down debt.

If you have ever seen the film version of *Barbarians at the Gate,* then when the actor playing Henry Kravis[2] says 'debt tightens a company', it is the Theory of the Efficient Firm to which he is referring. Note that the theory is concerned only with the return on equity, and ignores important practical factors, such as the greatly increased risk of financial failure attendant upon a company with high borrowings (see below).

Leverage or gearing

We have just seen how having debt within a capital structure can enhance returns. For this reason, the extent to which debt operates within a company will be referred to either as 'leverage' (after the idea of using a fulcrum to multiply the pressure being exerted) or '**gearing**' (after the similar idea of using a smaller gear wheel to multiply the number of revolutions from a drive shaft). There is more than one way of calculating gearing, but the one that has become most universal is simply to divide the amount of debt into the total capital, thus:

$$\frac{debt}{debt + equity}$$

So that if a company had £100M of debt and £50M of equity, its gearing would be two-thirds, or 66.6%.

It is worth noting that both **Miller Modigliani** and the Theory of the Efficient Firm argue for (or at least validate) high levels of gearing, and both have been criticized for their possible influence on the events of 2007 and 2008. You will probably have noticed already that their approach is purely mathematical and they ignore (or assume away) various key practical issues.

In particular they ignore the extra risk represented by high levels of debt, except in so far as it may affect the interest rate that a bank may charge. If you are financed entirely by equity and you happen to have a bad year then you can simply decide not to pay a dividend that year. If, however, you are financed by debt and you cannot afford to make your interest payments, then you have just gone bust.

Conversion

Certain types of instrument carry the right either to swap the instrument for shares in the company, or to subscribe for new shares in the company at an agreed price. Where these rights are attached to another instrument, such as a bond or loan note, they are generally referred to as '**equity kickers**'. Examples include share options, warrants, convertible loan notes and convertible preference shares. Conversion rights can also be triggered under the terms of a bond issue should the company subsequently go into default.

Summary

- Companies can be financed only in one of two ways: by debt or equity. Debt may be further broken down into bank lending and bonds.
- Equity is literally a share in the company, in the sense of a share in the company's ownership. Ownership carries the rights of being kept informed about the company's affairs, voting at General Meetings, being paid a dividend out of profits at the discretion of the directors, and entitlement to a share of the company's assets on a winding-up. However, equity ranks behind debt in a winding-up, and so traditional finance theory tends to assume that in normal circumstances it should always be more expensive to issue equity than debt.
- In the case of a public company, where a quoted price is available for the company's shares, then the dividend yield can be calculated by putting the dividend paid in respect of each share over the share price, or the total dividend paid by the company over its market capitalization. Both calculations will of course give the same result.
- An overdraft or revolving facility is a flexible credit facility against which the company can draw for its day to day needs. However, it can be reduced or withdrawn at any time by the bank and thus makes certainty in financial planning impossible.

- Term loans will be for a fixed period of time and will typically be secured by a fixed or floating charge over the company's assets. Fixed charges may be general, or limited to specific assets. Repayment of capital will usually take place at the end of the term. Interest may be payable during the life of the loan or may be payable in one lump sum ('balloon payment') at the end along with the repayment of capital.
- Different levels of bank lending to the same company can be divided into senior and junior debt. Senior debt is secured, and takes priority over the company's assets in a winding-up. Junior debt is usually not secured, and even if it is, it has to wait for the senior debt to be repaid in full before it can go against the assets of the company. Because junior debt carries more risk, it is more expensive.
- Bonds are instruments, like shares, but represent debt obligations of the company. They have a fixed repayment ('redemption' or 'maturity') date when the principal amount must be repaid, and carry the right to receive interest (a 'coupon') from the issuer in the meantime.
- The Miller Modigliani theory states that a company's capital structure should have no effect on its valuation. This theory is false as it rests on various impractical assumptions.
- The Theory of the Efficient Firm states that a company should always borrow money and use the proceeds to buy back equity when it would be return enhancing to do so, taking into account the tax benefit of being able to pay loan interest before tax.
- Leverage, or gearing, is a measure of how much debt a company has in its capital structure relative to equity. It is calculated by $\dfrac{\text{debt}}{\text{debt} + \text{equity}}$ and expressed as a percentage.
- Various types of instrument can carry the right to buy or convert into equity. These rights are generally known as equity kickers.

Notes

1   The theory actually talks about return on assets, but this is a more convenient way to explain it.

2   Jonathan Pryce.

04
Accounting basics (1): the balance sheet

Now that we have seen how a company (corporation) is financed, it is time to consider the role of accounting. Accounting refers generally to the preparation of documents, by the company and/or its accountants, which record the sort of things that we were discussing in the last chapter. In some cases they may be all that we have to go on when considering the state of a company's finances. In other cases they may be what we are given to study in preparation for some form of discussion. In either case, it is clearly essential that we should be able to understand what they are telling us.

Sadly, as with so many things in finance, accounting is often taught in an unnecessarily complicated way, which leads to many people giving up in frustration and thus never gaining any sort of understanding of what they need to know. The objective of this book is to present the essentials of accounting in a straightforward way, stressing and explaining the underlying concepts and avoiding where possible the use of accounting terms. Where these *are* used (and obviously there are a certain number that you will need to know in order to understand what you have in front of you when you look at accounts) they will be fully explained. If you are still reading at the end of the chapter, then the book will have succeeded in its objective!

Broadly speaking, we can break accounting down into two different types, which each fulfil very different functions and objectives. These are: (1) financial and (2) management accounting. Let us consider the differences between them before we go any further.

Financial accounting: the basics

Financial accounting is what someone will mean if they talk loosely about 'the accounts' of a company. They will be prepared by the company's accountants, in consultation with the company's own internal finance personnel, and will, in many cases, be audited. We will consider auditing in more detail below. For the moment, let us simply note that it is a process by which a company's accounts can be certified as correct, according to recognized accounting standards, by an external, and thus hopefully independent, firm of accountants (often referred to these days simply as 'an audit firm').

The fact that they are, or may be, audited gives a clue to their purpose. They are intended to be relied upon by outsiders, and it is felt that these outsiders have a right to know that the accounts have been verified by some third party, rather than just being prepared by the company itself. Those outsiders most likely to be dealing with a company are banks and trade creditors, though in the case of a public company it is probably correct to think of shareholders as outsiders as well, given the separation of ownership and control. Thus, in terms of public companies, the providers of both debt and equity finance will be numbered among those who will be seeking to rely upon the financial accounts.

The two most important components of financial accounts are the **balance sheet** and the **profit and loss account** (earnings statement/income statement), each of which we will consider in some detail later.

Management accounts: the basics

Whereas financial accounts are prepared for outsiders, management accounts are prepared for insiders. Outsiders will never have any right to see them or expectation of doing so unless this is conferred by some sort of separate agreement; for example, it may be a condition of a loan agreement that the bank that has extended the loan has a right to delivery of a set of specified management accounts every quarter while the loan remains outstanding. Normally, however, outsiders will never get to see them; indeed, they will normally (and understandably) be viewed by the company as highly confidential information.

Their purpose is also very different. Whereas financial accounts are designed to give outsiders a view of the company's overall financial health, management accounts are designed to assist the company's executives in the taking of key management decisions.

This has another important consequence. The company has little discretion as to the form that its financial accounts may take; this will be laid down for it in a mixture of company law and accounting rules. However, while there are some recognized standard elements that will generally be encountered in management accounts, such as a cash-flow projection, they may take any form that those preparing them deem appropriate. In practice they will be tailored to match as closely as possible the information requirements of the particular decision being considered.

TABLE 4.1 Comparing financial accounts and management accounts

	Financial accounts	Management accounts
Audience	Outsiders (including shareholders)	Insiders (but restricted circulation)
Purpose	Convey a picture of the company's financial health	Assist with executive decision making
Required content	Balance sheet and profit and loss account	None
Verification	Audit by qualified outside agency (professional audit firm)	None
Status	In the public domain once released and filed	Confidential private information
When prepared	Annually or quarterly as required by law	At any time, but usually at regular intervals as decided by management

Financial accounts

Financial accounts portray two very different but complementary pictures. On the one hand, an outsider such as a lending banker will want know what the company's assets and liabilities are. For example, it may owe its various creditors $1 million, but if it owns the office building from which it operates, and this is valued at $3 million, then the bank will probably feel pretty relaxed about things – even more so if the company's own debtors (customers) owe it $2 million. However, if it owes its creditors $3 million, has no cash in hand, and is owed only $1 million by its debtors, the bank is likely to take a very different view of the situation.

On the other hand, the relative value of the business's assets and liabilities tells only part of the story. If it is earning high **profits** then it is likely to be able to service even quite large liabilities from incoming cash. In fact, as we will see later, just because a company is earning high profits does not necessarily mean that it is also enjoying strong cash-flow, but for the moment let us just note this point and pass on. Whatever the case, it must be right that as well as being interested in the company's assets and liabilities, an interested outsider will also want to know how it is doing in trading terms: is it making a profit, and if so, how much?

Basically, these two pictures are painted by the two required elements of any set of financial accounts. The balance sheet shows the company's assets and liabilities. The profit and loss account (which you may also encounter described as an earnings statement or income statement) does what it says on the packet: it shows the state of the company's trading activities and evaluates whether it is making a profit or not.

Actually, there is one very important difference about the way in which these two accounting documents are prepared, one that has been highlighted by a deliberate mistake in the last paragraph. We have just talked about whether a company is making a profit or not. We cannot answer this question without having to ask a second one: when? For example, the business might have been profitable last month, but has made losses in each of the previous six months. It is essential that we know exactly which period we are talking about.

Traditionally a profit and loss account will cover a period of one year and this may be described as either 'the year to' or 'the year from' a particular date. Or it may simply state the two dates at the beginning and end of the period (particularly if this is more or less than a year, as can happen, for example, if the company changes its accounting date). It is very important when looking at a profit and loss statement always to check at the top of the page the exact period for which it has been prepared. The accounting date, by the way, is the date each year in respect of which the accounts are made up (so that the profit and loss account would cover the year that comes to an end on the accounting date). Unsurprisingly, many businesses around the world choose 31 December as their accounting date.

So, the profit and loss account covers a *period*, usually of one year. A balance sheet, however, does not.

Just consider for a moment what would happen if you tried to draw up an accurate statement of a company's assets and liabilities over a period. You would come across an immediate and insoluble problem: the amount of its individual assets and liabilities will change from one day to the next. Suppose that today its outstanding amount due from its customers is $1 million. Tomorrow, a customer might pay an old invoice for $100,000, which means that the $1 million figure is no longer correct. It will have gone down by the amount received, and either the amount owed to the bank will have decreased by the same figure, or the amount of the company's cash will have increased. So, you might try to fix the various amounts at the beginning of the period and the end of the period, but that is the best you can do.

Accordingly, this is exactly what a balance sheet does. It is prepared not in respect of a period but *as at a particular date*. This will of course be the accounting date. Thus the balance sheet for the last year will tell you what the assets and liabilities were at the beginning of the period (since the end of the last period must have been the same moment as the beginning of the current period) and this year's balance sheet will show you the position at the end of the period (year). This is why accountants frequently describe the balance sheet as a snapshot. It captures a particular moment in time, just as a photograph does.

Even if you were never to learn another thing about accounts, this is a very important point to grasp. A balance sheet will be a correct picture of the company's affairs in respect of the day on which it is prepared. There is no guarantee at all, however, that it is a correct picture of the situation prevailing either the day before or the day after. This is a large part of the challenge facing financial analysts; their work consists of ascertaining exactly what has changed between one balance sheet date and the next, and when, how and why.

Balance sheet

So, we now know that the balance sheet will show the company's assets and liabilities as they were on the accounting date, which will be the last day of the accounting period, usually a year. Exactly how does it do this?

There are two important concepts to grasp about the balance sheet before we start. They are both based upon something called the **accounting equation**:

> Assets = capital + liabilities

Do not let the word 'equation' frighten you off. This is not some complicated mathematical proposition, but a statement of simple arithmetic, as easy as 2 + 3 = 5.

Can you see that if 2 + 3 = 5, then 2 = 5 – 3? Or that 3 = 5 – 2? In other words, that you can simply re-state the equation in order to find a solution for any one of its three elements? If so, you understand the principle of the accounting equation.

> If assets = capital + liabilities,
> then liabilities = assets – capital,
> and capital = assets – liabilities.

That is as far as we need to go with this. If you are confused, just go back and look again at the example of 2 + 3 = 5. However, hopefully you will *not* be confused, in which case congratulations! You have now learnt not one but two of the most important principles of accounting.

A note on equations

It is a natural reaction to panic when faced with an equation. It is because it reminds us of maths, and we remember that we couldn't do maths at school. It is a basic fault of finance lecturers that they tend to throw equations and formulae at their students without thinking about the effect this may have. This is because they are mathematicians, and it just happens to be the way they think about things themselves. For the same reason, they have no conception of the blind terror that mathematical symbols arouse in most people.

However, equations have much more to do with everyday logic than they do with complicated arithmetic. Let us take the simple equation:

> A = B + C

Since what is on each side of the 'equals' sign must (by definition!) be equal to each other, can you see that it makes no difference which way round we state it? In other words,

> A = B + C

is exactly the same as

> B + C = A

This is important because we need to be able to 're-state' the equation. This is just a mathematical term meaning 'find an answer for a different component of the equation'. In other words, 're-state for B' simply means 'instead of finding what A is equal to (which we already know, because the equation tells us), find what B is equal to'.

Well, most people find it easier to plan for an outcome that starts with 'B =', so being able to switch the two sides of the equation as we have just done is a handy starting point. In fact, we are already very close to our desired solution. All we need to do is to get rid of that pesky 'C', and we're there. This is where we meet the only rule you need to know and remember, and a very simple one it is too:

You can do whatever you like to one side of an equation, provided you also do exactly the same to the other side.

Again, this is simple logic, not maths. If each side of the equation must be equal to the other, and I start off with 100 apples on each side, then if I take 3 apples away from the left-hand side I must also take 3 apples away from the right-hand side so that each side now has 97 apples.

In order to get rid of the 'C' from the left-hand side, I need to deduct it. Fine, I am allowed to do that. But only so long as I also deduct it from the right-hand side. So my equation now becomes:

$$B = A - C$$

Note that to remove something from one side of an equation, you have to look at whatever mathematical function is operating upon it, and do the opposite. So, to get rid of something that is being subtracted, you need to add it. To get rid of something that is multiplying, you need to divide by it instead, and vice versa. So:

$B - C = A$ would become

$B = A + C$ because I have added C to both sides.

$B \times C = A$ would actually be stated mathematically as $BC = A$ and would become

$B = A$ divided by C, which would be stated as $B = \dfrac{A}{C}$, because I have divided both sides by C.

B divided by $C = A$ would be stated as $\dfrac{B}{C} = A$ and would become

$B = A \times C$, which would be stated as $B = AC$, because I have multiplied both sides by C.

A note on mathematical notation

By custom, certain things are represented mathematically as follows:

One value 'over' another means that the number on top is being divided by the number beneath the line, thus $\dfrac{A}{B}$ means 'A divided by B'.

So, if A = 24 and B = 3, then:

$$\frac{A}{B} = \frac{24}{3} = 8$$

Placing two values next to each other without any sign in between them means that they need to be multiplied by each other, thus AB means 'A multiplied by B' (which is of course the same thing as B multiplied by A, so that AB = BA).

So, this time:

$$AB = A \times B = 24 \times 3 = 72$$

So, what are the two important principles of the balance sheet that we can derive from the accounting equation? The first is that any balance sheet must have two sides, one representing 'assets' and the other 'capital + liabilities'. The second is that each side of the balance sheet must have the same value; in other words, it must 'balance', hence its name. It may be helpful to think of a balance sheet as an old-fashioned pair of scales. Just like a pair of scales, it has one container on each side. Just like a pair of scales, when the weight (value) in each container is exactly the same, then it will balance. In fact a pair of scales was originally called a balance, hence the expression 'to be weighed in the balance'.

So, we know that we need to prepare a document that is set out in two halves, one on each side. We also know that one of the sides will feature assets, while the other will feature capital and liabilities. Just what sort of things would actually belong in these categories?

Let us start by thinking about **assets**. These are divided into two different types of asset for accounting purposes: fixed and current.

Fixed assets are those that cannot easily be turned into cash. In accounting terms, the two main requirements for qualifying as a fixed asset are that the thing should have a long life, and/or that it was not bought for the purpose of being re-sold. So, good examples of fixed assets would be an office or factory building, the plant (machinery) used in the factory, or the furniture and fittings in the office. Slightly more surprisingly, perhaps, another example would be any motor vehicles being used in the business, even though in everyday terms we usually think of these as short-term, wasting assets.

Perhaps you can think of other assets that would be classified as **current assets**? These should be things that have a short life and so are likely to be quickly used up, or that represent cash, or that can readily be converted into cash. The most obvious ones are stocks (in a manufacturing business), debtors (it is assumed that these debts owing to the business will be discharged within a reasonably short time), any money held as cash (in most businesses today typically only the contents of the petty cash box), and money showing as a positive balance on any bank account.

What about capital? In any business, however constituted, this will be all the money that has been introduced into the business by its owners. In the case of a company, this will represent its issued share capital. This is the amount that has been paid to the company by shareholders in return for shares in the company. Things can be a little more complicated than this in reality, since we are required to draw a distinction between the amount paid for the nominal price of a share (its face value) and the price actually paid for it by the shareholder, but let us ignore this for our present purposes.[1] Similarly, we might find in the 'Capital' section, described as 'Reserves', amounts retained from profits either for specific purposes (perhaps to settle a particular debt that will fall due for payment during the forthcoming year) or generally.

Just like assets, **liabilities** are subdivided into **long term** and **short term**, and here things are really simple; we simply look at when the company is likely to need to discharge the particular liability. The general rule is that if this date lies more than one year in the future, then we are allowed to describe it as long term. If it is less than one year in the future, then we must treat it as short term. The rationale is hopefully obvious: long-term liabilities are likely still to be in existence at the date of the next balance sheet, while short-term ones are not. So bank loans or bonds that have a fixed term (period) or repayment date with more than one year left to run will be long-term liabilities. An overdraft facility, which is usually repayable on demand or on short notice, will be a short-term liability, as will any amounts currently owed to trade creditors, such as suppliers.

So, we are now able to prepare our balance sheet, along with some figures by way of example:

FIGURE 4.1

Example balance sheet (1)
as at 31 December 2011

Fixed Assets	£	Capital	£
Office furniture and fittings	1,000	Share capital	900
		Reserves	570
Current Assets	£	Long-term Liabilities	£
Stock	600	Bank loan (2 years)	1,000
Debtors	620		
Bank	700	Current Liabilities	£
Cash	50	Creditors	500
	2,970		2,970

... and that is essentially that. Except that it's not. For reasons best known to themselves, the accountants decided to take this perfectly simple and logical structure and start messing around with it. Despite the fact that a balance sheet has two sides to it, they decided to present it vertically rather than horizontally, so that now nobody would guess that it actually has two sides to it at all. To make matters worse, they decided to net current assets and short-term liabilities off against each other to create a new line in the accounts called 'net current assets'.

So in order to create a layout that you will recognize when you see it, we need to re-state our balance sheet as you will see it below.

However, you are urged most strongly always to think of a balance sheet in its pure and simple form. No matter how complicated the figures with which you are presented, it will always be possible to re-state them in this way, and you will always find it easier to think in terms of a balance sheet that has two sides, each of which must balance with the other, and which follows the simple outline of the accounting equation. Indeed, even senior investment bankers have been known to jot down figures in this way when considering capital structures, complete with a 'right' and a 'left' hand side to the balance sheet.

Of course, if you are tasked with preparing some sort of complex financial exercise then you will almost certainly not be able to present your figures in this way, and you will have to follow the prescribed format. However, even then it does no harm at all to remember that what you are looking at is essentially an artificial layout designed by accountants, and that it does no more than place an arguably unnecessary layer of complexity on top of what is really a very simple situation.

So, please don't do what the accountants want you to do, which is to panic and run away, thinking that only accountants can understand accounts. Just take a long, hard look at the second example and compare it calmly with the first. You will see that it really does comprise nothing more than the same numbers, just differently expressed.

You will also see that the two parts of the balance sheet still balance. This is because the only real difference is that short-term liabilities are now being deducted from the left-hand side of the balance sheet rather than added to the right-hand side. In mathematical terms, we have deducted the same amount from both sides of the equation.

FIGURE 4.2

Example balance sheet (2)			
as at 31 December 2011			
Fixed Assets			£
Office furniture and fittings			1,000
Current Assets	£	£	
Stock	600		
Debtors	620		
Bank	700		
Cash	50	1,970	
Creditors: amounts falling due within one year			
Creditors	500	500	
Net current assets			1,470
Total assets less current liabilities			**2,470**
Creditors: amounts falling due after more than one year			
Bank loan			1,000
Capital and Reserves		£	
Share capital		900	
Reserves		570	1,470
			2,470

Valuation

Valuation has become a very important and, at times, controversial topic in recent years. Briefly, how can we know, as outsiders, that the values placed on assets by those who have prepared a balance sheet are correct?

Well, the first very important thing to understand is that accountants, when they prepare or audit accounts, do not represent that the value that they place on an asset is 'correct'. This may come as something of a shock, so let us be clear what is meant by this. What accountants *are* representing, particularly when they sign an audit certificate, is that a set of accounts is 'true and fair'. This does not mean the same thing as 'correct'; in other words they are not guaranteeing in any way that on the balance sheet date you could take, for example, a motor vehicle, and sell it for the amount of cash that is stated in the balance sheet as its value.

What the accountants are guaranteeing is that they have arrived at that valuation (1) in accordance with all appropriate accounting standards and regulations, and (2) consistently. Consistently, that is, not just with other assets held by the same company, but with all similar assets owned by all similar companies. Thus, a cynic might argue, if the motor vehicle in question has been valued incorrectly, then at least you can rely on the fact that all similar motor vehicles owned by other companies in the same line of business have been valued in exactly the same incorrect way.

It is difficult to limit discussion of valuation to manageable proportions for our present purposes, since whole books have been written about it for professional accountants. Briefly, accounting traditionally has been dominated by something called the historical cost convention. This requires that the starting point for any asset valuation should be 'cost' (the amount that the company originally paid for it). This basic principle is modified by the concept of 'impairment', which says that if you become aware of something that adversely affects ('impairs') the value of the asset, then you should **write the asset down** to whatever new (lower) figure seems reasonable to take account of this impairment in value.

In addition to this, both tax and accounting regulations in different countries require that certain types of assets, typically those that are regarded as 'wasting' (which means they can normally be expected to lose some of their value naturally as one year succeeds another), must be written down in some concrete, pre-defined way, perhaps by losing 25% of their value every year. Motor vehicles would be a good example of this principle. In fact, there is frequently a difference between what tax regulations require and what accounting standards deem to be fair, which is why a separate set of accounts is typically prepared for tax purposes.

As for writing the value of assets up, rather than down, this has normally been dependent on obtaining an independent report from a professional expert, which the auditors then act upon by agreeing that certain assets may be entered in the balance sheet at a higher value than that of the previous year. Property (real estate) companies are an excellent example of where this revaluation process can form a very important part of any external financial analysis.

Gradually this traditional approach has been reformed and refined, as accountants started grappling with some fairly obvious issues. To what extent, for example, should one take account of inflation? What about assets that are intangible but nonetheless a vital part of the company's business, such as intellectual property rights or brand recognition? What about assets in respect of which the company has transferred the legal title, but on terms of deferred payment? How should one deal with the problem of a pension scheme funding deficit in the balance sheet of the sponsoring company? Possible answers to these questions, and various others, have been gradually absorbed into accounting practice, and any reader who wishes to pursue this area in more detail is recommended to any of the standard introductory works on accounting.

Before leaving the subject, however, we should be aware of one very important issue that has still not been fully resolved: the extent to which assets held as investments should be 'marked to market'. At first sight, it seems eminently sensible that investments should be valued at their current market value, but two problems have emerged, neither of which seems to have been anticipated by the accounting profession. First, what happens to assets in respect of which no public market exists? Second, what should one do during periods of extreme abnormality in public markets, such as we saw in September 2008 when at one stage it was effectively impossible to sell corporate bonds, almost irrespective of price? Issues such as these have sparked an intense debate within the accounting profession, with one faction maintaining that it is always possible to assess the 'fair value' of an investment, and others now openly disputing this – a very recent development.

Auditing

As explained above, the whole concept of auditing is that it is an independent process carried out by expert professionals. Their scrutiny of the paper trail leading to each entry in the accounts, and challenging of assumptions made by those who run the business, can, when finally they sign the audit certificate, give immense comfort to outsiders who then have to rely upon those accounts for whatever reason as providing an accurate view of the company's finances.

All of that, of course, was before the infamous Enron scandal, which probably destroyed confidence for ever in the infallibility and sanctity of the audit process. We should note for the sake of completeness that while Arthur Andersen, the audit firm concerned, was originally convicted of obstruction of justice, that conviction was subsequently overturned by the US Supreme Court on the grounds that the trial judge had misdirected the jury. However, the facts behind the auditing of Enron and various other companies disclose three significant issues.

First, many companies had resorted to off balance sheet funding structures, setting up related parties such as limited partnerships, the ownership of which could be juggled in such a way that their accounts did not have to be consolidated with those of the company. In this way the ownership, the financial liabilities and the right to the income stream of various assets could effectively be hidden from outsiders.

Second, while in many countries accountancy firms were not also allowed to perform lucrative consultancy and corporate finance work for their audit clients, the spirit of this sensible precaution was being broken by the provision of such services through related vehicles. This meant that the audit team was no longer purely independent, but could be subjected to at least moral pressure not to make too many problems when challenging the accounts.

Third, much important audit work was being performed by very junior staff, many of whom were not yet even professionally qualified. In many cases not only did they not understand the complex transactions that they were being asked to monitor, but nor did those nominally supervising them.

These are all issues that the accountancy profession recognizes and is moving to deal with, though the third one is so deeply rooted in the traditional way of doing things that it seems unlikely that significant changes will be made. To be fair, there would be very significant cost implications in doing so.

It is clearly right that outsiders should be entitled to rely upon the figures with which they are presented in financial accounts, and the audit process is a vital part of this. However, at the same time there is a growing move away from the requirement to audit accounts. In the UK, for example, many small private companies are now exempt, while in other countries, such as Russia, private companies do not even have to file their accounts with a public registry.

In the next chapter we will move on to look at the other main component of financial accounts, the profit and loss account. Later, though, we will come back to the balance sheet as we examine the concept of working capital.

Summary

- Financial accounts are prepared for outsiders so that they can evaluate the extent to which they may wish to have financial dealings with the company. Management accounts are prepared for insiders to assist with executive decision making.
- Financial accounts normally have to contain both a balance sheet and a profit and loss account. Furthermore, the way in which each of these documents must be prepared and laid out is also laid down by law or accounting standards. Management accounts may take any form that those preparing them decide upon.
- Financial accounts are required by law to be issued on certain dates, usually once a year, although special rules may apply to public companies whose shares are listed on a stock exchange. Management accounts may be prepared at any time, but traditionally either quarterly or monthly.
- The balance sheet is based upon the accounting equation, assets = capital + liabilities. This equation may be re-stated for each component thus: capital = assets – liabilities, and liabilities = assets – capital.
- Because of the accounting equation, every balance sheet must have two sides to it, and the two sides must balance (be equal).
- Assets are divided into fixed assets and current assets. Fixed assets are those that are expected to have a long life and/or were not bought for the purpose of re-sale. Current assets are all those that do not qualify as fixed.
- In the case of a company, capital will usually be represented by called-up share capital. However, two other items may commonly be found. Reserves are past earnings that have been retained within the business. The Share Premium Account is a technical accounting requirement when shares are issued at more than their nominal face value.

- Liabilities are divided into long term and short term according to how long they are likely to endure, the break point for which is normally one year.
- Balance sheets are no longer presented horizontally, so it is not immediately apparent that they have two 'sides', but in fact they do and any balance sheet, no matter how complicated, can if desired be represented in the historic manner. Readers are encouraged to do so whenever possible.
- Valuation of assets is dealt with pursuant to accounting standards, but is also influenced by taxation law. The traditional approach has been to use cost as a starting point, with the current value being written up or down as appropriate.
- The audit process is designed to inspire confidence in outsiders that they may safely rely upon the financial accounts of a company, though this confidence was badly shaken by the Enron and other corporate audit exposures. In many countries smaller companies are no longer required to have their accounts audited and in at least one country (Russia) are not even required to file them with any public registry.

Notes

1   For the curious, the difference between the two is generally posted to something called the Share Premium Account.

05
Accounting basics (2): the profit and loss account

We now turn to the second component of any standard set of financial accounts. This is called the profit and loss account (commonly abbreviated to P&L), but depending on the country in which you live you may find this being described as an earnings statement or an income statement. Please do not worry about this – they are all just different names for the same thing.

In the next chapter, the last on accounting matters, we will turn back to the balance sheet and look again at things like creditors and debtors. This is because we need to look at **working capital**, on which they have a significant impact, and we could not do this in the last chapter because it requires an understanding of earnings (**profit**). For *that* we need to know about the P&L account.

So what is a P&L, and what does it tell us about the company? We can answer this question by recalling two key differences between a P&L and a balance sheet. First, whereas the balance sheet tells us the relative values of the company's assets and liabilities, the P&L is designed to tell us if the company is actually making money in the operation of its business and, if so, how much? Conversely, might it actually be losing money instead? Second, whereas a balance sheet is a snapshot of a particular moment in time, a P&L relates to what happens over the course of a whole period, traditionally one year.

It might be helpful to think of a soccer game. A balance sheet is the equivalent of taking a photograph of a particular moment in the game. It will be a perfect record of where every player was on the pitch at the second when the photo was taken, but only for that one precise second. The P&L is not concerned with showing where the players are at any particular time, or even with how many there are on each side. It is concerned instead with showing how many goals were scored during the game as a whole, and consequently whether the result for any one team was a win, a loss or a draw.

Turnover

The first thing that the P&L will tell us is the **turnover**, which is an accounting term for how much money the company has received during the course of the year from its customers. This can also be known as sales, or even sometimes as revenue or revenues, but again these are just different names for the same thing. Turnover is not the same thing as profits, though.

From the money it receives from its customers, the company will have to pay all sorts of liabilities to third parties before it can assess whether it has made a profit and, if so, how much. Obvious examples would be the rent on an office or factory, and the wages it pays its staff. In the case of a manufacturing business, it will also need to pay for raw materials or components to turn into its finished products.

Though this appears to be a simple and obvious point, it is in fact a very important one and a potential source of much misunderstanding, such as when somebody says something like 'We are a three million dollar business'. A good general rule to apply is that unless someone specifically uses the word 'profit', then they are almost certainly talking about turnover (sales).

It is also worth noting that the word 'turnover' can be used in a non-accounting sense to refer to the rate at which people come and go, and this can be applied in particular to staff and customers. High staff turnover suggests poor morale and/or bad workplace practices, while high customer turnover can be indicative of a lack of customer satisfaction with the company's products or services.

Profit (or earnings)

Profit (earnings) is what is left over after all the company's expenses have been deducted from its turnover (sales). Sadly, this number can be negative, in which case the company has made not a profit, but a loss.

In assessing its profits a business will not only take account of the expenses it has actually paid, but also of accounting items such as **depreciation**. It is these accounting items, which do not represent sums of cash actually paid out, which are stripped out of a set of accounts when calculating cash-flow rather than profit.

Depreciation represents an assumed fall in the value of any assets held for use in the business, and is usually calculated in accordance with any relevant accounting standards. As well as appearing in the P&L as if it were an expense that the business has paid during the accounting period, it also features in the balance sheet as a reduction in the value of the business's assets since the last balance sheet date. We will examine shortly how this works.

The word 'profit' is itself capable of a number of different meanings and we therefore have to be very careful always to define exactly what sort of profit we are describing, and be sure to ask other people to do the same.

This is actually a very complex subject, with different types of profits being stated after deduction of different types of expense, or ignoring different types of income. For our purposes, we will keep things very simple and consider only three broad categories of profit. Irritatingly, one of these, the first in fact, is also capable of some ambiguity.

Gross profit

This is often used in the sense of 'profit before payment of tax', just as we have already seen when referring to shareholders' dividends, which are declared before tax (the gross dividend) but paid after deduction of tax (the net dividend). However, this usage is not correct when we meet it in the context of a P&L account.

Gross profit is really only applicable to manufacturing businesses, though it can also be a useful measure when looking at wholesale and retail businesses, which have to buy in their stock before they can sell it on to their customers. It refers to the profit that a company has made after deducting only the cost of the raw materials or components that we mentioned earlier.

There is a set formula for calculating this amount to be deducted. First you look at the previous year's balance sheet and find the figure for 'stock'. This becomes your figure for opening stock. (Again, this is a deliberate simplification, since there can be various types of stock.) Then you add to this the cost of the stock you have purchased during the year covered by the present P&L (purchases), together with any associated transport costs (carriage inwards). Finally, you deduct the figure for stock from this year's balance sheet (closing stock). Whatever figure results from this process becomes the cost of goods sold, and is deducted from the sales to arrive at the **gross profit**.

An example might be helpful. The accompanying excerpt from a P&L account shows the opening lines that you might expect to see in the case of a manufacturing business.

FIGURE 5.1

**Example profit and loss account
for the year ended 31 December 2011**

	£	£	£
Sales			186,000
less Cost of Goods Sold			
Opening Stock		34,000	
add Purchases	71,000		
add Carriage Inwards	2,450	73,450	
		107,450	
less Closing Stock		36,000	101,450
Gross Profit			84,550

Profit before tax

This is what many people understandably but incorrectly call 'gross profit' (because it is stated before, or 'gross of', tax). You may wonder why accounts should bother to state the level of profit before tax when the company still actually has to pay the tax, and thus you might well think that the only meaningful measure is the amount left over afterwards, out of which the directors might decide to make a distribution (pay a dividend) to the shareholders. There are, however, two main reasons why profit before tax can be a useful measure to have.

First, you might be studying to what extent the company has grown its annual profits over time. In this case, it is extremely unlikely that the rate of corporate taxation has stayed the same throughout the several years you have under review. Therefore the only way in which you can validly measure management performance is by looking at profit *before* tax, since otherwise the results of your analysis would be corrupted by changes in tax rates, something of course over which management had no control.

Similarly, you might be trying to compare the performance of this company with competitors in different countries. Again, the relevant tax rates are most unlikely to be the same. In practice, the situation will be even more complicated, as different tax practices can lead to different deductions being made from turnover in arriving at the profit figure; different levels of depreciation on assets such as plant and machinery would be a prime example.

The second situation where profit before tax is useful is if you are trying to arrive at a valuation of a company for the purposes of buying it. Should you be planning to buy the company largely with bank debt, such as, for example, a private equity firm might do, then in many countries around the world you would be able to reduce very significantly the amount of taxation that would be payable, since you might be able to arrange matters in such a way that the interest payable on the bank debt could be deducted from the company's turnover as an expense, thus leading to a much lower figure for taxable profit. In fact, a private equity firm would go even further than this and look not at profit at all, but rather at something called **EBITDA**, which we will consider below. This is a measure not of profit but of cash-flow, but the principle remains valid.

Profit after tax

This is sometimes referred to as 'net profit' because it is 'net of' (after payment of) tax. It is also sometimes called 'profit (or earnings) available for distribution', since dividends (distributions) can only be paid out of profit once the business has paid tax on that profit.

Profit after tax is of limited use for analysis purposes. It cannot be used to compare businesses in different countries, for not only is the rate of taxation likely to be different, but so too are the rules governing the basis of assessment. Similarly, it can be of limited use even when comparing the results of the same business over different years, since again rates, rules and allowances may change from year to year. Nor is it of great use when valuing a business of which you are planning to take control, since you could use that control to change its capital structure (for example by introducing

TABLE 5.1 Financial accounting statements

	Balance sheet	Profit and loss account
Also known as		Income statement, earnings statement, P&L, statement of revenue and expense
Records	Assets and liabilities	Turnover of the business and various deductions from this, only some of which will represent actual cash payments
Designed to show	The ability of the business to pay its liabilities on any given day (liquidity)	The profit or loss of the business for accounting purposes (profitability)
Time basis	A snapshot of a single day	A record of a period, usually a year
Important distinctions	Treats assets and liabilities as either short term or long term	Treats profit and loss items as either operating (relating directly to the business process) or non-operating

more debt) and thus reduce the amount of tax payable, as loan interest in tax is deductible (paid before tax).

Why then should we use it at all? For two main purposes. The first is in analysing dividend policy. As we will see in a later chapter, this is a matter of calculating how much dividend a business chooses to pay its shareholders relative to the amount of profit available for distribution. In this situation, using anything other than profit after tax to analyse the directors' decision would clearly be unreasonable. They can only pay dividends out of money that is available for that purpose. We will deal with this specifically in Chapter 13.

The second purpose is in assessing a business's solvency (basically, its abilities to meet its obligations) in income rather than asset terms. For example, we may know how much a business has to pay in loan interest each year, and be curious as to how much money may be available for the purpose. This is a very complex subject, and we will see in a moment that a measure called EBITDA is commonly employed to calculate the cash-flow of a business. However, this ignores, amongst other things, the payment of tax.

Why should this be? It is said, after all, that the only two things that cannot be avoided in life are death and taxes. Well, EBITDA assumes that you can change the capital structure of the business (eg introduce more debt) and by doing so alter the amount of tax that may be payable (because loan interest is tax deductible). Indeed, EBITDA is commonly modelled in so-called leveraged transactions (for example, leveraged buyouts or real estate (property) deals) precisely to see just how much debt the business or asset can afford to service.

This is fine if you are the owner of the business. However, if you are a minority shareholder (stockholder), or a banker to the company, or a supplier who is extending credit to it, then you will be much more concerned with its net cash-flow, since taxes do unfortunately have to be paid. In other words, EBITDA could be said to be the conceptual or potential cash-flow of a business, since the amount of tax payable can be changed, whereas any calculation grounded on profit after tax will show the actual cash-flow, since it assumes that the amount of tax payable cannot be changed. Hopefully this will become clearer once we have looked at the relationship between profit and cash-flow.

Profit and cash-flow distinguished

One thing that we need to be very clear about is that the P&L account tells us about what profit the company is making, but not about its cash-flow. Cash-flow is a very important concept in finance, and many people believe that it is a much more accurate indicator of both the health and the value of the business than profit might be. Please note that elsewhere in the book we will also be using the word 'cash-flow' in the sense of a single cash payment or receipt, but this will hopefully be obvious from the context.

What is cash-flow?

Just as the name suggests, it refers to the flow of money in and out of a business, and how we might attempt to measure it. If you look at your bank balance at the beginning of the year, and then again at the end of the year, the difference between the two will be your annual cash-flow. That is to say that if you start with your opening balance, add all your inflows during the year (your income), and then deduct all your outflows (your expenses or outgoings), the resulting figure will be the same as your closing bank balance. (If it isn't, you've made a mistake somewhere!)

Why isn't it the same as the business's earnings (profits)?

There are two reasons for this. First, accounting standards demand that when calculating its profit, a business must take into account various items of a non-cash nature. Depreciation is a good example. If a motor car is used in the business, the accounts may require that some percentage of the current value of this as stated in the last balance sheet be written off to reflect the fact that the vehicle loses value as it gets older and incurs higher mileage. An asset of this kind is known as a **wasting asset**.

The important thing to understand here is that although the business is required to set this depreciation off against sales like any other business expense when calculating profit, it is not really an 'expense' at all in the sense of a liability that has been discharged by making a cash payment, such as payment of staff wages or payment of an insurance premium in respect of the business's factory. No money has changed hands at all, yet the depreciation is set off against sales as though it has.

Why? Well, like many accounting issues, this one is largely tax-driven. Clearly a day will come when the business will need to buy a new vehicle to replace the existing one. You might think that this would represent a legitimate expense of the business, and that the fairest way of dealing with this would simply be to set the purchase price off against the sales of the business during the year in question. You would be correct. Unfortunately, tax authorities are not remotely concerned with what is fair, but only with what generates the maximum tax revenue. Thus, rather than allowing you to reflect the reality of your income and expenditure, they grudgingly allow you to claw back in each succeeding year some small part of what you should have been allowed in the first place. These chunks of depreciation clawed back from the taxman are often called **capital allowances** or **writing-down allowances** when they occur in business taxation, and strictly speaking for tax purposes they should be thought of as being set off not against sales in arriving at profit, but against profit when calculating liability to tax.

Incidentally, one thing you need to be aware of is that capital allowances vary widely between different countries, and sometimes even within a single country, where there may be special rules for development areas. In attempting to revive a run-down region, for example, a government might offer 100% writing-down allowances on factory plant and machinery as an inducement to businesses to establish factories there, thus providing employment. This can be a very important factor if you are attempting to compare the cash-flow of businesses in different countries. For example, Germany has always traditionally offered very generous writing-down allowances on plant and machinery in order to encourage manufacturers regularly to upgrade their factories and remain competitive, whereas the UK has not, with predictable results for the UK manufacturing sector.

The second reason why cash-flow is different from profit relates to the reason why people might want to look at cash-flow in the first place. Briefly this was driven by two factors, both of which emerged during the 1980s. The first factor was a growing recognition that when conducting company valuation exercises, the only valid 'value' of a business was the **Net Present Value** of its future cash-flows, a concept that we will examine in a later chapter. The second factor was the birth and rapid growth of the leveraged buyout (LBO) industry, which was not concerned with analysing how much a business was 'worth', but with how much they could afford to pay for it. This in turn depended upon how much debt could be squeezed into the deal, which in turn depended upon how much loan interest the business was capable of servicing (paying).

Of course, earnings are affected both by loan interest and tax. Since this would make any debt analysis exercise based on earnings a circular process, it was thought better to work on the basis of cash-flow, and model the business according to the capital structure (mix of debt and equity) that you actually intended to use. In order to arrive at as pure a cash-flow measure as possible, you needed also to exclude accounting but non-cash items. This is how people arrived at **EBITDA**.

EBITDA as a measure of cash-flow

EBITDA stands for Earnings Before Interest, Tax, Depreciation and Amortization. **Amortization** is very similar to depreciation and is indeed often confused with it. Strictly speaking, amortization relates to intangible assets such as intellectual property (copyright, patents, trademarks, etc), while depreciation relates to tangible assets such as buildings and machinery.

Calculating EBITDA is a fairly straightforward process provided that the business is required to file properly detailed accounts. However, you may have to root around a little for the required information. Earnings, interest and tax will generally be in the body of the P&L, whereas depreciation and amortization details will often be contained in the notes at the end. Incidentally, a convenient starting point is available in **EBIT** (yes, you've guessed it, Earnings Before Interest and Tax) since many business accounts state this as **operating profit**.

One important point to be aware of is that, unlike many of the other accounting components that we have been exploring, EBITDA is not a recognized **GAAP** (generally accepted accounting principles) measure, which means there are no hard and fast rules about exactly how to go about it. This in turn means there is no guarantee that any two analysts will arrive at exactly the same figure.

For example, in addition to non-cash items such as depreciation, you will also have to consider the following. Accounting often spreads a cash payment that is made or received in one period into one or more other periods as well, depending upon the nature of the associated income or expenditure. For example, if a business pays a year's rent in advance on its factory in April, but its accounting year ends in December, then four-twelfths of that will be held over into the following year's accounts. Similarly, accounting practice will usually assume that all invoices issued during the year will count towards turnover, regardless of whether the business has actually been paid by the customer or not. Thus in preparing any cash-flow calculation you will need to decide how best to treat these items.

Even though the financial accounts of large business entities such as public companies now also typically contain a cash-flow statement, you will need to make quite sure that you fully understand what it is telling you, and how to treat this. For example, it may contain income from a non-trading source, such as investment income.

TABLE 5.2 Factors present within a profit and loss account that will affect cash-flow

Apportionment	A portion of some income or expense carried over to a period other than the one in which the payment was actually made
Earnings basis of accounting	Assumes that all invoices issued by the business represent cash that has or will be received by the business
Depreciation	Notional diminution in value of tangible assets used by the business
Amortization	Notional diminution in value of intangible assets used by the business

TABLE 5.3 Factors that may be disregarded for some cash-flow purposes

Interest	Because the amount of debt present within a company may be changed by decision of the directors. It may also be possible to re-structure the company's debt so that even if the amount remains the same, a lower rate of interest may be payable.
Taxation	Because in most jurisdictions the amount of interest payable by a company, and thus the amount of debt within it, will have a direct impact on the amount of tax payable.

Analysing the P&L

Return on capital

This is a basic but very valuable tool, which measures what return a business is delivering to its shareholders. It is calculated by:

$$\frac{\text{EBIT}}{\text{share capital and reserves}} \times 100$$

This is sometimes also called **return on equity** or **return on capital employed (ROCE)**, though in the latter case strictly speaking any outstanding debentures should also be taken into account. This is rarely an issue in practice, and may be safely ignored for our purposes.

Return on capital can be used to compare the return the shareholders are making on this investment relative to other assets in which they could invest instead. It is also a good way of comparing two businesses in the same sector, particularly if one is trying to choose between them as possible investments. If a business has a higher return on capital, one would expect it to have a correspondingly higher valuation; if not, then it may represent a bargain, and since there is rarely any such thing as a genuine bargain, this would be the signal for further analysis.

Return on capital is something with which the directors should also be concerned, since they will wish to attract new shareholders and deliver the best possible return for their existing ones. Frequently this point is overlooked during strategic discussions. For example, if a particular factory has very poor margins (see below), but could be closed and re-developed as a supermarket, this is an alternative that needs to be considered. By using the sale price to buy back shares, the capital employed in the business could be significantly reduced, thus resulting in a higher return on capital even with reduced EBIT.

Remember in using this ratio: (1) that EBIT will be affected by the level of borrowing (gearing) within the business; and (2) that it can be affected by changes in asset numbers, values, or depreciation policy. Thus, it is a good starting point for analysing a business, but by no means provides a full answer. For that, we need to dig more deeply, employing various tools and making use of everything they have to tell us. We will meet some of these in the chapter on working capital, but for now let us think about how we can analyse the business's **margins**.

Gross margin

This indicates the most basic level of profitability being achieved by sales (or turnover).

It is calculated as:

$$\frac{\text{gross profit}}{\text{sales}} \times 100$$

A very low **gross margin** suggests either that the company is not charging enough for its products, or is being forced to pay too much for its raw materials. However, bear in mind that gross profit will be heavily influenced by stock levels, so you need to check whether these have been rising or falling relative to sales (we will explore this further in the chapter on working capital).

A low gross margin may also suggest that the business is obsessed with sales rather than profitability, being prepared to discount their prices heavily in order to sell more product. In these cases, a business tends to be led and/or dominated internally by people whose background is in sales and marketing.

Net margin

This takes us to another level since it will include all a business's operating overheads, so naturally there will be a big difference between the gross and the **net margins** in the case of a manufacturing business. It is calculated as:

$$\frac{\text{EBIT}}{\text{sales}} \times 100$$

This is a very valuable analysis tool, showing the business's real level of profitability. Remember that we are here taking into account all the company's overheads, so look for signs that they may have opened newer, larger premises or taken on more staff. In fact a business that is operating within a very rapidly growing market will probably be loss-making for this reason. That does not mean it is being badly run; on the contrary, it can be an indication that the directors are doing exactly what they should be doing to safeguard the company's strategic position (though it would raise obvious questions about running out of cash).

Remember too that net margin takes no account of interest, so it will present a lowly geared company as performing equally with a highly geared company. This is a good example of where you need to use different analysis tools in combination with each other. It would clearly be relevant to look at return on capital (above), but also at liquidity, which we will examine in the chapter on working capital.

Summary

- The profit and loss account is the second standard component of any set of financial accounts.
- It shows the profitability of a business over a given period (typically one year) by starting with the turnover (sales) of the business and then deducting certain items from this.
- While some of these items relate to sums of money actually paid or received by the business during the period, others do not. For this reason it is necessary to draw a distinction between profit and cash-flow.
- Cash-flow is calculated by adding back any non-cash items that have been deducted.
- A common measure of cash-flow is EBITDA. In addition to depreciation and amortization, this also adds back interest and tax, since both of these items will be dependent upon a company's capital structure and it is within the control of the directors to change this.
- The P&L can be used to measure return on capital.
- Other useful analysis methodology is to calculate the business's gross and net margins to measure different levels of profitability.

06
Working capital and further financial analysis

When we looked at the balance sheet of a business we saw three key components of something called working capital: stocks, debtors and creditors. Actually, the technical accounting definition of working capital is the difference between **current assets** and **current liabilities**, but it is also used in a more general sense to mean the money that is tied up in the business, ie the money that is needed on a daily basis to allow the business's operations to function.

This is one reason why the balance sheet is so useful as part of a set of financial accounts. An outsider, particularly one who is looking to extend either a loan facility (such as a bank) or trade credit (such as a supplier) to the business, can examine it and use it to analyse various aspects of the business's financial health. Let us look at two ways in which we can measure a business's **liquidity**. We will meet the word 'liquidity' in two different senses in this book. When it is applied to an asset or investment, it means the ability to turn that asset instantly into cash (so gold and government bonds are liquid, whereas real estate (property) is not). When it is applied to a business, however, it means the ability of the business to pay its debts in the short term.

The current ratio

The current ratio looks at the short-term (current) liabilities on the balance sheet. Remember, these will be those that fall due within one year, and will include bank overdrafts and trade creditors. It then looks at the short-term (current) assets of the business, and expresses one relative to the other by dividing current assets into current liabilities thus:

$$\frac{\text{current assets}}{\text{current liabilities}}$$

If we think about the constituent parts of these two balance sheet categories, then what we are usually talking about is:

$$\frac{\text{stocks} + \text{debtors} + \text{cash}}{\text{creditors} + \text{overdraft}}$$

Two things are important to understand here. The first is that we are concerned only with the short-term situation; that is why we are allowed to exclude long-term liabilities. The second is that we are assuming a particular situation occurs that in practice would almost never happen; we are assuming that all the business's debts and liabilities would suddenly have to be paid tomorrow. In practice that would happen only if the business effectively committed an act of insolvency and became subject to some insolvency regime such as receivership or liquidation. That is, however, precisely the purpose of the ratio. If we lend this business money (which is effectively what we are doing if we supply it with goods or services on credit) and it falls into insolvency (bankruptcy), what are the chances that we will get our money back?

There is of course another assumption that the ratio implies, and one that is even more unrealistic in practice: that we could turn all our current assets into cash tomorrow. Stocks of finished goods might have to be heavily discounted in order to be sold in a hurry (usually called a **fire sale**), and the figure will also include stocks of raw material and work in progress. We might be able to sell the former back to our supplier at a loss, but the latter would have no effective commercial value; who wants a half-built television or washing machine? As for debtors, anyone who has ever worked in the credit control department of a business will know at first hand that it can take weeks or even months to persuade some customers to pay up, and if they know that the business is or is likely to become insolvent, then they become even more reluctant; a canny debtor in that situation might for example ask for a discount for prompt payment, or for forgiveness of other outstanding invoices.

The current ratio shows us something very valuable about the state of the business's finances. The result obtained by applying the ratio should always be greater than one. Even in the case of a service business, which will not carry stock, we would hope that this would always be so.

If it is not, then the business is said to have a **working capital deficiency** or a **working capital deficit**. This is serious, as it would appear to show that the business may be unable to pay its debts as they fall due, and in most countries the directors would come under a legal duty to meet and discuss the situation. It may be, for example, that the shareholders might be prepared to introduce new capital into the company, thus boosting the cash reserves. If no such solution could be found, they would then usually come under a duty to call a meeting of the company's creditors, which may in some circumstances rank as an act of insolvency, and might also give a lending bank the right under its loan agreement to appoint a receiver (for a discussion of insolvency, see Chapter 17).

In summary, then, the current ratio is a useful accounting tool, though it makes some rather unrealistic assumptions.

The acid test ratio

The acid test ratio, also sometimes known as the **quick ratio**, attempts to deal with this problem by excluding stock from the picture. The acid test ratio is thus:

$$\frac{\text{current assets} - \text{stocks}}{\text{current liabilities}}$$

If what you are after is a real measure of short-term liquidity, then this seems sensible. As we will see below, there could be various reasons for high stock levels, some good, but mostly bad. In any event the assumption that these can quickly and easily be turned into cash feels wrong.

Ideally, the figure arrived at by applying this more demanding ratio will still be a positive number, a value greater than one. This shows that the business can pay its short-term debts as they fall due without having to sell any stocks. If it is less than one then this raises obvious questions. The managers of the business would argue that in reality stocks of finished goods will be being sold from day to day and that the proceeds of those sales (the turnover) will be available to pay creditors; in accounting terms, stocks will reduce and debtors increase. This is true, but it is highly likely that at the same time new stocks of raw materials will have to be ordered, or the business's manufacturing or assembly operations will grind to a halt.

So, if the result is less than one, life becomes much more complicated. A lending bank, for example, would now have to get into detailed sales and cash-flow modelling, looking at the various margins in the profit and loss account and seeing how sales translate into profit, and profit into cash-flow.

Long-term liquidity

Remember that both these ratios only deal with the short-term liquidity of a business. It may seem strange to think that there may be such a notion as long-term liquidity, since 'liquidity' seems almost by definition to be concerned with the here and now. It asks the question 'What would happen if a business was suddenly called upon to pay all its debts at once, tomorrow?'

It may be better, therefore, to think in terms of a business's long-term financial health generally. Much of this will depend on its strength within its market relative to its competitors, and how this is likely to change over time. These are essentially qualitative and subjective matters, not sensible of calculation. However, one thing that we can do using the financial accounts is to calculate the level of gearing, which we have already seen how to do:

$$\frac{\text{debt}}{\text{debt} + \text{equity}} \times 100$$

We can use the resulting percentage to monitor two things: (1) whether the level of gearing has changed over time (has the company for example been taking on more debt to boost its return on equity?); and (2) how the business compares to its competitors. A business that is highly geared may be operating at a high level of capital efficiency, but it is less able to withstand a sudden downturn in trading (perhaps because of a recession) or to react to a sudden need for capital.

Another useful metric is what is called **interest cover**. We calculate this by:

$$\frac{\text{EBITDA}}{\text{loan and overdraft interest}}$$

Notice that there is no 'x 100' here, as this measure is ordinarily used as a ratio, but there is nothing to stop you calculating a percentage should you wish to. This is a measure used by lending banks when deciding how much money a business might borrow, and it will usually form part of the loan agreement. There may for example be a covenant that the business will not allow interest cover to fall below 2, or 1.6, or some such number.[1] This is of particular importance in leveraged (highly geared) transactions such as leveraged buyouts. Note that this is a cash-flow calculation, and so will be unaffected by things like depreciation policy. Remember too that EBITDA is not a GAAP measure, and so there is no universal agreement on exactly how it should be calculated.

It's time now to take a closer look at working capital. There are various measures that the directors will use for their own monitoring purposes as they attempt to manage working capital. Fortunately, some of them rely purely on information that is published in the financial accounts, which means that we outsiders can use them too.

Working capital

We have already mentioned the three main components of working capital: stock, debtors and creditors, but it is easy to overlook cash. Let's start with that.

Cash

Cash management is one of the primary duties of the finance department of any business. Running out of cash is obviously every business's worst nightmare, for unless fresh cash can quickly be sourced either through a line of credit or by issuing new shares, then insolvency is almost certain to ensue. Without cash, one cannot pay one's creditors.

However, as we saw in an earlier chapter, having too much cash can also be a bad thing, at least when viewed from the point of view of the world of finance. Remember the Theory of the Efficient Firm. If the business has too much cash for its present needs then it makes sense to buy back shares, thus reducing the amount of share capital and increasing the return on equity. The Theory of the Efficient Firm of course goes further than this, advocating that a business should even be prepared to borrow in order to buy back shares. So, as with so many things in finance, there is a trade-off. Hold cash and you improve your liquidity, but at the expense of return on equity.

Seek to boost the return on equity by returning cash to shareholders, and you render the business more vulnerable to sudden and unexpected shocks.

There is a practical consideration here too, at least in the case of public companies. You may often read about such a company (corporation) having a **cash pile**. This means what it says: they have a lot of cash piled up at the bank. Often they will seek to justify this by describing it as a **war chest**, suggesting that they are out shopping for other businesses to buy, and that this is cash they have specifically set aside for that purpose. Ironically, however, it can simply serve to make that company itself an attractive acquisition target. Particularly in recent years, when so many public companies have been acquired by way of leveraged transactions, a company with a great deal of cash and very little debt has obvious attractions, whereas one with little cash and a great deal of debt is relatively unattractive, since there is little scope for borrowing yet more money. So, using spare cash to buy back shares does not just make sense in financial theory, but also from the point of view of the law of the jungle that stalks the merger and acquisition (M&A) market.

Stock (inventory)

There are two ways in which we can think about how efficiently a business is making use of stock, and they are really just different ways of looking at the same thing. The first is called inventory (or stock) turnover (by the way, stock and inventory are two words for the same thing). Stock turnover measures how many times the amount of stock in the business gets used up in the course of a year; how many **turns?**

We measure this stock turnover ratio by taking the cost of goods sold and dividing it into the closing stock thus:

$$\frac{\text{cost of goods sold}}{\text{closing stock}}$$

However, there is a growing trend to use not closing stock but average stock thus:

$$\frac{\text{cost of goods sold}}{\text{average stock}}$$

Where average stock $= \dfrac{\text{opening stock} + \text{closing stock}}{2}$

So, this stock ratio (or average stock ratio as appropriate) measures the number of turns; that is to say the number of times a year that stock is turned over.

The second way in which we can express how efficiently a business is making use of stock is to measure the stock days, which gives us the number of days it takes to turn the stock over once. This is calculated as:

Average stock ratio × 365

Please note that there are a number of issues to look out for here, which are listed in the box.

Issues with stock analysis

Please be aware that any form of stock analysis is open to manipulation. Business managers are well aware that this is one measure used to analyse their performance and the unscrupulous can deliberately run stocks down towards the end of the year, thus leading to an artificially low closing stock figure, only to ramp this up again in the first few weeks of the following year.

Any really meaningful stock analysis often requires figures that are not publicly available, for example a breakdown of different types of stock (raw materials or components, work in progress and finished goods), how these might fluctuate during the year, and how they are allocated between different products or plants. For this reason, while stock analysis is a sound and useful exercise, its limitations should be borne in mind.

Some people use sales instead of cost of goods sold as the top part of the ratio, and indeed some databases of business information operate on this basis. So, you should always check which version of the ratio is being discussed or presented, and when you are performing this analysis yourself it probably makes sense to run both methods. In this way, you will always have available whatever figure it is you need for comparison purposes.

A low number for stock turnover (or a high number of stock days, if that is the measure you are using) would obviously be a cause for concern. It could indicate inefficiencies in the scheduling of raw material purchases, inefficiencies in the manufacturing process that is leaving large amounts of work in progress lying around, or finished goods that cannot be sold, perhaps because customer tastes have changed or because of cancelled orders. These would all be things you would wish to investigate further.

A high number for stock turnover or a low number for stock days would on the face of it be an encouraging sign of business efficiency, but again there is a trade-off here. If you keep your stocks very low, there is always a danger of the dreaded stock-out, which means that you may be unable to fulfil a customer's order. This would result not just in lost sales, but also in damaged goodwill with your customers.

Stock management has for some time been recognized as a key area of potential business and financial efficiencies. A variety of techniques have been developed to pursue these. More sophisticated manufacturing systems are one. **Just in time** (JIT) manufacturing is another. Under JIT in its purest form a product is not manufactured or assembled until a specific customer order is received; the computer business Dell is a well-known example of this. In Japan, where the technique was pioneered, the philosophy extends right the way through the process chain to the ordering of components. Here obviously a very high degree of trust in your suppliers is required. Note that in Japan strikes are almost unknown and businesses in a particular sector tend to work together with their customers and suppliers in very tight networks known as *keiretsu*. It is difficult to see how the purest form of JIT could be employed without these two factors being in place.

Debtors

Debtors are the remaining positive element in working capital. Remember that when we look at the balance sheet, any debt that is owing to a business is treated as an asset, just as any debt that the business itself owes to a third party is treated as a liability. Debts will one day be turned into cash. At least, that is the theory on which accountancy proceeds; a certain number of debts each year will go unpaid, but there is an important distinction to draw here.

If a debt remains unpaid at the end of the year, it simply gets stated in the balance sheet as part of the debtors figure, and is carried over to the next year. Remember that a balance sheet is a snapshot of a single moment in time. It captures the debts that are outstanding at that particular moment and is not concerned with exactly when the debt arose, or when it may be settled.

If, however, the business decides that a particular debt will not be paid (either because there is a rogue debtor who refuses to pay and the amount involved does not merit the expense of trying to collect the debt through the courts, or because the debtor has become insolvent) then it becomes a **bad debt**, and will be deducted from the debtors figure at the next balance sheet date. It will also become an allowable deduction when calculating that period's taxable profits. In most jurisdictions, businesses are also allowed to claim back any sales tax that they may have paid on the relevant invoice in expectation of receiving it from their customer, at least where the customer has become formally insolvent.

We can measure **debtor days** quite simply:

$$\frac{\text{debtors}}{\text{sales}} \times 365$$

The debtors figure will of course be the figure in the closing balance sheet for the period, while the sales figure will come from the P&L for the period.

Note that strictly speaking we are concerned with sales that have been made on credit, but except in the case of a retail business there will usually be little, if any, difference between overall sales and sales made on credit. Incidentally this is one reason why retail businesses make such attractive candidates for LBO transactions; they should always be very efficient in terms of working capital when compared with businesses in other sectors.

One of the ways in which a business can seek to improve its working capital efficiency is to **squeeze the debtors**. Again, there is a trade-off here. On the one hand it is simple common sense to try to get your customers to pay their invoices as quickly as possible, and this is something that is often not done as well as it might be. If you are a large business with lots of small customers, then this is something that can be enthusiastically pursued without any great danger. If, however, you have a very small number of large, powerful customers then great care must be exercised. The number of days that they take to pay their invoices will usually have been agreed at the start of the relationship, or maybe at the beginning of each year, and any attempt to change it may lead to the loss of the customer, leaving a huge hole in the business's sales. Believe it or not, there are some businesses that have just one very large customer, and here all bargaining power clearly lies entirely with the latter.

So, a low number for debtor days is generally a good sign, as is a smaller number compared to the previous period. Yet you need to be aware of the possible trade-offs: a rapid reduction might lead to an equally rapid reduction in the business's customer base.

Nor can market dynamics or economic conditions be ignored. In a rapidly growing sector, the imperative is to gain as much market share as possible, as quickly as possible, and relatively generous credit terms may be offered to gain a lot of customers in a hurry. In an economic recession businesses find themselves trying to juggle two mutually irreconcilable factors: nervousness as to customers possibly becoming insolvent grows, promoting tighter credit controls, yet sales are falling, prompting the easing of credit controls to gain more customers or bigger orders from existing customers.

Just to make matters even more complicated, the banks usually choose this time unilaterally to reduce, or even remove altogether, business overdraft facilities. Nobody ever pretended that working capital management is easy. On the contrary, it is becoming increasingly recognized as one of the most important of business skills. Good or bad working capital management can literally make or break a business.

Creditors

We have looked now at all the 'good' elements of working capital, all the things that sit on the top of the current ratio. It is now time to look at the 'bad' element, which sits underneath.

We can measure **creditor days** in much the same way as we did debtor days. By the way, these are also known as **days payable**, since creditors can also be referred to as 'accounts payable'. This is an unfortunate phrase that can be a source of confusion as it uses the word 'accounts' in the US sense of a either a specific business relationship or an invoice, both meanings that are not well recognized elsewhere.

$$\frac{creditors}{cost\ of\ goods\ sold} \times 365$$

As will hopefully be obvious by now, the creditors figure comes from the balance sheet while the cost of goods sold figure comes from the P&L.

Here a high number is a good sign, and usually an indicator of a company's power relative to others with whom they do business. Perhaps in no other area is the difficulty of operating a small business better illustrated. A small business may find it difficult to get credit at all, and even if it does so will be expected to pay promptly, usually within 28 days, or risk both losing that supplier and gaining a bad credit rating. A large business, on the other hand, might well take over 100 days on average to pay its invoices, thus essentially treating its suppliers as a source of free funding for its own advantage.

Changing the subject, there is an obvious issue here. All of these ratios that we have been examining date back many decades and are fully appropriate only to manufacturing businesses rather than to service industries. Stock days will clearly be redundant in such a case, while with creditor days vital elements that we require (such as 'cost of goods sold') will simply not exist in the financial accounts. In the case of a service company, the analysis *can* be performed by substituting 'purchases on credit' for 'cost of goods sold', but this will usually involve a more detailed breakdown of the numbers than publicly available accounts will allow. For example, temporary staff may be provided on credit by an employment agency, but that figure may just appear in the same category as the salaries of permanent staff.

There is another issue with the ratios that some readers may already have spotted. Do they really deal adequately with the reality of being an ongoing business (what accountants refer to as a **going concern**)? What about the staffing costs of the business, for example? Most employees are paid monthly in arrears; thus they are effectively providing their services to the company on credit. Does it not seem strange, therefore, that they should not be taken into account alongside trade creditors?

This seems particularly true in the case of the liquidity tests. If a company is to remain in business throughout the year it will have to pay its staff. If it finds itself unable to do so at the end of any month then it will have to file for insolvency just as it will if it finds itself unable to pay a trade creditor. So why is it that the recognized tests completely ignore this fact? Incidentally, even if the business were to close its doors tomorrow, it would still have to pay its staff their statutory minimum redundancy entitlement, so why is this not taken into account as a contingent liability?

The truth of the matter seems to be that while accountants claim to be applying a going concern basis, they may not have properly thought through just what such an approach should entail. Just as they have struggled to come to terms with the reality of asset valuation, so they have failed to reflect the reality of the ongoing liabilities that a business assumes every day that it decides to stay in operation, or even if it decides not to.

Summary

- From a commercial point of view, working capital is the money tied up within the business in debtors, creditors and stocks. From an accounting point of view, it is the current assets of the business less its current (short-term) liabilities.
- Where the value of a business's current assets is less than its short-term liabilities it is said to have a working capital deficit, or working capital deficiency.
- We can seek to measure the working capital efficiency of a business by calculating its stock days, debtor days and creditor days. However, these should be viewed as rough guidelines rather than precise indicators, since they can be influenced by many factors, not all of which will be within the directors' control.
- A business can attempt to improve its working capital efficiency by better stock control, **stretching its creditors** or squeezing its debtors. However, all of these tactics carry significant business risks.
- Accountants are required to view a company on a going concern basis unless presented with evidence to the contrary. However, it is not clear that the full implications of this have been thought through in terms of accurately representing working capital. It is strongly arguable, for example, that both actual and contingent staffing costs should specifically be taken into account.

Notes

1 You can come across interest cover calculated the other way around, in which case you would of course be looking for a number less, rather than greater, than one.

07
The time value of money

At some stage during the early 15th century, somebody in Florence initiated the most crucial development ever to occur in the history of the visual arts: the discovery of perspective. The credit is usually given to the great architect Filippo Brunelleschi, who is perhaps best known for the revolutionary dome of Florence cathedral, today one of Europe's outstanding tourist attractions.

It is difficult to over-state the significance of his discovery. Previously all paintings were flat, or two-dimensional, the great 14th-century religious paintings in Sienna being good examples of this phenomenon. Given that artists seek to represent the world around them (or, at least, they did then), and that the real world is not flat, it is perhaps only surprising that Brunelleschi's innovation came as late as it did. From now on, the notion of perspective would be accommodated automatically into any artist's worldview. No longer would figures or buildings in the background of a painting be the same size as those in the foreground, but smaller, just as they would appear to be in real life.

There are two direct parallels here with the world of finance and, just as perspective revolutionized the world of art, so both of these aspects of finance are crucially important. One of them we will leave for a later chapter, but let us concern ourselves now with what is arguably the most important concept in finance. Perversely, it is perhaps the least well understood. It is called the time value of money.

Looking down the time tunnel

If we were to look down a long but large tunnel, such as a road tunnel, and see two identical motor cars, one just in front of us but the other a long way off in the distance, the one that was further away would seem considerably smaller than the one immediately ahead. So, if we were asked to draw a sketch of the scene, perhaps as a witness to an accident, that is how we would represent them. Understand this simple truth, and you also understand the idea of the time value of money.

Suppose now that instead of a road tunnel that stretches away into the distance, we were looking down a time tunnel, perhaps as a scene from a science fiction film. If we were now looking at something, such as a car, at the other end of the tunnel, something that was perhaps 10 years away into the future, the director of the film would almost certainly depict this as being much smaller than something that was immediately in front of us, something that was in the present or very near future. In other words, they would be representing something that was further away *in time* as being much smaller, just as if it were in fact further away *in space*. Well, in finance we do exactly the same.

How to think about future cash-flows

Let us think back quickly to something that was said earlier in this chapter. We talked about an artist representing something that was far away as being smaller than that which was near, in the foreground. We said that this was because this was how they would appear to be in real life. The key words here are 'appear to be'.

Suppose that you wish to draw a very simple picture that features only two objects, two children, each of whom is exactly a metre tall. If we have them both directly in front of us, we can see very well that they are exactly the same height as each other. Yet if we now put one of them on a conveyor belt and let them travel away into the distance, they will look shorter and shorter than the other child whom we have kept with us as they travel progressively further away. Finance works in exactly the same way.

Suppose now that instead of two children who are exactly the same height as each other, you have two bank notes of equal value to each other; two 10 dollar bills, for example. If we hold one in our right hand and the other in our left hand we can see clearly that each of them is worth exactly 10 dollars. Now keep hold of one, and put the other one on the conveyor belt, but this time let it travel away into the *future*, rather than into the distance. Remember, we know that both of them have the same value, but consider a very important question. Is it right that we should continue to *represent* them as if they had the same value?

We can answer this quite easily by asking another question. I am planning to give you a cash gift of 10 dollars. Would you rather have 10 dollars today, or 10 dollars one year in the future? Of course you will answer that you would rather have 10 dollars today.

There are all sorts of reasons why this is the only logical answer. You might be killed in a road accident next week and thus not be around to collect and enjoy the 10 dollars in a year's time. If you have the 10 dollars today you can invest it, perhaps by putting it in a savings account, and thus it is likely to be worth more than 10 dollars in a year's time. Finally, we have to consider how inflation might affect the situation. You will not be able to buy as much of anything with a 10 dollar bill in a year's time as you can today. In financial terms, its purchasing power will be less, because prices will have risen with inflation.

Thus, while both bank notes still have the same face value, we are clearly right to regard the one that has travelled into the future as being somehow less valuable than the one we are still clutching in our hand. How should we represent this for financial purposes?

Discounting

There is a way in finance of distinguishing between the **present value** and the **future value** of a cash-flow. You are about to receive a cash gift as a present. This represents a cash-flow; 10 dollars will be flowing to you from a third party. Incidentally, it would also represent a cash-flow if it was you who had promised to pay the 10 dollars to somebody else. In that case it would be an outflow (cash flowing away from you) whereas in this case it will be an inflow (cash flowing towards you).

If we receive a cash-flow today of 10 dollars then clearly its *present* value is 10 dollars, since today is the present. Similarly, if we were to receive that cash-flow in one year's time instead, then its *future* value would be 10 dollars, since one year ahead lies in the future. We have just seen, however, that we must treat receiving 10 dollars in the future as if it were less valuable than receiving 10 dollars today, in the present. Therefore the *present* value of that future cash flow must be some amount less than 10 dollars. How might we try to calculate this, and why might we need to?

Let us deal with the second point first. Suppose instead of being offered the choice we have been considering up to now, you were offered instead the chance to have 1 cent today or 10 dollars in a year's time. This time, logic clearly operates in favour of waiting one year, and taking the chance of getting killed in a road accident in the meantime.

Yet if someone were to offer you $9.99 today, rather than 1 cent, you would take it. Put in financial terms, you would reckon that the present value of that future cash-flow, whatever it might be, would be less than $9.99 but more than 1 cent, so either way you would be getting a good deal.

So, if accepting $9.99 today would be a good deal, and so would rejecting 1 cent today, there must be a price at which your decision would change. That price would be the present value of the future cash-flow. Incidentally, this is exactly the sort of decision that has to be made on a routine basis in the world of finance and investment, so let us think about how we might go about arriving at an appropriate value.

We know that the present value of the future cash-flow will be less than its future value, and we know that its future value is 10 dollars. Thus, the present value must be less than that, which means we need to do something to 10 dollars that will reduce it in value. We are going to do this by multiplying 10 dollars by a number that is less than one. This lesser number is the **discount factor**. Thus:

Future value × discount factor = present value

The discount factor

So, the question now becomes: what is the discount factor? You will be glad to know that this question can be answered very easily, though sadly the ease of the answer is usually concealed behind what looks like a very forbidding mathematical formula. Let us leave that for later. If you can understand what is happening, then the formula can take care of itself.

The answer is that we first choose a **discount rate** to use, and we then perform a very simple calculation. We take 100 and divide it by a number that is equal to 100 plus the discount rate.

Calculating the discount factor

$$\text{Discount factor} = \frac{100}{100 + \text{the discount rate}}$$

So, if the discount rate were to be 10%, then the discount factor would be:

$$\frac{100}{110} = 0.909$$

Note

The financial notation for finding the discount factor is usually stated as:

$$\frac{1}{1 + r}$$

... but you will find it much easier to think of the simplified version above!

The discount rate

So, in order to find the discount factor, we need to know which discount rate to apply. How do we arrive at the right discount factor to use? Well, here we leave the realm of mathematics altogether for, you see, there often is no 'right' discount rate to use, certainly not in the sense of there being one right answer, with every other answer being wrong. So, how do we arrive at whatever discount rate we should use? Easy – we choose it ourselves!

Yes, it really is as simple as that. Of course, it has to a sensible choice, but as long as it can be defended with some rational argument then any rate will do. For example, you might decide that you would invest the 10 dollars if you had it today, and you know that your savings bank is currently offering an interest rate of 5%, so you choose 5% as the discount rate to reflect the added value that you are foregoing by *not* having the money available for investment today. (Incidentally, this value foregone is known as an **opportunity cost**.) Or you might focus more on the diminished purchasing power of 10 dollars in a year's time and settle upon, say, 3.8% as the discount rate if this seems a common assumption of the likely rate of inflation over the next year.

Most frequently, the rate chosen will have some very close relationship with how much it costs an investor to raise money, because of course this process will usually be applied to some financial investment or project rather than a simple gift. These will always involve at least one cash *out*flow in the beginning, for which you will be compensated by one or more *in*flows later on.

WACC

So, if a corporation was considering whether or not to build a new factory, something that would involve considerable capital expenditure in its early stages, it would be entirely reasonable to use its **weighted average cost of capital** (WACC), since this is how much it would cost the corporation to raise the necessary money. Remember, we looked at the raising of debt and equity finance in an earlier chapter. The cost to the corporation of issuing new equity (shares, stock) will be the additional dividend that it has to pay, while the cost of new debt will be the amount of additional loan interest that it has to pay. The phrase 'weighted average' means that we have to take into account how much of the total cost of capital each of these two elements represents. In other words, we have to add the amount of equity and debt together to see what proportion of the whole each represents. If, for example, equity represents 40% of capital and debt represents 60%, then we take 40% of the cost of equity and add it to 60% of the cost of debt.

Weighted average cost of capital (WACC)

Again, this is actually a simple calculation but it can seem off-putting by virtue of the formula involved. Let us look first at a worked example and then note the more formal statement of the principle below.

Simple example

A business wishes to calculate its WACC. It currently has borrowings of $120M and issued share capital of $80M. It is paying interest on its borrowings of 7%, and dividend to its shareholders of 6%.

The first step is to find the amount of total capital:

Total capital = debt + equity
Total capital = 120M + 80M = 200M

The next step is to add together the cost of equity and the cost of debt. In order to find these, we have to use the appropriate proportion of the total capital contributed by each of equity and debt.

We know that the proportion of total capital represented by debt is 60%, because:

$$\frac{120}{200} = \frac{60}{100}$$

(simply dividing both the top and the bottom by 2)

And we know that the proportion of total capital represented by equity is 40%, because:

$$\frac{80}{200} = \frac{40}{100}$$

(again, simply dividing both the top and the bottom by 2)

So we take 60% of the cost of debt and add it to 40% of the cost of equity to find the WACC:
60% of 7% is 4.2%, and 40% of 6% is 2.4%, so WACC = 6.6%

More complex example

This, however, ignores the effect of tax. Because loan interest is paid before tax, we must adjust the rate of interest used in our WACC to reflect this. Let us assume that the business is paying tax at 30%.

Whenever loan interest is paid, it is deducted from the profits of the business before calculating its tax liability. Thus any interest paid reduces the taxable profits of the business by an equal amount. This means that some amount of tax would have been payable but for the existence of the loan interest, but will not now be paid. This has to be set off against the headline cost of debt to arrive at an effective rate taking into account the tax advantage.

So, the effective cost of debt is not 7% but 70% of 7% (because 30% of this would otherwise have been taxable as profits), which is 4.9%.

So the tax-adjusted WACC would be 60% of 4.9%, plus 40% of 6%, which is 5.34%.

Formula

$$WACC = \frac{E}{V} Re + \frac{D}{V} (Rd \times 1 - T)$$

Where:
E is equity
D is debt
V is E + D
Re is the cost of equity
Rd is the cost of debt, and
T is the tax rate.

Hurdle rate

Just as a business might use its WACC as a logical discount rate in assessing a business project, so an investor might use some appropriate **hurdle rate**. This is essentially the minimum return that they would normally be prepared to accept for an investment of this nature. In the case of an investment fund, this will be the minimum return that the fund manager feels their own clients will be prepared to accept, plus any amount that the manager is planning to charge by way of fees. This may in turn be related to some hurdle rate within the fund itself, which the manager is obliged to achieve before being allowed to charge higher fees by way of performance-related remuneration.

Finding the present value of a cash-flow due in more than one year

So we now know how to calculate the present value of a cash-flow that we are due to receive in one year's time, and hopefully you will agree that it's not that difficult. In fact, the most difficult part is probably choosing which discount rate to use, which is nothing to do with mathematics at all.

Let's now turn our attention to the problem of calculating the present value of a cash-flow that is going to occur in the more distant future – say perhaps in three years' time instead of one year's time. Again, you will be glad to hear that there is a very straightforward way of doing this. You simply repeat what you have already done, but this time raise the discount factor to the **power** of the number of periods (in this case years) for which you wish to discount.

A note on powers

How powers work

Any time you see a little number in what is called superscript (in other words, above another number or symbol), it simply means that you multiply the full-size number by itself the number of times given by the smaller number.

For example, 3^2, which we would describe as 'three **squared**', means 3×3, and of course

$3 \times 3 = 9$.

And 3^3, which we would describe as 'three cubed', means $3 \times 3 \times 3$, and of course

$3 \times 3 \times 3 = 27$.

And so on. Incidentally, for any power above 3 we would simply say 'three to the power of' or 'three raised to the power of' whatever number we were using.

Example using a discount factor

Let us suppose that we want to find a discount factor using a discount rate of five. We have already seen that we would do this as follows:

$$\frac{100}{105} = 0.9524$$

But suppose we now want to find the same discount factor, but this time raised to the power of four. This would be expressed as:

$$\left(\frac{100}{105}\right)^4$$

Calculators have a rather nifty little button these days, which is marked ^, and which you can use to calculate a power. First, simply carry out the calculation within the brackets:

$100 \div 105 = 0.9524$

Then press ^4 = and you will see the answer, which is 0.8227. If you want to check this by doing the same thing in longhand, then:

$0.9524 \times 0.9524 \times 0.9524 \times 0.9524 = 0.8227$

The formula for multi-period discounting

Now that you already understand what is being done, hopefully the formula will not seem forbidding.

To find the present value (PV) of C_t, a cashflow occurring in t years' time,

$$PV = C_t \left(\frac{1}{1+r}\right)^t$$

Where C is the future value of the expected cash-flow,
t is the number of years into the future when it is expected to occur,
and r is the chosen discount rate. Remember, all this is saying is:

Step 1: calculate the discount factor by dividing 100 by 100 plus the discount rate.

Step 2: now raise the resulting number to the power of t, t being the number of years into the future when the cash-flow is expected to occur, and thus the number of periods for which you wish to discount.

Step 3: multiply the amount of the expected cash-flow by the number resulting from Step 2.

So, if we wish to find the present value of a cash-flow of $10, which we expect to receive in 5 years' time, discounted at a rate of 8%, then:

we first find the discount factor for one year:

$$\frac{100}{108} = 0.9259$$

Then we raise the discount factor to the power of 5:

$$0.9259^5 = 0.6805$$

Finally, we multiply the cash-flow by the discount factor to find the present value:

$$10 \times 0.6805 = 6.80$$

Finding the Net Present Value of multiple cash-flows

There is only one thing left to cover in looking at the basic concept of discounting, although in the next chapter we will be looking at a few specialized applications of this. We have looked so far at how to find the present value of a single cash-flow occurring in the future. In reality, though, very few investment situations will take this form. It is much more likely that we will be faced with multiple cash-flows, all occurring at different times. Not to worry! As we will see, we can use exactly the same techniques that we have already employed to find the present value of any number of cash-flows. Because this is taking something that relates to any number of cash-flows, but reducing them all to a single present value, it is known as the Net Present Value, or NPV.

The quickest way to understand what happens here is to see each of the individual annual cash-flows as ... er well, individual annual cash-flows actually. Work out the present value of each, then add up all the present values and the total will be the Net Present Value. And yes, it really is as simple as that. Let's take a look at an example.

Net Present Value example

Question

White Smile Corporation is considering whether to renew for five years a lease that is just about to expire on its distribution facility in Germany. A premium of 1M euros will be payable on the grant of a new lease. Thereafter, the facility is expected to generate the following net inflows (all figures in €000s):

Next year	€120
In Year 2	€365
In Year 3	€630
In Year 4	€825
In Year 5	€910

White Smile has asked you to calculate the Net Present Value of this project in order to help it decide whether to renew the lease. It informs you that its weighted average cost of capital is 6.5%.

Answer

First we need to calculate the discount factor for Year 1. Remember, this is just:

$$\left(\frac{100}{100 + r}\right)$$

So our Year 1 discount factor will be:

$$\frac{100}{106.5} = 0.9389$$

To find the discount factor for Year 2, $0.9389^2 = 0.8815$
To find the discount factor for Year 3, $0.9389^3 = 0.8277$
To find the discount factor for Year 4, $0.9389^4 = 0.7771$
To find the discount factor for Year 5, $0.9389^5 = 0.7296$

Now we just apply these:

TABLE 7.1

	Year 0	Year 1	Year 2	Year 3	Year 4	Year 5
Cash-flow	-1000	120	365	630	825	910
Discount factor		.9389	.8815	.8277	.7771	.7296
Present value	-1000	113	322	521	641	664

Now, by adding up the present value of each year's cash-flow, we can find the answer

NPV = €1.261M.

An even easier way...

If you are setting all of this up in a spreadsheet, then all you need is the Net Present Value function, which in Excel is:

=NPV(rate, range of cash-flows)

For rate you input the chosen discount rate as a percentage.

For range you highlight the cells that contain the present values (in the above example, the third line of figures).

Why is it important to be able to find the NPV?

There are two answers to this. One is rather basic and the other slightly more complicated, but each provides us with an important principle of finance.

First, if we are using our cost of capital or our investment hurdle rate as a discount rate, then any project or investment that has a positive NPV is an attractive one for us to pursue. Whatever the value of the business or investment fund may be today, then assuming the projections we have used actually come to pass, the value of the business or investment fund will be higher at the end of the projected period. This gives us our first principle:

Where an investment modelled at an appropriate discount rate produces a positive NPV, it should be accepted. Where it produces a negative NPV, it should be rejected.

However, real life is much more complex than this, and rather than a yes/no decision as to whether to accept one particular project, reality often demands that a choice be made between competing projects where, for example, there is insufficient capital available to pursue them all. Here another measure comes into play as well, but we will leave that for the next chapter. So far as NPV is concerned, the common-sense approach is to accept the available projects in descending order of their NPV. In other words, we accept the highest NPV first, and then come down the list accepting each in turn until we run out of available capital. So, our second principle is:

In the case of competing projects, both of which have a positive NPV, the project with the higher NPV should be preferred.

Please note that in practice this second principle is subject to all sorts of qualifications. If the project with the higher NPV would require a much larger investment than the other, for example, then the risk-budgeting process would have to be considered. Similarly, NPV ignores strategic business issues, public relations concerns, and legal and regulatory issues.

Compounding

Before we leave discounting, we should briefly consider compounding, which is its mirror image. With discounting we are considering how future values should be diminished. With compounding, we are considering how present values may be enhanced. Each demonstrates the time value of money, but working in different directions.

Suppose that at the beginning of the year you place $10 on deposit in a savings account that pays a 5% rate of interest. Let us ignore tax to keep things simple. How much do you have at the end of the year? Answer: $10.50.

You can arrive at this by calculating 5% of $10, which is 50 cents, and adding it to the $10. You can also do the same thing slightly more efficiently (from an arithmetical point of view) by multiplying $10 by the compounding equivalent of the discount factor. Remember, though, that we are doing things the other way round here, so this time the top of the factor has to be higher than the bottom, since we want to make the number bigger, not smaller. So here we use:

$$\frac{100 + r}{100}$$

$$\frac{105}{100} = 1.05$$

$$1.05 \times \$10 = \$10.50$$

Just as for discounting, we can do this over multiple periods by raising the factor to the power of the number of periods involved. Let's assume that we wanted to know how much the money would be worth if we left it in the savings account to accumulate for three years. In other words, we want to know the compound return. •

A note on compound returns

If I put $10 in a savings account at 10% rate of interest, then during the course of the year I will earn $1 of interest. However, if I leave the money sitting in the account then the interest that I earn during the second year will not be $1, because the starting value (the opening balance) of the account at the beginning of the second year will be not $10, but $11. The interest in Year 2 would therefore be 10% of $11, which is $1.10, so the closing balance at the end of the year, which will be the same as the opening balance for the next year, will be $12.10, and so on with each successive year.

For this reason, a compound return is sometimes referred to as interest upon interest, and this is in fact a very good way to think about it. If, in our above example, we were to withdraw our interest every year and spend it, we would only be earning a simple return. As we will see in a later chapter, a bond is a good example of a simple return, paying out an annual sum of cash. It is a simple return because this is paid out, not reinvested, and so there is no opportunity to earn 'interest upon interest'.

Thus a compound return should be much more attractive and desirable to an investor than a simple return of the same percentage rate. If you plot a compound return example, such as the one above, on a graph you will find that the value of your capital is expressed by an upward curve, whereas with a simple return it goes up in a straight line. The former is clearly preferable.

The opposite is also true, something that is often over-looked. Assume now that you are not the investor *earning* the return, but the investment or investment manager *providing* the return. Clearly it is much more difficult to supply a compound return of, say 10%, than a simple return of 10%, and for this reason we should value that investment or investment manager more highly.

This time, because we are compounding for three years, we need to use:

$$\left(\frac{100 + r}{100}\right)^3$$

$$\frac{105}{100} = 1.05$$

$$1.05^3 = 1.157$$

$$1.157 \times \$10 = \$11.57$$

Sunk costs

Before we move on, a quick note on what are called **sunk costs**. Because we are looking down the time tunnel into the future from today onwards, whatever happened in the past is immaterial. It is behind us so we cannot see it, since we are looking forwards. Thus if we are evaluating the NPV of a project on which certain costs have already been incurred in the past, we ignore those costs. This may seem instinctively wrong, but if you think about *why* we perform NPV calculations then hopefully it may seem less so.

Remember that in many cases we are looking to choose between competing uses for a limited amount of capital. We make that decision, rightly, on which is likely to produce future cash-flows of the highest NPV. Thus we would evaluate a brand-new project and an existing one directly against each other. Of course, we may well want to use a higher discount rate for the new project if we feel that it is subject to greater uncertainty, but in cash-flow terms we look at both starting today. It is the NPV that is of concern to us, not the overall return on investment over the life of the project. It may actually be advantageous to close down the existing project and divert new investment elsewhere. It is only by ignoring sunk costs that we can properly make such decisions.

Incidentally, one of the most frequent mistakes in business is to ignore this basic principle of finance. The next time you hear someone say something like 'But we've spent X on this already', reach for this book and explain to them why sunk costs are irrelevant. If that doesn't work, try hitting them over the head with it.

Payback periods

Payback calculation is another commonly used project analysis tool. Briefly, it means calculating the length of time that the project or investment is likely to take to pay back your initial capital in full. It used to be widely employed, particularly by those who did not understand discounting and present values. It is nonetheless a useful tool, and it would be wrong to brand it as simplistic. Similarly, however, it would be wrong to use it in isolation. It would clearly be illogical to accept a project only because it had a short payback period if another one had a dramatically higher NPV.

Perhaps payback period may be better viewed as a means of evaluating the uncertainty of a project, and thus the appropriate discount factor that should be used. If one project may take 10 years to pay back its capital, while another may take only five, that argues not for automatically accepting the latter, but for modelling both sensibly against each other, with a hefty premium on the discount rate of the former to represent the higher return that we would expect in order to reward us for accepting the greater degree of uncertainty. It is in fact routinely used in this way, for example, when evaluating infrastructure projects.

Summary

- When cash-flows occur in the future, they are assumed to be of less value than cash-flows of the same value occurring in the present. Discounting is a way of assessing their present value.
- Discounting is performed by multiplying the future value of the cash-flow by a discount factor.
- The discount factor is found by using 100 / 100 + r, where r is the chosen discount rate.
- The discount rate can be any choice that can be rationally supported according to the purposes for which the analysis is being performed. The inflation rate and the savings rate are two possible examples.
- Where the analysis is being performed for business or investment purposes, then it is customary to use the organization's weighted average cost of capital (WACC) or target rate of investment return (the hurdle rate).
- Discounting over multiple periods is achieved by raising the discount factor to the power of the number of periods involved.
- A Net Present Value for a project or investment is found by modelling the present value of each individual year's cash-flows, and then adding them together.
- In principle, we should accept any project that, if discounted at an appropriate rate, shows a positive NPV.
- In principle, in the case of competing projects that cannot all be accepted, we should choose the projects with the highest NPVs.
- Compounding is the opposite of discounting, showing how the present value of a capital sum will grow in the future if invested at a given rate of compound return.
- Costs that have already been incurred in the past (sunk costs) should be ignored when calculating the NPV of a project.
- Payback period is also a relevant consideration, but it should be used sensibly, and never in isolation. It may be better thought of as a tool in assessing the relative uncertainty of a project, and thus the appropriate discount factor to be employed.

08
Special uses of discounting

N ow that we understand the basic principles of discounting and compounding, it is time to turn to two or three particular applications of them, which we can use to arrive at meaningful answers in various special situations. As always, though, it is important that we should first understand the *what* and the *why*, before we dive into the *how*. Let's start by examining something that the world of finance calls an **annuity**.

Incidentally, with final salary (**Defined Benefit**) pension schemes being closed down left, right and centre, this is something that in the future is going to play a vitally important role in everybody's life. You see, a switch to money purchase (**Defined Contributions**) pension schemes means that on retirement you are given whatever pot of pension money you have managed to accumulate, and are obliged to buy an annuity with all or most of it, depending on which country you live in. Sadly, almost nobody understands how annuities are calculated (and thus how they are priced) – a good example of a decision of vital importance to our lives that cannot be made on an informed basis without some understanding of finance.

Annuities

What is an annuity?

An annuity is a fixed sum of money that is paid each year for a certain number of years, hence its name, from the Latin '*anno*' for 'year'. So a 10-year annuity of $1,000 means that you would receive $1,000 a year every year for 10 years, after which the payments would stop.

The amount of years (sometimes called a 'term of years') may be fixed in some way other than by a number. For example, the money purchase pension schemes referred to above usually result in an annuity being granted either for the lifetime of the annuitant (the person receiving the money), or for the joint lifetime of them and their partner, in which case the payments will stop only when they are both dead. This is a sensible arrangement conferring both financial security and peace of mind.

Though it is now much less common than it used to be, you will also find annuities being granted under the terms of someone's will, and in the case of an annuity to a wife, it may stipulate that it is for her lifetime or until she remarries, which is another way of fixing the term of years. This sort of annuity attracted a lot of criticism over the years, the argument against it being that the husband was trying to control his wife's life from beyond the grave. It is of course a staple of Victorian fiction, perhaps most famously in George Eliot's *Middlemarch*, in which the misanthropic Edward Casaubon adds the vicious codicil to his will that his wife will lose her inheritance if she marries a certain named individual. Romantics everywhere will be happy to learn that our heroine ignores the provision and marries him anyway, thus sacrificing her fortune but gaining (we trust) her happiness.

This sort of annuity of course became open to abuse with the arrival of the permissive society, since a couple could simply live together without getting married. Thanks to the poet Philip Larkin we can date this change in social mores exactly. Sexual intercourse, he informed his readers, began in 1963, noting sadly that this all came rather late for him as he was born in 1922. In consequence, the wealthy weasels of the legal profession began to advise their clients to add the words 'or cohabit'. This of course raises the prospect of lengthy and expensive legal proceedings to determine whether a couple are actually cohabiting or not, which suits the members of the legal profession just fine, since they are likely to become even wealthier in the process, whatever the outcome.

Why should we want to find the present value of an annuity?

Suppose that you are the sort of feckless young Regency buck who is likely to feature in literature of the best bodice-ripping variety. An elderly uncle, of whose existence you were but dimly aware, dies on his sugar plantation in the West Indies and, apart from making provision for a few mulatto mistresses and the statutory mad wife locked in the attic of his country estate in Gloucestershire, leaves you an annuity of £100 a year for 10 years.

Your initial feelings of joyful surprise give way, however, to a rather unworthy irritation that the old boy should not have made it a lump sum, since you have many debts of a rather pressing nature, and are anxious to discharge these before nasty, rough-looking men come looking for you to do very unwelcome things to the softer and more delicate parts of your anatomy. As you bemoan your fate to your drinking buddies that evening, one of them looks up from the barmaid's cleavage and tells you to go and see that nice Mr Rothschild, who is an absolute wizard with annuities, and will surely have the answer to all your problems. So you duly go in search of that nice Mr Rothschild, and he spares you enough time from financing the Napoleonic Wars and saving the Bank of England from a nasty run on sterling to offer you a lump sum today in exchange for signing over to him the right to receive your annuity for the next 10 years.

By now you will be astute enough, dear reader, to know what that nice Mr Rothschild is up to. He has worked out the present value of the annuity, and has offered the feckless young man a lump sum that is large enough to be tempting to a cash-strapped man about town, but is considerably less than that present value. Sadly, as feckless young men tend not to read books of this nature, he is oblivious to this fact, thanks Mr Rothschild kindly, pockets the folding stuff he is offered, and goes off happily in search of the more pressing of his creditors.

How do we find the net present value of an annuity?

Since an annuity is simply a stream of cash-flows occurring in different years, we could simply discount each year's cash-flow to a present value, and then add all of these up to find the NPV, just as we did in the previous chapter. With a 10-year annuity this would be just about manageable, but suppose it was, say, a 50-year annuity instead? Any such exercise would rapidly become a very lengthy and tedious calculation. Wouldn't it be so much easier if there was some convenient shorthand method available? Well, there is.

The bad news is that it involves a formula. The good news is that the only input values you need are the amount of the annuity, the number of years for which it is going to run, and the discount rate. All of these we will know, the first two because we will be told them and the third because we choose it ourselves.

Step One

The first bit will sound very familiar, as we have done something just like it before. We take the number 1 and add the rate to it. Next we raise it to the power of the number of years.

Remember that in the last chapter we showed exactly this same principle but using the number 100 instead of the number 1. This was because many people find it simpler to work with numbers in this way rather than adding a percentage rate to 1, which is what the formula really requires. However, this time we are in danger of getting some unmanageably large numbers if we use 100 instead of 1, so it is important that we should now understand the idea behind adding a discount rate to the number 1.

The key is to remember that 5% expressed as a number is 0.05, just as 50% (which is of course 10 times as large) is 0.5. 75% would be 0.75, 90% would be 0.9 and so on. Thus, if we add 5% to 1 we get 1.05. This is the stumbling block that prevents many people from properly understanding discounting and compounding. Hopefully this explanation will allow people to grasp the fact that percentages are not some arcane mystery, but actually quite simple.

The reason that we used 100 in the last chapter was in the hope of making things clearer by making them bigger. If you think about it, if we make everything 100 times bigger then 1 becomes 100, and 0.05 becomes 5 (if it's easier to think in these terms, remember that to multiply by 10 we move the decimal point one place to the right, and to multiply by 100 we move it two places to the right). Thus:

$$\frac{1}{1.05} = \frac{100}{105}$$

Can you see that they are effectively the same thing? Try the division for yourself. Both return the same answer: 0.9524.

So, let's continue. To remind you of the first step, we take the number 1 and add the rate to it. Next we raise it to the power of the number of years.

Assuming a £100 annuity for 10 years, and assuming that Mr Rothschild's cost of capital is 5%:

$$1 + 0.05 = 1.05, \text{ and}$$

$$1.05^{10} = 1.6289$$

Step Two

We take the number 1 and divide it by the result of Step One.

$$\frac{1}{1.6289} = 0.6139$$

Step Three

We take the result of Step Two and subtract it from 1.

$$1 - 0.6139 = 0.3861$$

Step Four

We take the amount of the annual payment, and divide it by the discount rate.

$$\frac{100}{0.05} = 2,000$$

Step Five

To find the Net Present Value of the annuity, we multiply the result of Step Four by the result of Step Three.

$$2,000 \times 0.3861 = 772$$

Yes, it really is as straightforward as that. The accompanying note shows the formula. It might be helpful to look at it in conjunction with the above step by step process. Can you see how we are starting within the innermost brackets and working our way outwards? See how terrifying the formula seems when we look at it in isolation, and yet how simple the process really is when you adopt a step by step approach.

The annuity formula

We find the present value of an annuity by:

$$PV = \frac{A}{r}\left(1 - \frac{1}{(1+r)^n}\right)$$

Where:

PV is the present value

A is the annual amount payable

r is the discount rate, and

n is the number of years for which the annuity is to be paid.

Note: In some books you may see C used instead of A, and i instead of r. It is submitted that the above notation is more sensible and thus also easier to remember.

Incidentally, do you think that Mr Rothschild offered the young man nearly £800 for his annuity? It doesn't seem very likely, does it?

Calculating the present value of an annuity using Excel

Using an Excel spreadsheet, there is a very convenient shorthand method of calculating the present value of an annuity using the PV financial function. First, construct a simple three-cell section containing respectively the discount rate (r), the number of years (n) and the annual payment (A). Now, in the cell that you wish to use to calculate the present value, type:

=PV(r,n,A)

If you do this using the values:

$r = 5\%$

$n = 10$, and

$A = 100$

then you should arrive at the answer that appears in the text: 772. Note, however, that there is one important difference. The Excel function calculates the price you should be prepared to *pay* for an annuity, not the amount for which you should be prepared to *sell* it. Thus it will return a negative figure: -772, since it thinks of this as a potential negative cash-flow, an outflow. To correct this, simply insert a minus sign at the front of the formula thus:

=-PV(r,n,A)

(Remember that if we multiply one negative number by another negative number, the answer will always be a positive number.)

Perpetuities

What is a perpetuity?

A **perpetuity** is an annuity that will last forever. Instead of being bound by a term of years, the payments stretch away down the time tunnel to infinity itself. Of course, there are very few instances where this actually happens in practice. An undated government bond would be one example, though strictly speaking these are not 'perpetual' since they can be redeemed by the government at any time. Another possibility might be the income stream that might be expected from land once it is built upon, subject to regular repairs and rebuilding. However, the 'perpetual' nature of this, at least in respect of residential property, has been seriously eroded by leasehold reform in certain countries, most notably the UK.

Nonetheless, the calculating of perpetuities is a valuable function in finance. In particular, there are arguments for their use when assessing the value of a business.

How do we calculate the present value of a perpetuity?

Step One

Choose your discount rate and divide it into the amount of the annual payment. So, if we wanted to discount a perpetuity of 100 by 5%, then:

$$\frac{100}{0.05} = 2,000$$

Step Two

There is no Step Two. The present value of a perpetuity of 100 discounted at 5% is 2,000. Yes, it really is that easy. Incidentally, can you see that dividing something by 5% is the same thing as multiplying it by 20 (because 5% goes into 100% 20 times)? If not, don't worry.

How do we deal with payments that may grow over time?

What happens when we have a regular payment that does not stay the same, but grows over time? For example, suppose our young man's uncle had been concerned to protect his nephew against the effect of inflation by stipulating that his 10-year annuity would increase by 3% a year.

There is a very simple rule here, which uses something called the **Gordon Growth Model**, named after the man who developed it. Simply put, this says that whenever we are using a discount rate to value either an annuity or a perpetuity, we should deduct the anticipated rate of growth from the discount rate before applying it as appropriate. While this principle holds equally true for both annuities and perpetuities, it is easier to see it at work on a perpetuity since this is so much the shorter process. Imagine a perpetuity of 100, which again we want to discount by 5%, but this time we are anticipating that the amount payable will increase by 3% a year.

Step One

We deduct the growth rate from the discount rate:

$5 - 3 = 2$

Step Two

We use this new rate in our present value calculation in place of the original one:

$$\frac{100}{0.02} = 5,000$$

So, by building in an assumption of growth then, not surprisingly, the present value has also grown. Again, can you see how dividing by 2% is the same as multiplying by 50 (because 2% goes into 100% 50 times)?

The Gordon Growth Model

The model was created in 1959 by Myron Gordon, who was at that time an Associate Professor at MIT, as a means of valuing public companies. It assumes that the value of a company is the Net Present Value of all its future cash-flows to its shareholders; in other words, the dividends that it generates.

   Like most models developed by finance academics it is difficult to reconcile with what happens in the real world, but when studying finance you just have to learn to ignore this. Its shortcomings are obvious. To state but a few:

- It assumes that investors hold shares only for dividends, rather than in the expectation of capital gain driven by investor sentiment.
- It assumes that the base amount of future dividends is known and will remain constant.
- It assumes that the company's dividend policy will never alter.
- It assumes that the rate of growth can be known, and will remain constant.
- It requires a growth rate that is less than the cost of capital.

A simplified form of the model may be stated thus:

$$V = \frac{D}{(k - g)}$$

Where V is the value of the company,
   D is the amount of dividend paid by the company,
   k is a constant, representing the company's cost of equity, and
   g is the anticipated rate of growth of D.

In considering perpetuities in general, the formula will often be seen as:

$$PV = \frac{C}{(r - g)}$$

Where C represents the annual payment,
   r is the discount rate originally chosen,
   g is the anticipated rate of growth, and
   $(r - g)$ is the discount rate actually applied in the calculation

The Internal Rate of Return

Calculating an **Internal Rate of Return** (IRR) gives us the compound return of a series of cash-flows over time. We will learn more about compound returns a little later, but for the moment let us look at what an IRR is and how to calculate it.

We saw that an NPV is usually calculated as part of what might be called 'go/don't go' decision making, and is effective in that whenever a positive NPV is calculated then in principle it makes sense to undertake the investment or project. There are situations, however, where the NPV is not really seen as such a useful measure (though it probably still *is*; we are talking here about custom and attitudes). For example, when assessing the likely performance of a cash-flow based investment, such as an infrastructure project, or the likely performance of an investment fund containing several or many investments, investors seem more comfortable with the concept of what *return* they will make, rather than a dry old NPV. In part this is because they are used to investment returns being expressed in percentages although, as we will see, this can itself give rise to huge misunderstandings.

Another issue is that NPV does not always tell the whole story, at least not if you use it as a single headline number without showing people the full workings (which many boards of directors or trustees seem unwilling to look at anyway). Two projects may show exactly the same NPV but require very different amounts of capital, or show very different cash-flow profiles over time. As a headline number, then, IRR works better, particularly if your audience is not one that is willing or able to dive into the minutiae of your analysis.

How do we calculate an IRR?

There is good news and bad news here. The good news is that we proceed exactly as if we were calculating an NPV, setting out the actual amounts of cash-flows anticipated over the life of the investment or project in the years when they are expected to occur. Incidentally, the only requirement that must be followed in every case is that the initial cash-flow has to be negative. Normally this will not be a problem as the cost of the investment will be paid up front, but it is worth looking out for, since you may sometimes have to change the polarity of what is happening. For example, the initial cash-flows of an investment fund will usually be positive, as it draws down its investors' money prior to making investments. One way around this is to look instead at the investors' cash-flows, which will of course be negative in the first instance as they pay their capital into the fund.

Our investment fund worked example makes a fundamental point that it is very important to understand and remember. Both NPV and IRR calculations operate upon *cash-flows*, and only upon cash-flows. Thus unrealized gains and losses, where investments may have been written up or down, are not taken into account. You wait until the investment is actually sold, and then you enter into your workings the amount of cash actually received at that point.

The bad news is that although the set-up of our calculation is exactly the same, the execution is different. Only qualified bad news, though, since calculating an IRR is exactly the opposite of calculating an NPV, so if you understand one you must also understand the other.

Remember that when calculating an NPV we *choose* a discount rate in order to *calculate* an NPV? Well, when calculating an IRR, we do the opposite. We *choose* an NPV in order to *calculate* a discount rate.

The NPV that we choose is zero, so the discount rate we are after is whichever one will reduce the NPV of all the cash-flows to zero. There is only one way to calculate this, which is by running the calculation over and over again with a different discount rate each time until the NPV result is zero. This is known as **iteration**, which means doing the same calculation again and again, and it is the only method by which it is possible to calculate an IRR.

Calculating an IRR with Excel

As you can see in the text of this chapter, the only way to calculate an IRR is by iteration. Fortunately, a computer does this very well and extremely quickly compared to a human being. It is important to realize, however, that this is *all* the computer is doing, albeit very efficiently.

Remember that in order to calculate an IRR, on the computer just as much as manually with a calculator, you first need to produce a stream of cash-flows. This means that you have to arrange all the cash-flows, whether positive or negative, of a particular year in the same column and add them all up to arrive at a net cash-flow for each year.

Then you can run the Excel IRR function, which is '=IRR(guess,range)'. 'Guess' is voluntary and may usually be safely ignored. 'Range' involves highlighting the cells in which the stream of cash-flows appear. At the risk of stating the obvious, these should all be adjacent to each other in a continuous sequence.

Remember that the first cash-flow must be negative. This is the most frequent cause of an error message.

An IRR represents the compound return of an investment or project over its lifetime, and is probably the most useful tool in our financial toolbox. IRRs also illustrate the most important feature of the time value of money. If you try running some IRR calculations on any series of cash-flows you will find that you have to add larger and larger numbers each time you extend the cash-flow series by a further year. This is because the effect of what happens in later years is much less than what happens in the first few years. Remember the time tunnel: the later cash-flows are treated as being much smaller, by being discounted over more periods.

Annuities and DC pension schemes

We will return to the concept of an IRR when we discuss compound returns generally in a later chapter. For the moment, let us turn as promised to the matter of annuities purchased pursuant to Defined Contribution (money purchase) pension schemes. Here, the way in which an annuity is priced can make a very real difference to somebody's life.

With companies around the world either withdrawing or talking of withdrawing Defined Benefit (final salary) pension plans and leaving their employees instead with only DC cover, this is an issue that is likely to grow every more significant in the future. Yet, worryingly, many pension fund members do not seem to have woken up to the very severe changes in their personal circumstances that this may cause.

Let us take the same notional individual in each case. They are retiring age 65, and are expecting pension provision for themselves and their spouse for the rest of their joint lives. Their salary on leaving employment is £60,000. In each case, the survivor of the two dies in 30 years' time.

Case One

In the first case, they are a member of a DB scheme and entitled to an index-linked pension of two-thirds final salary for life, or half final salary for joint lives. They decide on the latter option. Incidentally, 'index-linked' in this context means that it will increase each year automatically in line with inflation.

So, our two pensioners receive an annual amount of £30,000 initially, increasing each year by the rate of inflation. Can you see that because the amount increases by the rate of inflation, and the rate of inflation would be the most likely discount rate for us to choose (because we would be concerned as to how the purchasing power of £30,000 would diminish over time), then the present value (today) of each future payment will always be £30,000? So, the cost in present value terms to a third party (the pension fund) of providing that pension will be:

£30,000 × 30 = £900,000

So, arguably, this also represents the value to our pensioners of that pension entitlement.

Case Two

In the second case, the company that employs our pensioner closes the DB scheme just before their retirement date and credits them instead with the value that their pension contributions have accrued over the years. Let us say for the sake of argument that this is £300,000.

Our pensioner scans the financial press and discovers that a joint life index-linked annuity will yield about 3.5%. So, their annual income will be:

£300,000 × 3.5% = £10,500

So we can see that our two pensioners will now only be receiving just over a third of what they might otherwise have been expecting.

Why so little? If you run the annuity formula on a 30-year annuity of £10,500 at 3.5% you will find that the present value is roughly £193,000. On the other hand, the present value of a *perpetuity* of £10,500 at 3.5% is exactly £300,000. So why is the annuity provider selling an annuity for the price of a perpetuity?

The answer, they would argue, is inflation risk. While they would have to be pretty poor investors not to make a return of 3.5%, if they are unable to make a return of 3.5% *plus the rate of inflation*, there is a chance they could suffer a loss. It is for the reader to decide whether forcing the annuitant to take a hit of over a third of the present value of their pension pot is a fair price to charge for this risk, whatever it might be.

Where it comes to non-index linked (level) annuities, the situation is much more clear-cut. Suppose that our couple are both aged 65 and decide to take out a level annuity. Again, they consult the financial press and find that the appropriate rate is 6.6%. In other words, their pot of £300,000 will now produce an annual income of £19,800.

This sounds a lot better – as long as they are ignorant of annuity calculations like our young man who was desperate for ready cash. The present value of supplying an annuity of £19,800 at 6.6% for 30 years is about £256,000. In order to bring the present value up to £300,000 it is necessary to increase the term of the annuity from 30 years to 95 years, so that the annuity provider would only lose money if the last surviving annuitant reached the ripe old age of 155.

Again, the annuity provider would argue that they are taking a risk. If they are unable to generate a compound return of 6.6%, then they stand to make a loss, and the difference between £300,000 and £256,000 is designed to give them some sort of safety margin. Yet this time they do not need to worry about inflation. They only need to make 6.6% in absolute terms, not real terms, and how difficult is that? For example, staying with our UK example, the 10-year total return on the FTSE 250 index to May 2010, a period that included two stock market crashes, was 7.7%.

Whatever the case, while these are all matters of commercial judgement, and thus it is impossible to say for certain that they have got their figures wrong, it does seem appropriate to suggest that those providing annuities understand present value calculations, while those who are forced to purchase their products do not.

Calculating the compound return (IRR) earned on an investment fund

At the beginning of Year 1, Bob buys 100 units in a mutual fund for $9.56 each. At the end of the same year, he receives a cash distribution of $48. At the end of the next three years he receives $46, $53 and $38 respectively. At the end of Year 1, the redemption value of his units has fallen to $9.51. At the end of the next three years respectively, the quoted redemption values are $9.48, $9.50 and $9.52. He redeems his units towards the end of Year 5 at a price per unit of $9.53, but just before any distribution is paid for that year. Calculate the IRR on his investment.

When looking at a problem like this it is very easy to panic and fall into the trap that has been set for you. Trap? Yes. There is a red herring in this example, something that is completely irrelevant for our purposes, and that we should be ignoring completely. What is it?

The redemption values during the lifetime of the investment. Remember that an IRR is a measure of the compound return represented by *cash-flows*. Therefore, in order to calculate an IRR we must first construct our stream of relevant cash-flows. Unrealized gains or losses, while treated as being very important in calculating periodic returns or in calculating asset values for accounting purposes, are completely irrelevant when it comes to looking at compound returns based upon cash-flows.

So, we must begin by setting out all relevant cash-flows, since these are what we need to find the IRR. To make the calculations easier, let's assume that all cash-flows take place at the end of the year in which they occur.

TABLE 8.1

	Year 0	Year 1	Year 2	Year 3	Year 4	Year 5
Outflows ($)	-956					
Inflows ($)		48	46	53	38	953
Net cash-flow	-956	48	46	53	38	953
IRR (%)		?				

Once we have set out the relevant cash-flows we must check to see if we satisfy the one basic requirement for calculating an IRR. Yes, the cash-flow of the first period is negative. So we can proceed.

Remember that what we must do is to discount the cash-flows of each period by the same discount rate each time many times over, changing the discount rate each time, until we find the discount rate that produces a Net Present Value of zero. That discount rate will be the IRR. The recommended method is to start with a rate that is obviously too large, then use one that is obviously too small, and work inwards. Let's see how this works out in practice.

Let's take first 20% and then 2%. Remember that in each case we are going to calculate our discount factor as $\frac{1}{1+r}$ or, if it is easier for you to think in these terms, $\frac{100}{100+r}$. So, in the first case, our discount rate will be:

$$\frac{1}{1.2} = 0.8333$$

In the second case, our discount rate will be:

$$\frac{1}{1.02} = 0.9804$$

In each case, of course, we will raise our discount rate to the power of the number of years over which we are discounting, so if we are discounting at 20% for three years then the discount rate will be 0.83333 = 0.5786, and so on.

TABLE 8.2

Discounting at 20%

	Year 0	Year 1	Year 2	Year 3	Year 4	Year 5
Net cash-flow	-956	48	46	53	38	953
Discount factor	1.0	0.8333	0.6944	0.5786	0.4822	0.4018
Discounted cash-flow	-956.00	40.00	31.94	30.66	18.32	382.91

If we add all these DCFs together, we get a negative NPV: approximately minus $452. So, we have obviously taken too high a discount rate, as we suspected, and need to try a smaller one.

TABLE 8.3

Discounting at 2%

	Year 0	Year 1	Year 2	Year 3	Year 4	Year 5
Net cash-flow	-956	48	46	53	38	953
Discount factor	1.0	0.9804	0.9612	0.9423	0.9239	0.9058
Discounted cash-flow	-956.00	47.06	44.22	49.94	35.11	863.20

This time we get a *positive* NPV of about $83, so in this case we know that our discount rate was too low and should be increased. So we would try again, perhaps with 10% and 3%, and then again, perhaps with 8% and 4%. In order to save time, the final answer should be 3.89%.

Summary

- There are three specific applications of discounting that must be learnt: annuities, perpetuities and IRRs.
- An annuity represents the payment of a fixed sum of money every year for a certain number of years.
- A perpetuity represents the payment of a fixed sum of money every year forever.
- In each case, a present value can be calculated, though this will of course be directly affected by whatever discount rate is chosen. Someone looking to sell an annuity will argue for a low discount factor to justify a high price. Somebody looking to buy an annuity will wish to use a high discount rate, resulting in a low price.
- In each case, it is possible to build into the present value calculation an assumption that, rather than staying the same each year, the annual payment will grow by some specified percentage.
- In either case, we calculate the Net Present Value by choosing a fixed discount rate by which to discount all the relevant cash-flows. Thus the NPV is found by reference to the discount rate.
- An IRR represents the compound return on a stream of cash-flows. The only essential requirement is that the first in the series of cash-flows should be negative.
- We calculate an IRR by choosing a fixed NPV (zero), instead of a fixed discount rate. In this case, the discount rate is found by reference to the NPV. The discount rate that produces an NPV of zero is the IRR, and is found by iteration (performing the calculation over and over again using a different discount rate each time).
- It is important to remember that an IRR is a pure cash-flow return measure, and therefore non cash-flow items, such as unrealized gains and losses, are irrelevant.

09
Risk

As we discussed in the first chapter, there are three main problems that get in the way when trying to learn about finance. One is that finance academics seem to believe that finance is simply a branch of mathematics, and thus frighten us off with all manner of terrifying formulae. The second is that, perhaps because of this, they never take the trouble to explain the concepts that lie behind the formulae. The third problem is that they sometimes ascribe to a word a completely different meaning from that applied to it by the rest of us who speak the English language.

The word 'risk' is a perfect example of this. Many who have studied finance as part of a wider course of study, perhaps for an MBA, finish their finance lectures just as unhappy and confused as they were at the beginning. Not because they are unable to master the calculations that are required of them, but because they are totally unable to see what useful function they serve. This is entirely the fault of those who teach finance, who seem to have lost sight of two essential truths that apply to those who seek to impart knowledge. First, your primary duty is to communicate; if you cannot communicate, or even worse if you confuse, frighten or simply bore your audience, then you cannot hope to teach them anything.

Second, if you use a word in a specific sense that is known only to you, then it is almost inevitable that you *will* simply confuse your audience. It is like setting up your own secret society with its own ritualistic phrases, but never allowing anybody else to join. It may make you feel very superior, but at the expense of nobody being able to understand what you are talking about. Sadly, in many fields, not just finance, the use of obscure and even self-invented language by academics seems to have become obligatory. 'If you can't understand what I'm saying,' the message seems to be, 'then it's because you're very stupid and I'm very clever.'

Understand this difference of meaning, and you are a long way towards understanding risk. Understand risk and you are a long way towards understanding finance, since risk is its most basic and essential building block. When we measure the 'risk' of an investment in a finance class, or as part of some financial analysis, we are not measuring the risk of that investment at all, but something completely different. Yes, that is a nonsense but we have to do it anyway. It is like knowing the words of the Lord's Prayer even if you don't actually believe in God. Since the world of finance refuses to use 'risk' in any sensible everyday sense, then we have to make the effort to understand what they *do* actually mean by it.

It is sometimes referred to as 'financial risk', presumably to make a distinction with the everyday meaning, but even this is unhelpful, since there is much financial risk that falls outside this very narrow specialist usage. A good example would be default or counterparty risk, but others would include terrorism, interest rates, inflation, and even the weather.

What do we mean by 'risk'?

Look up the word 'risk' in a dictionary and you will find some such definition as 'The chance that something unpleasant or unwelcome may occur'. If we risk going out without a raincoat, for example, then the unpleasant thing that may occur is that we get soaked to the skin if it does actually rain. We may try to assess the chance of this actually happening by listening to the weather forecast or gazing at the sky. Or we might seek to remove the risk by carrying an umbrella. Alternatively, we might decide simply not to take the risk at all, by staying at home instead.

What does the world of finance mean by 'risk'?

In a word, volatility. More precisely, the volatility of historic returns. Let us explore what this means, and how we go about calculating it.

What is 'volatility'? Well, it conveys the idea of change. In chemistry, for example, it refers to the readiness with which a solid or liquid changes into a gas. In more everyday speech we talk of a person being 'volatile' meaning that they have rapidly changing moods and/or are prone to change their mind rapidly. We talk of a situation being 'volatile' when there is a chance that it could change suddenly and dramatically with explosive consequences; the chance of a mass demonstration turning into a riot, for example.

In finance, 'volatility' could also be thought of as conveying the idea of change, in that it expresses the extent to which the rate of return of an asset moves within a certain range over time, with the worst return usually being a negative number and the best return being a positive number. We can calculate this sort of volatility by using mathematics, or more specifically statistics. It is important that we should understand the underlying principles here, and exactly what processes are being used.

Again, this is something that quite understandably frightens people off. Again, though, it is something that, when stripped of the jargon and the Greek symbols, we can reduce to simple logic and arithmetic that anybody can understand. Let's start by looking at the idea of an **average**, or **mean**.

Calculating an average or mean

An average and a mean are two different words for exactly the same thing, by the way. Which one you choose to use will depend partly upon which shore of the Atlantic Ocean you were inhabiting as you grew up, and partly upon the level to which you studied maths. Finding an average is one way of handling data, perhaps data that have been collected from a **sample**. So, in order to illustrate what happens, let's put together a notional sample of data. Imagine that we have been asked to find the average height of a group of 10 schoolchildren. As a first step we physically measure their heights and record the results in centimetres. We will end up with something like Table 9.1.

TABLE 9.1 Height data sample

Name	Height (cm)
Maria	148
Gaston	180
Xavier	154
Carol	153
Peter	173
Samantha	161
Lisa	155
William	176
James	178
Francesca	156

Number of observations: 10
NOTE A collection of data such as this is called a sample. Each item of data within the sample is called an observation.

Calculating the average is really very easy. We simply add up all the individual observations and then divide by the number of them. So, in this case, the heights of the individual children add up to 1,634 centimetres, and when we divide that by the number of children (10) we arrive at an average height of 163.4 centimetres. Again, please note that when dividing by 10, all we have to do is move the decimal point one place to the left. It may help to think of 1,634 as 1,634.0 or even 1,634.00, which are simply different ways of expressing the same number. While all are mathematically valid, we of course tend to leave off any zeros to the right of a decimal point when using a number for everyday purposes.

TABLE 9.2 Calculating an average or mean

	Individual observations
	148
	180
	154
	153
	173
	161
	155
	176
	178
	156
Total	1,634
Divide by number of observations	10
Average (mean)	163.4

NOTE Note that there is no individual observation that is the same height as the average. The average is simply a calculated mathematical output.

Calculating volatility

So, we have our average, or mean. We now need to turn to the idea of volatility. Once again, finance has unfortunately not chosen a particularly good word to describe this, since as we have seen, in most other fields it carries a strong sense of 'change'. In finance, however, it describes the extent to which individual observations tend to cluster around the average. If we are thinking in terms of perhaps the annual returns of an investment over time, then it may be more appropriate to think of 'movement' (particularly if the return is based purely upon the price of an asset such as gold as it goes up and down), or 'uncertainty of outcome'.

It is essentially the latter that finance attempts to calculate – the range within which the return of an asset is likely to fall when measured for any particular year (or quarter, or month, or even day). This range is expressed as a distance from the average, whether greater or lesser.

It may help to express this graphically. If we think of the average return of an asset when measured over the last 20 years being 6.3%, then if we take two different observations, say 2.4% and 8.1%, then they will lie to the left and right of the average respectively. The first will be 3.9% away to the left, while the second will be 1.8% away to the right.

FIGURE 9.1 Distance from the average (or mean)

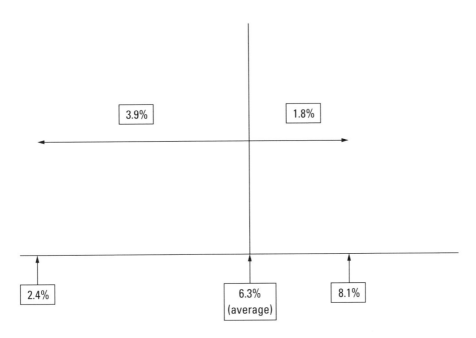

So, if we think of all the individual observations of our children's heights being positioned in the same way, some of them will lie to the left of 163.4 cm, while others will lie to the right of it. As mentioned above, in this case no observation will fall exactly on the average. This is common in sampling of this nature. For one thing, we are only recording the heights in discrete intervals of 1 centimetre, while the average includes a portion of a centimetre.

What we need to do is to find some measure of the likely width of the whole sample when viewed in this way; how closely or distantly are the observations likely to cluster around the mean? By the way, statisticians call this dispersion. To do this, we turn again to the same technique that we used when calculating the average. This time, we measure the distance of each observation from the average (whether to the left or right), add up all the distances and then divide again by the number of observations. So, let's try that with our sample.

TABLE 9.3 An attempt at calculating dispersion

Name	Height (cm)	Distance from average (163.4)
Maria	148	-15.4
Gaston	180	16.6
Xavier	154	-9.4
Carol	153	-10.4
Peter	173	9.6
Samantha	161	-2.4
Lisa	155	-8.4
William	176	12.6
James	178	14.6
Francesca	156	-7.4
Total	*1,634*	*0*

Huh? How can that be right? Can you spot what has gone wrong with our process?

Some of the observations are to the left of the average and the difference will therefore be a negative value, while others are to the right and will thus be a positive value. If we simply add them all up, the positives and the negatives will cancel each other out, as they have in the calculation we have just performed. Clearly, therefore, if we are going to perform any meaningful calculation we have to find some way of getting rid of all the negative signs, and expressing instead the distance each observation is from the average, be it positive or negative. Take a moment to think about how we might do this.

The answer is that we square the distance of each observation from the average in order to arrive at something called the **Variance**. Don't panic! We have already met the concept of powers when we considered discounting. Remember that squaring a number is simply raising it to the power of two; in other words, we multiply the number by itself.

So, $2^2 = 2 \times 2 = 4$, and $3^2 = 3 \times 3 = 9$, and so on. Why do we do this?

If we multiply a negative number by a negative number, we get a positive number. One way of remembering this is that if we multiply numbers that both have the same sign then the result (product) will always be positive, whereas if we multiply two numbers, one negative and the other positive, the result (product) will always be negative.

TABLE 9.4 Multiplication: the battle of the signs

Multiply one number...	...by another number...	...and the product will be
+	+	+
+	-	-
-	+	-
-	-	+

Rule: where two numbers sharing the same sign are multiplied by each other, the product will be positive; where two numbers with different signs are multiplied by each other, the product will be negative.

Product

The product is what we call the result arrived at by multiplying two or more numbers by each other. For example, the product of 2 and 3 is 6.

So, in this way we can make sure that all our Variances are positive numbers, which gets around the inconvenience of the positives and the negatives cancelling each other out. See Table 9.5, which shows this next step in the process.

TABLE 9.5 Calculating variance (1)

Name	Height (cm)	Distance from average (163.4)	Variance (distance^2)
Maria	148	-15.4	237.16
Gaston	180	16.6	275.56
Xavier	154	-9.4	88.36
Carol	153	-10.4	108.16
Peter	173	9.6	92.16
Samantha	161	-2.4	5.76
Lisa	155	-8.4	70.56
William	176	12.6	158.76
James	178	14.6	231.16
Francesca	156	-7.4	54.76
Total	1,634	0	1,322.40

NOTE If performing this exercise with a calculator, most now have a key marked ^{2}. If not, they may have a key marked ^ or x^y, after which you key 2 to raise the number to the power of two (which is the same thing as squaring it). In each case you will usually need to press = afterwards.

If using Excel, then there is no specific function as such. We simply use the power symbol ^. So, assuming that the distance from the average had been calculated in cell B12, we could find the Variance by '=B12^2'.

Now we simply take the average of all these calculated Variance figures in order to arrive at the Variance of the sample. Please see the note under Table 9.6.

TABLE 9.6　Calculating variance (2)

Name	Height (cm)	Distance from average (163.4)	Variance (distance²)
Maria	148	-15.4	237.16
Gaston	180	16.6	275.56
Xavier	154	-9.4	88.36
Carol	153	-10.4	108.16
Peter	173	9.6	92.16
Samantha	161	-2.4	5.76
Lisa	155	-8.4	70.56
William	176	12.6	158.76
James	178	14.6	231.16
Francesca	156	-7.4	54.76
Total	1,634	0	1,322.40
#	10		
		Sample Variance	132.24

NOTE 1 When calculating the Variance (and the Standard Deviation, which we have not yet met) of a sample, particularly one that is small when compared to the population from which it is drawn, it is customary to use the number of observations minus one. Having stated this point for the sake of completeness, it will not be mentioned again. When analysing long periods of financial returns, it can in any event be safely ignored. For example, in analysing the returns of the FTSE 100 index we would start in January 1984, when the index began, so the sample and the population would be the same. While this may not be strictly true in other cases, normally the period of sample data will be sufficiently long that it makes little difference.

NOTE 2 As you might expect, there is an Excel function for calculating the Variance of a sample. This is '=VAR(range)', where the range is the sequence of cells containing the observations, which would in this case be the values in the 'Height' column. Note that there is a limit of 255 individual observations for use with this function, but unless you are calculating daily volatility this is unlikely ever to be an issue.

This is fine, but it still leaves us with a very large number. This is of course because of the squaring exercise that we carried out. As well as the happy result of eliminating all the negative signs, it also had the less happy one of turning some quite small numbers into some very large ones. We need to find a way of undoing this, and we turn to the opposite process, which is known as a **square root**.

A root is the opposite of a power, and can be used in conjunction with any number, but we here only have to consider the square root, which is $\sqrt[2]{\ }$ (sometimes called 'root two'). The square of a number is the number multiplied by itself once, so $3^2 = 9$. The square root is the number that, when multiplied by itself once, produces the number to which the square root is being applied. So, the square root of 9 is 3, or in mathematical terms:

$\sqrt[2]{9} = 3$. (Incidentally, the square root can also be denoted simply by $\sqrt{\ }$.)

If we calculate the square root of the Variance of a sample, it gives us what is called the **Standard Deviation** of the sample.

TABLE 9.7 Calculating standard deviation

Name	Height (cm)	Distance from average (163.4)	Variance (distance²)
Maria	148	-15.4	237.16
Gaston	180	16.6	275.56
Xavier	154	-9.4	88.36
Carol	153	-10.4	108.16
Peter	173	9.6	92.16
Samantha	161	-2.4	5.76
Lisa	155	-8.4	70.56
William	176	12.6	158.76
James	178	14.6	231.16
Francesca	156	-7.4	54.76
Total	1,634	0	1,322.40
#	10		
		Sample Variance	132.24
		Sample Standard Deviation ($\sqrt{Variance}$)	

NOTE 1 Most calculators now have a √ key. Remember that this must precede the number to which you are applying it.

NOTE 2 The Excel function for calculating the Standard Deviation of a sample is expressed '=STDEV(range)', where 'range' is the sequence of cells containing the observations. In other words, it is possible to skip the calculation of Variance and proceed directly to the Standard Deviation.

So, we calculate the Standard Deviation of our sample as 11.499, which rounds to 11.50. Incidentally, Standard Deviation is customarily denoted mathematically by σ, the small Greek letter sigma, so now you will know what it means should you come across it. You will find that the world of finance is heavily populated by Greek letters, many of which trip spontaneously off the lips of investment managers as they make presentations. It is difficult to discern any useful purpose for these. They are designed to impress, but usually serve only to confuse.

Risk

You may not realize it, but we have now arrived at the world of finance's definition of risk. If we were looking at a particular investment, say some stock in the Coca-Cola Corporation, all we would have to do would be to substitute the annual returns of that stock, expressed as percentages, for the heights of our schoolchildren. We could then calculate the Standard Deviation of those annual returns, and that would be the 'risk' of Coca-Cola stock. For according to the world of finance, the 'risk' of any investment is simply the volatility of its historic returns, customarily expressed as one Standard Deviation. Understand this, and everything else in finance falls into place.

For the fundamental problem that faces many who study finance, such as students at business school, is often not that they do not understand the calculations themselves. As we have just seen, they are fairly straightforward once explained in simple terms. No, it is that they do not understand *why* they are being shown how to perform these calculations, because they cannot for the life of them see how they can really represent 'risk'. The teachers of finance, in their turn, for the most part do not understand this lack of understanding on the part of their students, since for them it is inconceivable that 'risk' could be anything other than a measure of the volatility of historic returns. They are transmitting on one wavelength, while many of their students are attempting to receive on another.

Since the world of finance is never going to accept that it is wrong, the solution is simple. Just pretend for the purposes of learning about finance that 'risk' is indeed what it says it is. You can think of finance as being like a state religion. You can choose whether or not to believe in it, but you have no choice but to understand what it is saying, and at least to pretend to believe in it – and the idea that the risk of any investment may be measured by the volatility of its past returns is an essential part of this.

Indeed, the idea that risk and historic volatility are one and the same is the foundation stone that underpins the whole mighty temple of finance. As we will see, every financial analysis tool, no matter how complex, starts from this one basic principle. Let's look at one of these before we move on.

The Sharpe Ratio

You will hear much talk of 'risk adjusted' returns. What does this actually mean? Well, we now know that really it means 'historic volatility adjusted returns', of course, but how do we actually measure this? One popular way is by using something called the **Sharpe Ratio**.

A ratio is simply one number expressed by reference to another. Here the two values that are used represent the return and risk of an investment respectively, or at least what is called the excess return of the investment, and that element of risk that is thought to attach to the excess return. Doubtless that all sounds rather confusing, so let's build up the concept piece by piece.

Finance believes in the existence of something called the **risk free return**. Rather like the discount rate, what this should actually be at any one time in any one situation can be largely a matter of personal choice. In the case of a US dollar investor, they might decide to take the rate currently being paid by the US Government on its Treasury Bills (T-Bills). In the case of a sterling investor, they might decide to take the rate currently being paid by the British Government on short-term government bonds (gilts). Traditionally it has been assumed that these rates are risk free in the sense that there is no risk of either the US or the British Government ever defaulting on their obligations, and being unable to pay their debts. Readers may care to form their own views as to the ongoing validity of these assumptions.

Let us assume that we are considering an investment whose average historic annual return is 3.4%. We now need to calculate the appropriate average risk free return over that same period, whatever it might be. Let's assume for the sake of argument that this comes to exactly 2%. If we take that average return and deduct the risk free return, then what is left will be the excess return. In other words, the excess return will be the total return minus the risk free return. This represents the extra return that an investor could expect to make by investing in this particular asset rather than in a risk free asset such as a government bond.

The excess return is one of the two numbers that we need in order to calculate our Sharpe Ratio. What is the other? Remember the traditional view of risk and the answer may be obvious. It is one Standard Deviation of the excess return.

In other words, you calculate the annual excess return for all (each of) the individual years in your sample, and calculate its Standard Deviation. This will give you the second figure that you need. The Sharpe Ratio is simply the excess return divided by its own Standard Deviation.

The Sharpe Ratio

The total return of an investment is usually represented as r for these purposes, and the risk free return as rf. Thus, in order to find the excess return, we deduct the latter from the former, so:

Excess return = $(r - rf)$

Remember that the Greek letter σ is commonly used to denote the Standard Deviation of a number. Thus, in order to express the Sharpe Ratio mathematically, we need:

$$\frac{(r - rf)}{\sigma(r - rf)}$$

Hopefully now that we understand what it is saying, this equation looks much less forbidding. If we substitute words for symbols, it is:

$$\frac{\text{the excess return of an investment}}{\text{the Standard Deviation of the excess return}}$$

Note please that it is the excess return that we use for the Sharpe Ratio, not the total return. This is a common mistake.

So, in our present example, we have an excess return of 1.4% (3.4% – 2%). Let's assume that when we run the Standard Deviation calculation it comes up with a figure of 5.2%. If we divide 1.4 into 5.2 we get 0.2692. This is not a very good result. Generally the higher a Sharpe Ratio is above 0.5 the more attractive it is, while the lower it is below 0.5 the less attractive it is. So a Sharpe Ratio of only 0.2692 suggests a high risk investment, for which we would be looking for a correspondingly high excess return in order to compensate us for that high level of risk. At first glance, 1.4% does not look nearly enough.

Summary

- The world of finance does not use the word 'risk' in the same sense as we use it in everyday life.
- In finance, it means the volatility of the historic returns of an investment, commonly measured by one Standard Deviation.
- In looking at a sample of the historic returns of the investment, we first calculate the average (or mean) return.
- Next we measure the distance of each individual observation from the average, and square it. If we take the average of these numbers it gives us the Variance of the sample.
- A square root of a number, A, is the number B, which when multiplied by itself produces A. So, for example, 3 is the square root of 9 since 3 × 3 = 9. The square root of the Variance of the sample is its Standard Deviation.
- For the world of finance, the assumption that the Standard Deviation of an investment's past returns is the same thing as its risk is central and fundamental, underpinning every financial model or tool ever developed.
- For example, the Sharpe Ratio measures the 'risk adjusted' return of an investment by dividing its excess return into the Standard Deviation of its excess return. We calculate the excess return by deducting the risk free return from the total return.
- A Sharpe Ratio in excess of 0.5 is regarded as relatively attractive, while a Sharpe Ratio below 0.5 is regarded as relatively unattractive.

10
Return

Risk and return are the left hand and the right hand of finance. There is general agreement that they are related although, as we will see in a later chapter, there are a number of different ways in which this relationship can be viewed. At the very least, everyone would agree that within any particular asset class there is always an inherent trade-off between the two; generally, a higher return can be earned only at the expense of also accepting a higher level of risk. Note the words 'within any particular asset class'; where we are looking to compare different types of assets against each other, the picture can be less clear.

It is therefore essential that we should understand exactly what the world of finance means when it talks of 'risk' and 'return'. We have already looked at the former of these terms. It is now time to turn our attention to the latter.

With 'return' we come to another word that poses problems. Like an elephant, we find it difficult to define it, but recognize one when we see it. It is difficult to hit upon a common meaning if we hunt through the dictionaries, and one has intellectual problems with many of the definitions offered. Princeton University, for example, defines it as 'The income or profit arising from such transactions as the sale of land or other property', while Wikipedia talks of 'the ratio of money gained or lost (whether realized or unrealized) on an investment relative to the amount of money invested'. The first definition surely takes too simplistic a view of modern investment activity, while the latter would ignore completely one particular view of 'return', which we will be considering in this chapter.

So perhaps it is better to start with a general idea of what constitutes 'return', rather than tying ourselves to any one particular narrow definition. Most people would probably say, if asked, that it represents the extent to which you might either gain or lose money (or value expressed as money) on one investment or any number of investments. Let us start from this basis. What we are actually going to be looking at in this chapter are the different ways in which return can be measured, but, as you will see, underlying these different approaches are some very different attitudes to just what constitutes a 'return' in the first place, or at least how investors might view this.

Periodic returns

What are periodic returns? The returns of a particular period. The period in question may be a year, a quarter, a month, or even just a day. It is necessary to amplify this rather basic statement a little, however.

First, if we are using periodic returns for any sort of analytical exercise then it is obviously important that they are all the same type of period. There is no point comparing the annual return of one stock with the weekly return of another. Even if you had all 52 weekly returns of the other stock for each year, you would encounter significant differences when calculating things like the Standard Deviation.

Second, periodic returns record the return observed in *one single period*. It does not matter over how many years you are analysing the return of a stock; each return figure that you use will be the return of one individual year, and have no direct relevance at all to any other year. It is this concept of representing only one single period (whatever that period might be) that lies at the heart of understanding periodic returns.

Third, assuming that we have any manner of periodic returns from which to select, the choice of which type to use (annual, quarterly, etc) will be determined largely by the type of analysis that we wish to perform and, to a lesser extent, by how many individual data points we can handle as a matter of practical reality. For strategic asset allocation purposes, for example, annual returns are commonly used, while with **Value at Risk** (VaR) modelling daily returns are employed.

It all depends what you want to do with the numbers. If, on the one hand, you are modelling what might happen if you hold a particular asset for a decade or two, then daily volatility is irrelevant. If, on the other hand, as with VaR, you are trying to establish how much money you might lose on a particular portfolio of stocks in any one day, at different levels of probability, then there would be little point in using anything but daily figures.

So, to recapitulate the single most important point: a periodic return figure is one that states the return of one particular period, and that one period only, whether it be a year, a quarter or whatever. This may seem a very obvious point to be reiterating, but it is such a fundamental assumption that people lose sight of the fact that they are making it, and in the process often blind themselves to other very valid ways of looking at return.

What can constitute 'return'?

There are really only two broad categories of return with which we need to concern ourselves, and the Princeton definition touches upon both. There will be a capital gain or loss that arises whenever we sell an asset that we have previously bought. Then there will be income of any kind that the asset generates while we hold it. This income type return may be called a **yield** or **running yield**, or in the case of instruments like bonds, a **coupon**. Again, however, we need to qualify this rather simplistic treatment of what is actually a more complex concept.

First, what happens if we make a gain or loss on the repayment of a loan, or the **redemption** of a bond (which is essentially the same thing)? It may seem strange to think of this as generating a gain or a loss, but in fact that will almost always be the case. We may have bought that loan or bond in the market from somebody else, and hopefully for less than its final repayment or redemption amount. Even if we have held it ourselves from inception, that final amount will form only part of the overall return that we wish to calculate. And should we treat this as part of the yield, or part of the capital gain? If we were indeed to adopt such a binary approach then this would be a difficult decision to make, and would depend largely on the particular circumstances of each individual case.

Second, many investment transactions today take the form not of buying or selling a particular asset, but of buying or selling *rights in respect of* a particular asset. This may take the form of buying a right to buy, or a right to sell, on a particular day and at a particular price. It may even take the form of paying money to someone in return for putting you in the same financial position as if you held a particular asset, even when you don't. This may all sound rather fanciful at this stage, but don't worry; all will be explained when we look at **synthetic** instruments such as **options** and **swaps**. For the moment, let us just note that in the increasingly synthetic world of investment a gain or loss can be realized when one of these instruments either changes hands or expires. In some cases, for example, an investor can decide simply to **write off** what they paid for such an instrument, rather than to exercise their rights under it, since to do so would incur an even greater loss.

Third, many gains or losses arise not on the sale or purchase of an asset, but on its revaluation for accounting purposes. This is where the 'whether realized or unrealized' part of the Wikipedia definition comes in. If you buy a share in the Coca-Cola Corporation today and tomorrow the share price goes down, then as far as the world of finance is concerned you have now made a loss on that investment. This is even though it is unrealized, because you have not actually sold it, and even though by the time you *do* actually sell it in the future you may well have made a gain. Incidentally, this concept of recognizing return by way of unrealized gains or losses is commonly known as **mark to market**, and can cause very significant problems during periods of market instability, particularly for investors that may be heavily regulated such as pension funds, insurance companies and banks.

Having explained the limitations of the approach, however, let us broadly adopt it, at least where the imperative to do so is convenient and clear-cut. Part of the usefulness of this binary approach is in its ability to separate out different asset types. Asset types such as equities, bonds, real estate, infrastructure and private equity produce income, whether predictable or not. Others, such as commodities, energy and gold, do not; hence the expression 'gold doesn't have babies'. As we will see, the traditional way in which return is calculated tends to gloss over this difference, with the result that asset types in the first category can be unfairly prejudiced. For example, we will see when we look at equities (shares or stocks) that the way in which dividends are treated when calculating return can make an enormous difference.

TABLE 10.1 Some examples of asset types, differentiated by their income-producing qualities

Income Characteristics			
Predictable (1)	**Fairly predictable**	**Unpredictable**	**None**
Bonds	Equities (2)	Private equity	Gold
Infrastructure	Real estate (3)		Oil
			Commodities

NOTE (1) Subject always to the risk of default.
(2) Though dividend policy is set by the board of directors.
(3) Subject to tenant default, or void periods with no tenant in place.

Annualized returns

We have seen that periodic returns, of whatever nature, record the return of one single period. So, what do we do when we want to look at the returns of more than one period? One answer of course is simply to use a longer period. If we want to look at lots of daily returns we might look instead at the return of the month, or quarter, or even year that they represent. There are many reasons, however, why this approach will not normally be appropriate (for example, we may wish to calculate the average and Standard Deviation). Frequently we will be looking at any number of annual returns, for example – perhaps the returns of a particular share in every year over 10 or 20 years. How do we approach this?

Annualized returns are the traditional tool used. What are these? Average annual returns. We have already seen how to calculate an average (or mean). We simply add up whichever periodic return figures we are looking at, and then divide the result by n, which you will know by now represents the number of individual observations (in this case, return figures).

TABLE 10.2 Average annual returns (calculating the arithmetic mean)

Year 1	Year 2	Year 3	Year 4	Year 5	Total
14%	8%	6%	3%	4%	35%
				Total / n	7%

Note that in this case $n = 5$ since that is the number of individual observations.

There really is no more to it than that. It is exactly the same exercise that we carried out when calculating the average (or mean) of the height of our schoolchildren.

Incidentally, this sort of average that we have just calculated is called the **arithmetic mean**. There is actually a different way of calculating an average, which is called the **geometric mean**, and mathematicians quite correctly argue that it is this, and not the arithmetic mean, which we should use when looking at investment returns.

If we want to find the average height of a schoolchild then it is perfectly valid to take a group of schoolchildren, add up their heights, and then divide the total by the number of observations, the number of children in the group. However, if we think about the way in which investment returns operate, and are usually stated, they are a percentage rate by which the value of an asset is increased (or decreased) during a given period. In other words, we are multiplying the starting value of our asset by the rate of percentage return. It is as if, instead of measuring the heights of all the children in a group, we measure them all once a year and want to know not the average height at a particular time, but the average rate of growth.

This argument is developed in the following box, which also shows you how to calculate a geometric mean.

The geometric mean

When we wish to find the average of a list of values, such as the average height of a group of schoolchildren as featured earlier, it is quite correct to add up the observations to find their total value and then divide by the number of observations to find their average or mean. If you think about the way in which investment returns work, however, there is an argument that this approach does not reflect reality. Suppose that we have an investment that yields a return of 14% in Year 1, 8% in Year 2, and 6% in Year 3. What is actually happening here in arithmetic terms?

The answer surely is multiplication, not addition. In Year 1 we need to multiply the starting value of our investment by 14% (or 0.14) to find the return or 114% (or 1.14) to find its closing value. Would it not then make more sense to use a multiplication-based approach for our calculations rather than one that works by means of addition?

The geometric mean is that tool. Unlike the arithmetic mean, which is what we have been using so far, the geometric mean multiplies all the numbers together and then calculates what is called 'the nth root' or 'root n' of that number. Remember that, just like powers, a root can have any value. We have only actually used the square root so far in this book, which is root 2, but here we will use the root of the number of observations in our sample.

Let's demonstrate this with the use of our example investment above.

The geometric mean of that investment's return over the three-year period in question will be:

$$\sqrt{(14 \times 8 \times 6)}$$

As always, we need to solve the numbers within the brackets first. $14 \times 8 \times 6 = 672$. All we have to do now is to find root 3 of this number (because we are working with three individual observations). You will find that this gives a solution of 8.76 as the geometric mean of the annual return.

If you calculate the arithmetic mean as:

$$\frac{(14 + 8 + 6)}{3}$$

you will find that it gives you a solution of 9.33. It is in fact the case that the geometric mean may be equal to or less than the arithmetic mean, but never greater than it, and there is a suitably impressive mathematical proof tucked away in a textbook somewhere to verify this.

Astute readers will at this stage doubtless be asking 'Ah yes, but what happens if one of your returns is negative? This could give some very strange results'. Indeed it could. In fact, as you rightly suspected, it is not possible to calculate a geometric mean for any sequence of numbers where one of them is negative.

There is a way around this, though. Suppose in Year 2 you suffer a negative return of 5% rather than a positive one of 8%. Think about what is actually happening. If we suffer a negative return of 5% we have reduced the value of our asset by 5%. It is now worth 95% of what it was worth before and, as we have already seen, this is the same as multiplying by 0.95. So, we can simply restate our three annual returns as 1.14, 0.95, and 1.06 respectively and proceed as before. This time we calculate:

$$\sqrt{(1.14 \times 0.95 \times 1.06)}$$

and you will find that once you calculate the bits in the brackets first this becomes:

$$\sqrt{1.14798}$$

which equals 1.047. In other words, the geometric mean of the annual returns is now 4.7%, since our asset value is increasing on average by that amount every year. So, you can see that it is indeed possible to handle negative periodic returns when calculating a geometric mean, provided that we re-state the percentage rates first.

Incidentally, the arithmetic mean would be:

$$\frac{(1.14 + 0.95 + 1.06)}{3}$$

which gives 1.05, or 5%. Can you see that we could also calculate the arithmetic mean as:

$$\frac{(14 - 5 + 6)}{3}$$

(which also gives 5%), since an arithmetic mean calculation can handle negative numbers?

So, we use an arithmetic mean when we want to know what the average is of a number of different values, but we use a geometric mean when we are multiplying by several (or many) different values (each one of which is called a multiplier) and we want to know the following: 'If we multiply all these different multipliers together, we arrive at a result – let's call it Y. If all these multipliers were to have the same value (let's call it Z) instead of each one being different, what would Z have to be, for our calculated outcome still to be Y?'

As you can see, this is subtly different and in principle the mathematicians are quite right. In practice, however, most investors and their advisers typically use the arithmetic mean, and only a cynic would suggest that this might be because it will always tend to produce a higher figure, thus flattering apparent investment performance. The Sharpe Ratio, for example, is almost always calculated using the arithmetic mean.

Compound returns

Regardless of what type of mean is employed when calculating it, however, an annualized return will always suffer from one very fundamental flaw, so fundamental indeed that some observers are now beginning to question whether it can ever give a valid view of reality at all. What is this flaw? That it ignores something that is so important that we have already spent a whole chapter considering it. *It ignores the time value of money.*

We have covered this already, but let us recapitulate a little basic arithmetic. So far, we have examined two ways of dealing with the annual returns of more than one year: an arithmetic mean and a geometric mean. Both produce an average return, commonly referred to as an annualized return. As we have just seen, the first works by adding the different returns together, while the second works by multiplication.

Now let's go back to the basic arithmetic. Suppose that in each case we have an investment that generates annual returns over a five-year period as follows:

TABLE 10.3

Year 1	Year 2	Year 3	Year 4	Year 5	Total
14%	8%	6%	3%	4%	35%

This may seem familiar; it is the same as an example we used earlier in this chapter. Now assume that we were to calculate either an arithmetic or a geometric mean. The former would add the numbers together as its first step, while the latter would multiply them. So what is wrong with these approaches? Well, remember that it does not matter *in what order* we add or multiply. (14 + 8 + 6 + 3 + 4) gives the same result as (4 + 3 + 6 + 8 + 14), while (14 × 8 × 6 × 3 × 4) gives the same result as (4 × 3 × 6 × 8 × 14). So, if we were to suffer a big loss in Year 1 of a 20-year period, each of these methods would treat it exactly the same as a big loss in Year 20. This is in blatant disregard of the time value of money.

The reality, as we saw when we considered discounting, is that we would be relatively unconcerned if we knew in advance that we were going to make a big loss in Year 20, but very concerned if we knew the same thing was going to happen in Year 1. That is because whatever happens in Year 20 is discounted by the relative discount factor raised to the power of 20, and will have a very low present value. Thus it will make relatively little impact on the Net Present Value of our return as a whole (our stream of cash-flows stretching out 20 years into the future).

You will find an example of the relative approaches in Table 10.4. Suppose that that we buy a share and hold it for five years. The return we make will be a mixture of the extent to which the share price goes up and down, and the dividend income that we receive from it. Let's assume that each year the share pays a dividend of 10% of its closing price at the end of the previous year. So, if it makes a return of +15% then it pays a dividend of 10%, and the remaining 5% represents an increase in the share's price. If it makes a return of -30%, then the share price has actually gone down 40%, but a 10% dividend has still been paid (in practice this would be an unrealistic assumption to make, but it will do for our present purposes). See how different the solutions are to the different calculations.

Different measures of return

TABLE 10.4A Annual returns

Year 1	Year 2	Year 3	Year 4	Year 5
50%	15%	12%	10%	-30%

TABLE 10.4B 'Annualized': arithmetic mean

Year 1	Year 2	Year 3	Year 4	Year 5	Total
50	15	12	10	-30	57
				Total / n	11.4
				Solution	11.4%

TABLE 10.4C 'Annualized': geometric mean

Year 1	Year 2	Year 3	Year 4	Year 5	Product
1.50	1.15	1.12	1.10	0.70	1.49
				$\sqrt[n]{Product}$	1.083
				Solution	8.27%

TABLE 10.4D Compound return: IRR of actual cash-flows

Year 0	Year 1	Year 2	Year 3	Year 4	Year 5
-1	0.10	0.10	0.10	0.10	1.00
(Closing price)	1.40	1.47	1.50	1.50	0.90
				IRR	8.31%
				Solution	8.31%

Can you see that the arithmetic mean would stay the same at 11.4% even if we switched the returns of Years 1 and 5? Similarly, the geometric mean would be unchanged at 8.3%. That is because annualized returns ignore the time value of money, whereas compound returns do not. With an IRR, by contrast, if you change the order in which a series of different cashflows occur, the IRR itself will change.

There are a further two important differences, which are really just different ways of expressing the same thing. If you think back to when we discussed IRRs you will remember that they can only be calculated on actual cash-flows. With compound returns, therefore, we look at the cash actually paid out and received by the investor, *when* it is actually paid out and received. Annualized returns do not do this. The other side of this coin is that annualized returns take account of gains and losses whether they have been realized or not, whereas compound returns, being concerned only with actual cash-flows, do not. This is where the Wikipedia definition at the beginning of the chapter is deficient; it assumes that something like an IRR is not a valid method of measuring return.

To be fair, this does no more than reflect prevailing practice. As you study finance, you are likely to come across only one example of compound returns being used, and this will be when you study bond yields. Apart from this one small area, it is as though the world of finance might never have heard of compound returns. It might be worth spending a few moments considering why this might be, since it is something that puzzles many people.

After all, compound returns appear to match perfectly the reality of what happens when someone makes an investment. There is an initial cash-flow going out when they buy the asset, a cash-flow coming in at the end when they sell it, and possibly some cash-flows coming in as income during the intervening period. Surely the only thing that the investor should care about is the addition or diminution of value that those cash-flows represent? Surely also it must follow that, if we are thinking in terms of cash-flows, then we *must* take account of the time value of money? Otherwise we would be saying that we do not care whether we receive a cash-flow today or one of equal nominal value in 10 years' time, which would clearly be a nonsense. We *do* care; in fact, we care very much.

The explanation lies in the fact that, as we have seen, finance takes a very artificial view of risk, and that this in turn requires annualized returns in order to be able to calculate it. Thus one artificiality leads to another. It is rather like one of those French farces where one little lie is told at the beginning of the first act, but then requires another lie in order that it should not be exposed. By the end of the third act, half the cast are engaged in full-blown deception plans, pretending to be people they are not, and lying about their whereabouts and backgrounds. So, in finance, the first lie (that all the material risk of an investment may be expressed by its historic volatility) requires another (that annualized returns are all that matter) in order to support it, and upon this unsteady foundation is built a confidence trick of global proportions.

If compound returns were to become universally adopted, then this would force a recognition of the fact that the traditional risk model is not fit for purpose, and the traditional risk model is the basic building block of finance. Discredit it, and you discredit countless thousands of books and learned academic research papers that have been written over the last half a century. The prospect of all of these being carried into university courtyards and consumed in vast bonfires is far too painful an image for their authors to contemplate.

Actually, for our purposes none of this matters very much. The object of this book is to explain finance theory as it is, not as it might be. The reason for pointing out what is wrong with it is that many people coming new to the subject struggle desperately to make sense of the underlying concepts. When they ask for clarification, their enquiries are met with a blank stare from the lecturer and a repeated explanation of the relevant formula, perhaps this time more slowly to accommodate an obviously backward intellect. If only somebody was to tell you at the beginning of the first lecture that they *don't* make sense, that they are not *supposed* to make sense, then everything would fall into place.

You are studying finance, not philosophy. You are not required to justify the conceptual framework of what you are being taught. Simply learn finance theory as an academic exercise, partly so that you can pass your exams, and partly so that you can understand what finance folk are talking about; both these things are important. It is just like having to study the Bible for a divinity exam when you don't actually believe in God.

So, just accept that annualized returns are the way to go. You might by all means enquire whether an arithmetic mean or a geometric mean has been used to calculate them; this might even earn you an admiring glance or two. But whatever you do, do not start enquiring whether the method of calculation used accurately reflects the reality of what actually happens in real world investment, and whether compound returns might not be a better way to approach this, and by the way if you are right what does this do to the traditional view of risk, please, Professor? Not unless you want to be branded as a persistent trouble-maker, that is, in which case please feel free to go ahead and upset people.

Summary

- 'Risk' and 'return' are the basic building blocks of finance. We have already examined risk. We now need to understand what is (or can be) meant by return.
- Return can be made up either of income, capital gain (or loss), or a combination of both.
- Return can be either realized, where it has been sold, or unrealized, where the investment has not yet been sold but its book value has been written up or down for some reason, perhaps because the investor is under an obligation to mark their assets to market.
- The traditional way for finance to look at returns, with the exception only of one type of bond return, is by way of periodic returns. These measure the returns that are made during a particular period, be it a day, a year, or whatever, but tell us nothing about what happened in any other period.
- Where we are looking at the returns of many different periods, the traditional approach is to take an 'annualized' return, which is an average.

- There are, however, two different ways of measuring the average. Strictly speaking, percentage returns should be quantified by way of a geometric mean, which will almost always result in a lower figure than the straightforward arithmetic mean – sometimes much lower.
- Both these measures are open to a fundamental objection, namely that they ignore the time value of money. It would seem more sensible to adopt compound return, such as IRR, as a measure of investment performance, since it accurately mirrors what happens in the real world. However, finance cannot do this as it would then be impossible to measure risk (volatility), since this process requires periodic returns.

11
Bonds (1): basic principles

We examined the basic features of bonds in an earlier chapter, but now that we understand such things as risk, return and discounting we can look at them in much greater detail. In particular, we need to focus on how investors should view bonds if they are either holding them already or considering buying some.

However, it is a little misleading to talk of 'bonds' in general as if they were a homogenous group. For while it is true that all bonds share certain similar characteristics so far as their legal structure as financial instruments is concerned, they can differ widely as far as investment issues are concerned. So, first let us consider how we might divide bonds up into different groups for study purposes.

How can we classify bonds?

There are two main strands to the classification process. The first is the type of issuer (whom we could think of as the borrower, since a bond is a debt instrument), and the second is the risk/return characteristics of the bond, which is in turn directly influenced by the first consideration – the circumstances of the issuer.

Type of issuer

Let us deal with the first point right away, since it is relatively straightforward. All bond issuers can be classified either as governments or corporations; thus bonds fall into two types: government bonds and corporate bonds.

'Relatively' straightforward, but not entirely so. Some confusion has arisen in recent years as to the precise status of certain types of issuers. What about what we might call 'para-statal' organizations, such as public bodies, businesses in state ownership, or even recently or partly privatized businesses whose liabilities may still enjoy a (frequently undefined) measure of government guarantee? Typically, such questions have tended to surface only when it is too late to do anything about them, namely once the issuer is seen to be incapable of honouring its obligations. While it always seems insufferably smug to seem to give advice with the benefit of hindsight, such issues should surely have been investigated and resolved at the time of issue.

Risk/return characteristics

This issue is not quite as clear-cut as it might be, since it depends partly upon who the issuer is, and that is of course part of the first leg of our approach. Briefly, there are a very small number of governments that are, as bond issuers, regarded as being so financially sound that their bonds are adopted as the legendary 'risk free' benchmark against which all investments denominated in their currency may be measured. US T-Bills for dollar investors, UK Government 'gilts' for sterling investors, a Japanese Government bond (JGB) for yen investors, and so on.

As we remarked earlier when looking at risk, the notional concept of a 'risk free' return may live on, but the reality does not. However, it is bonds issued by these governments, plus Germany, which are traditionally used for 'risk free' purposes in analytical exercises, such as calculating the Sharpe Ratio. These are traditionally called **prime bonds** in bond circles.

FIGURE 11.1 Risk versus return in bond markets

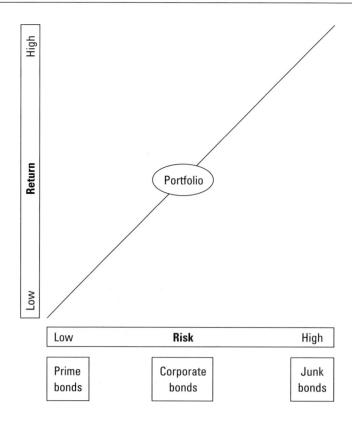

All other issuers, no matter whether they are corporate or governmental, are regarded as non-risk free. It is here that we meet and need to understand the concept of **unrewarded risk**. If we can choose between two investments that both offer the same rate of return, but one of which exhibits lower risk (no matter how we define or calculate this), then logically it is the one with the lower risk that we should choose. If we did otherwise, we would be exposing ourselves needlessly to more risk within our portfolio but without getting anything (such as a higher return) in exchange. This is called unrewarded risk, and clearly the rational choice would be to reject this rather than to accept it.

This means that in the world of finance and investment there is a constant trade-off at work between risk and return, and bonds are a perfect example of this. If we want a low risk bond portfolio then we would choose entirely from T-Bill type instruments, which would achieve our objective, but at the expense of the bond-holder having to accept a very low rate of return. If, on the other hand, we want a higher return, then we would have to buy bonds issued by corporations or by governments with non-prime status. Yes, these would indeed generate a higher rate of return, but at the expense of introducing more risk into our portfolio. Perhaps nowhere else in the whole world of finance is the relationship between risk and return so clearly demonstrated.

As you can see, our portfolio is nicely positioned at the moment, roughly in the middle of the risk/return relationship. There are three possible explanations for this:

1. We hold a **focused** portfolio composed entirely of mid-risk/mid-return corporate bonds;
2. We hold a **balanced** portfolio, with each part of the spectrum represented roughly equally;
3. We hold what is called a **dumbbell** portfolio, which has nothing in the middle but roughly equal exposure to both the low risk/low return and high risk/high return ends of the spectrum.

Financial theory says that we can slide our bond portfolio along the line at will. Buying more T-Bills or gilts, and selling other types of bonds in order to do so, will slide us down to the left, while doing the opposite will slide us up to the right.

It is extremely important that we should be able properly to assess the risk/return profile of a bond if we want to be able to position our portfolio exactly where we want it to be, and to avoid unrewarded risk. Let us look at unrewarded risk a little more closely. What exactly do we mean? It may be easier to think of this graphically represented, as in Figure 11.2.

Let us assume that we have targeted either a particular level of return (A) or a particular level of risk (B) for our portfolio. Clearly we would like to incur as little risk as possible consistent with achieving a return of A, and as high a return as possible consistent with accepting a risk level of B. The portfolio that meets these criteria is called the **efficient portfolio**.

As we saw earlier, we can change our mind about either the target return or the target risk, and slide our portfolio along the line in either direction. Thus we could construct any number of efficient portfolios, sitting at any point on the line. This line is known as the **efficient frontier** because it represents as far as you can possibly go in terms of chasing return without accepting a higher level of risk. So, it is not possible to construct a portfolio that sits above the efficient frontier, although it is possible to construct one that sits below the efficient frontier. If you do this, however, you have created a sub-optimal situation because you are now accepting unrewarded risk.

FIGURE 11.2 Risk versus return: the efficient frontier

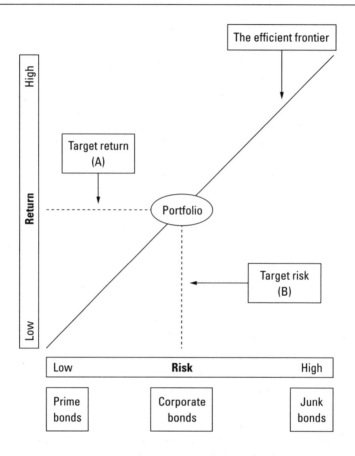

Risk ratings

Fortunately there are a number of commercial ratings agencies whose job it is to assess the risk inherent within bonds issued by different governments and corporations. These employ many specialist analysts who keep bond issuers under constant review and may from time to time re-rate an issuer either upwards (which is good) or downwards (which is bad). So, assuming that the ratings agencies have got things right, then you should be able to price a bond according to its risk rating. We will explore bond pricing in more detail in a moment.

Unfortunately there is no unanimity between the different agencies when it comes to the way in which they present their ratings, though two of them (S&P and Fitch) are identical in the upper quality ranges, and these two may therefore be conveniently taken as an example.[1]

FIGURE 11.3 Risk versus return: unrewarded risk

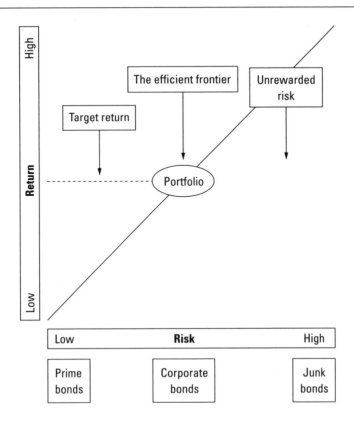

There is only one category of prime ('risk free') bonds: AAA. Below that are three categories of high grade: AA+, AA and AA-. Then there are three categories of upper medium grade: A+ and A-. Below this we move into lower medium grade, and below BBB we come to what are officially called non-investment grade bonds (because many institutional investors are not allowed to hold these instruments) or, colloquially, junk bonds.

What is the risk of a bond?

It may be remarked that it is in the world of **fixed income securities** (which broadly means bonds) that traditional finance theory seems to work best, most notably in the close relationship that we have just observed between risk and return. This is in fact richly ironic because it turns out that when it comes to bonds, finance does not actually apply the very artificial definition of risk, the 'risk as volatility' that we spent so much time learning how to calculate a little earlier, but a much more common-sense, everyday approach. So, far from validating traditional theory, bonds actually demonstrate all too clearly just how silly the traditional approach to 'risk' is.

TABLE 11.1 Bond ratings (long term)

Moody's	Fitch's	S&P	Classification
Aaa	AAA	AAA	Prime
Aa1	AA+	AA+	High grade
Aa2	AA	AA	High grade
Aa3	AA-	AA-	High grade
A1	A+	A+	Upper medium grade
A2	A	A	Upper medium grade
A3	A-	A-	Upper medium grade
Baa1	BBB+	BBB+	Lower medium grade
Baa2	BBB	BBB	Lower medium grade
Baa3	BBB-	BBB-	Lower medium grade
Ba1	BB+	BB+	Non-investment grade: speculative
Ba2	BB	BB	Non-investment grade: speculative
Ba3	BB-	BB-	Non-investment grade: speculative
B1	B+	B+	Highly speculative
B2	B	B	Highly speculative
B3	B-	B-	Highly speculative
Caa1	CCC+	CCC	Substantial risks
Caa2	CCC	CCC	Extremely speculative
Caa3	CCC-	CCC	In default – little apparent chance of recovery
Ca	CC	CCC	In default – little apparent chance of recovery
Ca	C	CCC	In default – little apparent chance of recovery
C	D	DDD	In default – no apparent chance of recovery
		DD	In default – no apparent chance of recovery
		D	In default – no apparent chance of recovery

The risk of a bond is held not to be the volatility of its historic returns (although if you were to carry out this calculation in respect of just about any bonds, even prime ones, you would find that they are actually very 'high risk' assets relative to their average historic return) but the chance that they may not actually be able for whatever reason to make the agreed payments, either of interest during the life of the bond, or capital at the end of its life. We can call this either **default risk** or **counterparty risk**. It is this risk, the risk of default, which the ratings claim to measure.

Of course, the risk of default grows greater with every time period that passes. Suppose that we are worried about the financial health of the issuer of a bond that pays interest (a **coupon**) every quarter, and is due to be repaid in full (redeemed) on **redemption**, or **maturity**, in five years' time. There must be some risk that the issuer will not make the interest payment for the current quarter. But that risk must be smaller than the risk that it will miss at least one of the forthcoming 20 interest payments. Similarly, the risk that it may not be able to redeem the bond at the end of its life must be greater still; after all, the redemption amount will be much larger than the interest payments, and there is another five years' uncertainty to take into account until the maturity of the bond. For this reason, short-term bond ratings are more forgiving than long-term ones.

So, with fixed income securities there is a direct link between the perceived risk of the issuer defaulting and the return that we are prepared to accept. If the perceived risk of default is high, then we require a correspondingly high return to reward us for being prepared to take that risk. Incidentally, the reason why it is probably sensible to use the phrase 'fixed income securities' is that some people restrict the meaning of 'bonds' to government bonds, and some even more narrowly to prime government bonds only. This is by no means universal, and for the purposes of learning about financial theory it is fine to talk about all these instruments as 'bonds', as is done in this book, but you need to be aware that in real life investment situations this more narrow meaning is sometimes applied.

Bond returns

We are now going to explore how we can measure bond returns but, as with everything in finance, it will be much easier to do this if we first think through exactly what it is we are dealing with. Let us think about a bond. It is almost always an instrument with a fixed life. That is to say, it has a pre-agreed redemption date on which the issuer (borrower) must repay the bond-holder (lender) the face value of the bond. There are one or two exceptions to this in practice; for example, the British Government still has some undated war loans outstanding, but we can ignore this for the purposes of learning about financial theory.

So clearly part of the return we expect from holding a bond will be this redemption amount. Were we to ignore the fact that at some stage we are due to receive a large capital sum this would make our return calculations most unrealistic. In fact, some bonds, known as **zero coupon**, pay no interest at all, and here the return will consist *only* of the redemption amount. You might wonder why anybody would ever be prepared to buy such a bond, and the answer is that it is issued at a much lower price than the redemption amount, but don't worry, all this will become clear when we look at bond pricing.

So there is a capital element to the return, but there is also an income element, known as the coupon, or the running yield. This is represented by the interest payments that the issuer makes periodically to the bond-holder, just as if they were paying interest to a bank on a loan. Remember that a bond is a debt instrument, not equity.

What happens if you buy an existing bond from another investor between interest payments? The answer is that you calculate the pro rata daily interest entitlement and take this into account. The resulting price is known as the **clean price**. The other, unsurprisingly, is known as the **dirty price**. A good way of remembering this is to think of a dirty breadknife. Because notional daily interest is not taken into account by the dirty price, it will go up and down on interest payment dates just like the teeth on a breadknife.

The running yield

Having just said that it is unrealistic to ignore the redemption value of a bond, we are actually going to begin by doing exactly that! Assume that we buy a $100 bond on the day that it is issued. Incidentally we would call this a **primary market** transaction, which simply means that we buy a brand-new instrument from its original issuer. It pays $5 interest per year, so this is the return that we will make on our investment (assuming we bought it at **par**, in other words at its face value):

$$\frac{5}{100} \times 100 = 5\%$$

However, suppose now that we decide to buy a bond that is not brand new, but may be a few years old. This is a **secondary market transaction**, since we are buying it not from the original issuer, but from whoever owns it at the moment. Since bond prices go up and down in response to various factors, it is almost impossible that it will still be trading at $100. No, we will buy it for some greater or lesser amount. If greater, then it is a **premium bond**, or trading at a premium; if lesser, then it is a **discount bond**, or trading at a discount.

So now we can no longer use the running yield, because we are paying some amount to buy the bond that is different from its face value. Now we need a different measure, called the current yield.

The current yield

The current yield is really easy to calculate. We simply take the actual interest paid by a bond each year, divide it into the current market price of the bond, and then express this as a percentage. Let us suppose that we have a US bond with a face value of $100 that pays $5 a year in interest, and is currently trading at $98.34:

$$\frac{5}{98.34} \times 100 = 5.08\%$$

What about the redemption amount, though? Well, there is something known as the **modified current yield** that takes this into account. You see, in this example we stand to make a profit at the end of the bond's life because we have only paid $98.34 for the bond, whereas we will actually be paid $100 on redemption. The modified current yield works by calculating the discount or premium that the market price represents relative to the redemption amount, dividing this by the number of years to redemption, and adding this to the current yield.

Let's illustrate this by extending our example. Suppose that our bond is due to be redeemed in three years' time. We know that we will make a capital gain of $1.66 ($100 – $98.34) in three years' time. This means that we are notionally making a third of this ($0.55 allowing for rounding) each year in addition to our interest yield. $0.55 is 0.55% of $100, so our modified current yield becomes 5.63% (5.08% + 0.55%).

Basic bond yields

$$\text{Running yield} = \frac{\text{annual interest}}{\text{face value}} \times 100$$

(Note: the face value of a bond is the same as its redemption value. If a bond is actually issued at its face value, rather than at a discount or premium to it, it is said to be issued at par.)

$$\text{Current yield} = \frac{\text{annual interest}}{\text{market price}} \times 100$$

$$\text{Modified Current yield} = \left(\frac{\text{annual interest}}{\text{market price}} \times 100 \right) + \left(\frac{(100 - \text{market price})}{\text{years to maturity}} \right)$$

Incidentally, the current yield, whether modified or not, illustrates one of the most fundamental and important aspects of bonds. Think back to the basic logic of arithmetic that we explored earlier. The current yield represents a mathematical expression, one of which (the annual interest payable) always remains the same:

$$\frac{A}{B} = C$$

Since one of these three values (A) always remains the same, then it must be the case that the value of B can only change if the value of C changes, and vice versa. Try it with some numbers. Let A represent 10. If you use 5 for the value of B then C will be 2. However, if you change B to 2, now C becomes 5. So, not only do they move relative to each other, but they move in opposite directions; as one goes up, the other goes down.

In financial terms, since (usually) the amount of annual interest remains the same throughout the life of the bond, then its market price and its yield share a direct mathematical link: as the price of a bond goes down, its yield goes up, and vice versa. We will examine this relationship in more detail a little later when we look at bond pricing. For the moment, let us simply note the principle, and a very important one it is too. In fact, if you could only remember one thing about bonds, then this might well be the thing to choose.

For any fixed income security, as its market price goes up, its current yield goes down. As its market price goes down, its current yield goes up. It must be this way, if you think about it, for the current yield simply represents the annual interest as a percentage of the market price. So, if the amount of interest is fixed, then as the market price goes down the interest must represent a greater proportion of it, while if it goes up then the fixed amount of interest must represent a smaller proportion.

FIGURE 11.4 Bond yield and price

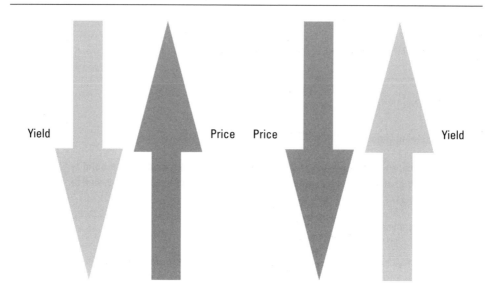

As you will doubtless already have spotted, however, neither of these current yield measures takes any account of the time value of money. For example, the modified current yield simply divides any premium or discount by the number of years remaining. As we have already discussed at great length earlier in the book, this does not reflect reality, for it ignores the time tunnel effect. If you are due to make a capital profit on maturity (by buying a bond at a discount to its face value) then you would much rather that the maturity date was tomorrow, rather than in three years' time. If, on the other hand, you have bought a bond at a premium to face value so that you are due to realize a capital loss on maturity, then you would prefer that the loss happened as far in the future as possible.

So, as with any type of investment, we need to think about compound, not periodic, returns. Most unusually, where bonds are concerned the world of finance actually accepts this. So, let us make the most of this rare opportunity where finance actually operates in the real world rather than in some parallel universe where time is not a relevant factor. In the next chapter we will move on to the idea of applying discounting to bond returns, which, as we will see, is also essential in looking at how bonds are priced.

Summary

- Bonds are debt instruments that are almost always issued at a fixed rate of interest and for a fixed period. The date on which they must be redeemed (repaid) by the issuer is known as the maturity date.

- Bonds may be issued both by governments and by corporations. Certain types of issuers, such as public bodies and nationalized industries, require careful examination to determine their status; is the debt actually guaranteed by the relevant government or not?
- A very small number of governments have traditionally been recognized as being of such unquestioned economic stability that their bonds are described as 'prime', and the interest rate payable upon them is regarded as 'the risk free rate' for the purposes of financial analysis.
- Because a bond is a debt instrument, the risk of a bond is seen as being the likelihood of the issuer defaulting, either upon the capital redemption payment or in respect of one or more interest payments. There are a number of ratings agencies that attempt to assess this risk in respect of each individual issuer, and publish their findings on a regular basis.
- The return on a bond is comprised partly of interest payments and partly of a large capital sum on redemption. Some measures of bond return, however, are concerned only with interest.
- The running yield looks at the interest yield offered by a bond when it is issued, by dividing the interest amount into the face value (redemption value) of the bond.
- The current yield looks at the interest rate currently offered by a bond, by dividing the interest amount into the market price.
- The modified current yield attempts to take capital value into account by including an annualized amount of the premium or discount represented by the market price relative to the redemption value. However, this measure takes no account of the time value of money.
- Because the amount of interest payable each year usually remains the same throughout a bond's life, this means that there is a fixed relationship between the price of a bond and its yield. As the price goes up, the yield goes down, and vice versa.

Notes

1   Note that there are separate ratings for short-term bonds. The ones we are considering relate to an issuer's long-term obligations, and are the ones commonly referred to in the media.

12
Bonds (2): discounting, redemption, pricing and valuation

As we have just seen, there are a number of ways in which we can measure bond yields, but none of the ones that we have considered so far take any account of the time value of money. So, how might we do this?

It is always a good idea when considering any aspect of finance or investment to stop and think about the reality of what is happening. If you can understand a situation at its conceptual level, then everything else, everything you need to actually start making some calculations, will fall naturally into place. OK, so what is happening when we buy a bond?

We pay a certain price for a piece of paper. That represents a negative cash-flow to us of that amount at time zero (today). In return, we expect to receive a stream of positive cash-flows at regular intervals over the next few years. Well, we have already met a perfect way of measuring the compound returns of that sort of pattern of cash-flows, namely an IRR. We can use this to calculate what is called the **redemption yield**, or the **yield to maturity**.

The redemption yield

As with so many things in finance, this is presented as a hugely complicated mathematical process but is really much simpler. The redemption yield assumes that the price of a bond is the same as the Net Present Value of its future cash-flows. In other words, whatever the discount rate that is used to calculate the Net Present Value, that will by definition be the yield to maturity so long as it produces a Net

Present Value that is the same as the current market price. That may sound confusing (and indeed it is – there is an easier way of doing this), so let us try to build up our thinking in a series of steps.

Step 1

As we have already seen, if we apply a discount factor based upon a particular discount rate to a stream of future cash-flows, that process will produce a Net Present Value.

Step 2

If we assume that financial markets are efficient, then the Net Present Value of those cash-flows and the market price of the bond will be the same. If it was otherwise then either the buyer or seller of the bond at that price would be getting a bad deal, and there would be what is known as an **arbitrage** opportunity.

Step 3

If we assume that the market price and the Net Present Value are the same, then it is as if all the bond dealers who are active in the market have effectively performed an NPV calculation for themselves.

Step 4

Whatever discount rate they have chosen to use is the one that produces the market price. All we have to do is to establish by trial and error (iteration) which discount rate they have used. This discount rate is the yield to maturity.

The complicated, traditional version, the one just described in Steps 1 to 4, looks at the present value of the bond, represented by its market price, and then all the cash-flows that can be expected from it. It uses iteration to find the exact discount rate that will produce a Net Present Value that is the same as the market price.

It is, however, possible to do this on a much more straightforward level, which also better reflects the reality of what is happening. Instead of taking the market price of the bond as the Net Present Value, let us assume that we buy the bond at time zero. Now we have a negative cash-flow representing the price of the bond and a Net Present Value of zero, which means that we can simply let Excel's IRR function do the work for us. Let us explore this with an example.

Assume that we buy a US bond with a face value of $100 for $96.54. It pays $5 interest every year, and is due to mature in exactly three years' time.

Option 1: set out the future cash-flows and use iteration to find the discount rate (r) that will produce a Net Present Value of $96.54.

TABLE 12.1 Bond relationships: how different factors move against each other

Year 0	Year 1	Year 2	Year 3
Interest	5	5	5
Redemption			100
Net cash-flows	5	5	105
NPV = $96.54			
r = 6.3%			

Option 2: assume a negative cash-flow of $96.54 in end Year 0/beginning Year 1, and calculate an IRR.

TABLE 12.2

	Year 0	Year 1	Year 2	Year 3
Interest		5	5	5
Redemption				100
Net cash-flows	-96.54	5	5	105
IRR = 6.3%				

Note: If you perform this exercise in Excel you might find that you are getting a lower discount rate for Option 1 (4.63% to be precise). This is because the Excel NPV function assumes that cash-flows occur at the end of the period. Therefore you must make sure that your first period in Option 1 is Year 1, not Year 0. Incidentally, the best way of executing Option 1 in a spreadsheet is to set up the rate (r) as a variable in a separate cell, and then just carry on changing this number until the NPV matches the market price. As we saw earlier, this is all the IRR function does anyway, albeit much more quickly.

As you can see, once we get the Excel entries set up correctly, both options give the same answer. It would be strange if it were otherwise, since we are just stating the same situation in different ways. In Option 1 we already own a bond worth $96.54 but hold no cash. In Option 2 we have cash of $96.54 but no bond. In order to put ourselves in the same position as Option 1, we would have to pay out the cash to buy the bond.

Bond pricing

If you understand the concept of a redemption yield then you will already also understand the concept of bond pricing, since each is based upon the other. However, let us go through it properly.

We have already learnt two very valuable principles that, if we apply them together, tell us everything we need to know about how to price a bond. The first is that the price and the yield of a bond are inextricably linked, so that if we know one we can work out the other. The second is that a bond can only be priced as a result of a discounting exercise. Let us first remind ourselves about *how* discounting works, and then think about exactly *what* we need to discount in this case.

How does discounting work and how is this relevant to bond pricing?

Think back to the earlier chapters in which we considered the basic principle of discounting. We saw that, no matter how complicated the particular situation might be, and no matter how terrifying the relevant formula, all discounting situations break down into a choice between two broad questions. This will be true regardless of whether we are looking to discount a single future cash-flow or a number of future cash-flows. The questions are:

1. Is this a situation where we need to calculate the present value, in which case we need to choose (fix) a discount rate? Or,

2. Is this a situation where we need to calculate the discount rate, in which case we need to choose (fix) the present value?

As we saw, trying to estimate the relative attractiveness of two different projects might be a good example of the first, while calculating an internal rate of return (IRR), such as a yield to maturity, would be a perfect example of the second.

All discounting situations must fall into one of these two categories; there are no exceptions to this. It is impossible to calculate discounting in any other way. Both discounting and compounding work with three factors: present value, future value and rate (whether a discount rate or an interest rate, which are essentially the same thing operating in different directions). In order to calculate any one of these, the other two must be fixed and certain.

With compounding, it is the future value that is unknown, so it is imperative that we know both the present value and whatever percentage rate we are to apply for compounding purposes. With Net Present Value calculations, it is the future value and the (discount) rate that are fixed, to allow us to calculate the NPV. With IRR calculations, it is the present value and the future value that are fixed, in order to allow us to calculate the rate.

So, how does this knowledge help us to price a bond? Well, what are we trying to find: the value at which we need to price the bond today, or at some time in the future? Today, obviously. Do we know what that value is? No, that's why we are trying to calculate it. So straight away we know what sort of discounting situation we are dealing with. We are trying to find the present value, in which case both the future value and the rate need to be fixed or the process cannot work.

Before we develop this thinking further, let's turn now to consider exactly what we need to value.

What do we need to discount in pricing (valuing) a bond?

Pricing and valuing a bond are of course the same thing, at least so far as financial theory is concerned. Finance says that market imperfections and irrational behaviour will be **arbitraged** away. What does this mean? A market imperfection can occur when an asset is priced either above or below its real value, perhaps because some market participants have a better level of knowledge about the asset than others (or think they do!). When this happens, because emotion rather than logic is driving events, as can happen during periods of market turmoil, it is an example of irrational investor behaviour. When either market imperfections or irrational behaviour happens, rational investors will seize the opportunity to take a profit either by selling or buying the asset as appropriate. As this occurs within the market, the price will automatically be adjusted back to the asset's real value. Incidentally, the logical outcome of this theory is that stock market crashes are impossible...

So we can safely assume that the exercise of pricing a bond is the same thing as the exercise of finding its value, and because we want to know what that value is today, then this means that the price of a bond today should be the same thing as its present value. What is it that we need to discount in order to find the present value? Let's try putting the question slightly differently: what value does a bond provide, on which we can put a price?

As we have already seen, a bond produces two different types of return. First, there is a series of interest payments that are made at fixed intervals during the life of the bond. Second, there is a capital sum, which will be equal to the face value of the bond, payable when it is redeemed on maturity.

Still with our discounting spectacles on, let's look at these two separate elements. First, we have a series of regular future cash-flows, the same amount being paid for a fixed number of years. Second, we have a one-off future cash-flow of a fixed amount occurring on a fixed date in the future.

We recognize the first of these straight away: it is an annuity. If we buy a 20-year bond on its date of issue that has a face value of $100 and pays 5% annually, then one part of what we have bought is a 20-year annuity of $5. The other part of what we have bought is the right to receive $100 in 20 years' time.

We know how to discount both of these things. So, if we discount both of them to find the present value of each, and then add the two present values together, then surely that must be the NPV of the bond, and thus also its price?

Yes, it is. If you take a look at the accompanying formula, which at first sight seems hideously frightening, you may notice that it looks strangely familiar. It consists of two elements that are added together, and if you look carefully you will notice that the left-hand element is simply the formula for an annuity, which we have already met, while the right-hand element is simply the present value of a single future cash-flow.

Bond pricing formula

Bond price = PV of interest payments + PV of redemption payment on maturity

PV of interest payments $= \dfrac{A}{r} \times \left(1 - \dfrac{1}{1+r}\right)^{n}$

Where A is the annual interest payment,
r is the discount rate, and
n is the number of years remaining until the maturity of the bond.

(A simplified statement of their formula appears below.)

PV of redemption payments $= M \times \left(\dfrac{1}{1+r}\right)^{n}$

Where M is the amount payable on maturity.

So bond price $= A \times \left(\dfrac{1 - \left(\dfrac{1}{1+r}\right)^{n}}{r}\right) + M \times \left(\dfrac{1}{1+r}\right)^{n}$

Don't panic! This formula is not nearly as forbidding as it looks. Think about what you already know:

   You know the amount of annual interest (A).

   You know the amount payable on maturity (M).

   You know the numbers of years to maturity (n).

So, the *only* thing you do not know is the rate (r), and you are allowed to make this up!

As we have already seen demonstrated at the conceptual level, the formula, daunting though it may seem, requires you to make up a discount rate with which to perform the calculation. Remember, if we want to calculate a present value then we must fix both the future values (which we know) and the rate (which we do not know). Yet we need a fixed rate for our calculation, so we have no choice but to make it up, just as we arbitrarily set the present value to zero when calculating an IRR. So, what rate should we choose?

What factors influence the choice of discount rate in bond pricing?

Assuming our bond is issued at a fixed rate of interest and for a fixed term (which most bonds are), then there are two factors that we need to consider. If we take a step back, at least one of these should be obvious, not least because we have already met it in the last chapter.

Remember that there is a fixed relationship between the perceived risk of a bond and the return that we will deem acceptable in order to justify buying it. We would expect a higher return from a BBB corporate bond than from an AAA government bond, because we would perceive there to be more risk of the issuer of the BBB bond defaulting.

Remember too that there is a fixed relationship between the yield of a bond and its price. Thus, the only way we can earn a higher return on the BBB bond is by paying a lower price for it in the first place. Assume that both bonds have a face value of $100, and that both offer the same rate of interest. If we are prepared to pay face value for the AAA bond, then we should only be prepared to buy the BBB bond if we can do so at some discount to face value. So, this means in turn that there must also be a fixed relationship between the perceived risk of a bond and its price.

Finally, as we have just seen demonstrated in this chapter, there is a link between the price of a bond and the discount rate that we use to calculate that price. So, the final link of our logic chain brings us to the conclusion that our choice of discount rate to use when calculating the price of a bond should be conditioned by the perceived risk of the bond. What is the risk of the bond? The risk that the issuer might default at some stage during the life of the bond.

So, the first factor that will influence pricing is the perceived risk of issuer default. We could try to analyse the financial health of the issuer for ourselves, or we could rely on the ratings agencies to do this for us. Let's try pulling this together by way of a worked example.

Bond Example 1

We are tasked with pricing a 10-year corporate bond that has a face value of $100 and pays annual interest of 5%. The bond is rated A+, and we are told that bond dealers are currently applying a discount rate of 3% to A+ bonds.

First, let's work out the present value of the interest payments:

$$A \times \left(\frac{1 - \left(\frac{1}{1+r}\right)^n}{r} \right)$$

$$5 \times \left(\frac{1 - \left(\frac{1}{1.03}\right)^{10}}{0.03} \right)$$

$$5 \times \frac{1 - 0.7441}{0.03}$$

$$5 \times \frac{0.2559}{0.03}$$

$$5 \times 8.53$$

$$\text{PV of A} = 42.65$$

Now, let's work out the present value of the redemption amount:

$$M \times \left(\frac{1}{1+r}\right)^n$$

$$100 \times \left(\frac{1}{1.03}\right)^{10}$$

$$100 \times 0.7441$$

PV of M = 74.41

So, the PV of the bond = 42.65 + 74.41 = 117.06

We would therefore price this bond at \$117.06, a premium to face value of \$17.06.

So, as you can see in Example 1, we first work out the present value of the annuity (the stream of annual interest payments) using our chosen discount rate. Then we do the same for the redemption payment that is due in 10 years' time. Then we add the two present values together to find the Net Present Value of the bond, which is also its price.

So far, so good; but we know that bond prices do not stay the same. On the contrary, they move up and down constantly. Small daily fluctuations tend to be the result of market activity. If lots of people are looking to buy Coca-Cola Corporation bonds on the same day, then obviously their price will move up a bit as a result of simple supply and demand. We will ignore these small daily movements, as they are part of normal market activity, but what about larger and longer-term movements? These can be caused by three things: market sentiment, a change of rating, and changing interest rates.

Market sentiment

When this occurs, the market's view either of bonds as a whole or of a particular type of bond suddenly changes. It has nothing to do with the individual issuer, but is more of what might be called a 'macro' view. A perfect example would be the period around September 2008 when the market for corporate bonds simply vanished completely. For a while it was almost impossible to sell *any* bond issued by *any* corporation, regardless of price.

Since, as we have already demonstrated, the only way in which the price of a bond can go down (and the yield go up) is by discounting using a higher rate, then what has effectively happened here as a matter of financial theory is that the market has decided that the discount rate being used until now does not properly reflect the risk of bonds generally, and that a higher one should be used. Similarly, as extreme market conditions ease and bond prices go up again, this can only mean that the market is now prepared to accept a lower discount rate.

Change of rating

Our second case differs from the first in that instead of the market's view of bonds as a whole changing, its view of one particular issuer is revised. This most often happens when one or more of the ratings agencies announces a downgrade; for example, during 2010 various governments were downgraded as bond issuers.

When this happens the perceived risk of that issuer (and hence of any bonds that it has already issued or that it may be seeking currently to issue) goes up; for example, a BBB bond would be regarded as higher risk than an AA bond. Investors will require a higher return in order to compensate them for this higher risk. The only way they can obtain a higher return (yield) is to pay a lower price. A lower price can in turn be achieved only by using a higher discount rate.

Let us see how this works out by looking at our second worked example.

Bond Example 2

We are tasked with re-pricing a 10-year corporate bond that has a face value of $100 and pays annual interest of 5%. The bond was originally rated A+, and we priced it at $117.06 using a discount rate of 3%. However, a downgrade has just been announced to BBB+, and we are told that a discount of 6% is felt appropriate for BBB+ corporate bonds.

As before, let's work out the present value of the interest payments:

$$A \times \left(\frac{1 - \left(\frac{1}{1+r}\right)^n}{r} \right)$$

$$5 \times \left(\frac{1 - \left(\frac{1}{1.06}\right)^{10}}{0.06} \right)$$

$$5 \times \frac{1 - 0.5584}{0.06}$$

$$5 \times \frac{0.4416}{0.06}$$

$$5 \times 7.36$$

PV of A = 36.80

Now, let's work out the present value of the redemption amount:

$$M \times \left(\frac{1}{1+r}\right)^n$$

$$100 \times \left(\frac{1}{1.06}\right)^{10}$$

$$100 \times 0.5584$$

PV of M = 55.84

So, the PV of the bond = 36.80 + 55.84 = 91.64

We would therefore re-price this bond at $92.64, a discount to face value of $7.36.

Changing interest rates

One aspect of bond returns has been deliberately withheld from the reader until now, to make it easier to learn about bonds step by step. Finance teaches that investors, and particularly bond investors, should not think about returns as absolute. In other words, they should not think about them in isolation, but relative to something else. What is that 'something else'? It is the so-called 'risk free' return, which we first encountered when we looked at the Sharpe Ratio. Remember that anything above the risk free return may be referred to as the excess return.

Remember this?

Excess return = r – rf

Where r is the return of an asset, asset type or portfolio that we wish to analyse, and

rf is the risk free rate.

As we saw earlier, traditionally the return available on prime government bonds was taken as the risk free rate, particularly if these were available in the investor's own currency. Incidentally, this explains in terms of finance theory what happened in September 2008. As the financial crisis gathered pace, the gap between the perceived risk of an AAA government bond and, say, an A corporate bond widened dramatically. At the same time, market dynamics were at work as investors sold corporate bonds at almost any price, driving their price down (and yield up) still further, and using the proceeds to buy prime government bonds, thus driving their price up and their yield down.

Incidentally, the efficient market theory says that in this situation all the rational investors in the world would buy corporate bonds and sell government bonds, laughing at all the poor fools who were doing the opposite, but as we all know this did not happen. Yet finance requires us to believe that all investors are rational and all markets are efficient...

But just as there is a relationship between the yield of a non-prime bond and the yield of a prime bond, so there is a relationship between the yield of any bond and prevailing interest rates. After all, it would clearly be a nonsense if an investor could borrow money at 3% and use it to buy AAA government bonds yielding 5% (not least because they could then lodge those bonds by way of security to borrow even more money at 3%...!). The rate at which a bank is prepared to lend money to a borrower must be higher than the risk free rate, since there will always be some element of default risk, no matter how reputable the borrower might be.

So, the pricing mechanism is actually a little more complex than that which we have previously presented. Rather than basing a discount rate on some absolute value, it is more likely to be based on some notional required excess return, expressed relative to the risk free rate. For example, you might require an excess return of 2% on a BBB+ bond, but of 3% on a BBB- bond. If the risk free rate was currently 3%, then your discount rate would be 5% for the BBB+ bond but 6% for the BBB- bond.

However, let's think again about how bond returns work. The interest rate that a bond pays is almost always fixed at the time of issue and remains the same throughout the life of the bond. If that yield was 5% and remained the same, then the sort of situation outlined above could very easily occur. In practice, what would happen is that the risk free rate (the AAA government bond yield) would fall until it was far enough below the rate of loan interest to make such a transaction unattractive. In order for the yield to fall, the price of the bond would have to rise. As the price of AAA bonds rose, so would the prices of all bonds, in order to preserve the differential excess return required for each grading.

Bonds generally speaking have a fixed running yield, as the rate of interest payable is fixed in advance. The rate at which banks are prepared to lend, and the contractual rate of interest payable on many loans, is not. The rate at which a bank is prepared to extend a fresh loan, or the rate payable on an existing loan with a variable rate of interest, will change according to central bank policy. In normal market conditions, for example, the Bank of England will announce a change to its base rate (the rate it charges to banks for overnight deposits), which will in turn alter LIBOR (London Inter-Bank Offer Rate), the rate at which the banks will lend to each other, and this will in turn alter the rate that banks charge to their borrowers.

This is one of the reasons why announcements of base rate are so eagerly awaited. In fact, some hedge funds effectively bet upon the outcome, since they know that if base rate goes up then bond prices go down, and vice versa.

TABLE 12.3

	Yield	Price	Interest rates	Rating
Yield		Opposite	Same	Opposite
Price	Opposite		Opposite	Same
Interest rates	Same	Opposite		N/A
Rating	Opposite	Same	N/A	

NOTE (1) Table of relationships assumes fixed income bonds issued for fixed periods.
(2) It is theoretically possible that prevailing interest rates could have an effect on rating. For example, if an issuer was already highly indebted, the rating agencies could be concerned about the increasing cost of servicing its (other) debts. In such a case, interest rates and rating would tend to move in opposite directions.

Bond durations

The **duration** of a bond is not the same thing as its maturity. It is a calculation of the moment in the bond's life that represents a tipping point so far as its future cash-flows are concerned. The moment when the present value of the cash-flows that remain to be enjoyed by the bond-holder until redemption is exactly the same as the present value of those that have gone before. As each interest payment is made, the duration will have to be recalculated, as the tipping point will have changed.

Imagine creating a makeshift see-saw for two children out of a plank of wood and an old oil barrel (without getting arrested for breaches of health and safety regulations). If one child was much heavier than the other, there would be no point putting the oil drum in the middle of the plank; the lighter child would head skywards and stay there, doubtless screaming loudly. In order to get the see-saw to work, you would have to position the drum much closer to the heavier child.

Bond durations are just the same. Each time an interest payment is made it is as if the lighter child just got lighter still, so you need to move the drum even closer to the heavier child in order to find the new tipping point. Thus a zero coupon bond, which provides only one cash-flow (on redemption), will be the only example of a bond whose duration is the same as its maturity. In every other case, the duration of a bond must occur before its maturity.

Because we are using present values, and because the time value of money means that what happens in the early years of a period has much more impact than what happens in the later years, this means that bonds that have high yields will have relatively short durations. Their tipping point will occur earlier than with a low yielding bond of the same maturity.

There is actually what looks like the formula to end all formulae that is used to calculate what is called the Macaulay duration of a bond, so-called (yes, you've guessed it) because it was invented by a Mr Macaulay. It is actually much less inaccessible than it appears, particularly if you notice that the bottom part of the formula is the same as that to find the price of a bond, which we have already worked our way through. Just to prove that it is actually much easier than it looks, please refer to the worked example. However, because it is a particularly tedious and cumbersome process, when doing this other than for the purposes of a finance exam, you might well prefer to use the Excel function. Unfortunately this is itself far from straightforward, so an explanation of this is also given later in the chapter.

Bond duration calculation

The Macaulay duration formula is:

$$\frac{\sum_{t=1}^{n} \dfrac{t \times A}{(1+r)^t} + \dfrac{n \times M}{(1+r)^n}}{P}$$

Where n is the number of (interest) cash-flows,

t is the time to maturity,

A is the amount of each (interest) cash-flow,

r is the rate (required yield),

M is the maturity/redemption/face value,

and P is the price of the bond.

Remember that we have seen previously that the price of a bond is calculated by adding together the present value of the remaining interest payments and the present value of the redemption payment on maturity.

$$A \times \left(\frac{1 - \left(\frac{1}{1+r} \right)^n}{r} \right) + M \times \left(\frac{1}{1+r} \right)^n$$

Worked example

Let's assume that we wish to calculate the duration of a $100 bond that has six years to run until maturity and pays 5% annually, in just one payment a year. Thus we have six cash-flows to consider: six yearly interest payments of $5.00 each plus one final cash-flow of $100 on maturity. Let's assume that the required yield is 6%.

Let's first see at what price the bond will be trading:

$$A \times \left(\frac{1 - \left(\frac{1}{1+r} \right)^n}{r} \right)$$

$$5 \times \left(\frac{1 - \left(\frac{1}{1+0.06} \right)^6}{0.06} \right)$$

$$5 \times \frac{1 - 0.7050}{0.06}$$

$$5 \times \frac{0.295}{0.06}$$

PV of interest payments = 5 × 4.9167 = 24.58

$$M \times \left(\frac{1}{1+r} \right)^n$$

$$100 \times \left(\frac{1}{1+0.06} \right)^{10}$$

100 × 0.7050

PV of maturity amount = 100 × 0.7050 = 70.50

So bond price = $24.58 + $70.50 = $95.08

OK, that's a useful revision exercise on calculating bond prices, and gives us the bottom part of the Macaulay formula, the price (P). Now, what about the top part?

You probably recognize the Σ sign from working with spreadsheets. It simply means that you add up all the things that fall under its operation. That is why, if you click on this symbol in Excel, it will suggest a range of values to be added together, which you can change or accept.

$\sum_{t=1}^{n}$ simply shows that we are required to add together all the cash-flows defined as n, starting with time period 1.

We know that t = 6, that A = 5, that r = 6%, that M = 100 and that P = 95.08. So, we have everything we need to apply to the formula. Let's do the top part:

$$\frac{1 \times 5}{1.06} + \frac{2 \times 5}{1.06^2} + \frac{3 \times 5}{1.06^3} + \frac{4 \times 5}{1.06^4} + \frac{5 \times 5}{1.06^5} + \frac{6 \times 5}{1.06^6} + \frac{6 \times 100}{1.06^6}$$

which is:

$$\frac{5}{1.06} + \frac{10}{1.124} + \frac{15}{1.191} + \frac{20}{1.262} + \frac{25}{1.338} + \frac{30}{1.419} + \frac{600}{1.419}$$

5.3 + 8.9 + 12.6 + 15.8 + 18.7 + 21.1 + 422.8 = 505.2

Now we divide this by the price to find the duration:

$$\frac{505.2}{95.08} = 5.31$$

Why is bond duration important?

Many of the people who hold bonds do not do so with a view to investment. This may seem a strange thing to say, but it can be explained in two ways. First, if we are talking about prime government bonds, they will logically (since they are seen as risk free, and there is thought to be a direct relationship between risk and return) never deliver an investment-type return, which we might define either as an excess return over the risk free return, or a positive return after the effect of inflation and taxes.

This is in fact an important point, to which we will return at the end of the book when we briefly discuss asset allocation. You will hear of people 'investing' in bonds, but if prime government bonds are what they are talking about, then this is not really possible. Prime government bonds may be a way of holding your money, but they are not really 'investments'.

Second, there are perfectly good and valid reasons for holding bonds that have nothing to do with investment, strictly speaking. Some people believe, for example, that prime bonds will always provide a hedge against inflation. Actually this is wrong, but that doesn't stop people believing it. If you are a taxpayer then prime bonds can *never* protect you against inflation. Even if you are tax exempt, then the best that can be said is that they *may* protect you for some period, depending on when you buy and when you sell. However, many people continue to believe what they want to believe, and to act accordingly.

More importantly, many institutions, such as pension funds, life insurance companies, banks and the treasury departments of large corporations, hold bonds as a way of matching their liabilities. This is starting to get us into some rather advanced territory, since it requires knowledge of various qualities and calculations of both bonds and liabilities that you are unlikely to meet unless and until you take a high-level specialist finance course, but let us note two ways of doing this, in simple terms.

The first is **cash-flow matching**. If you know that you have to pay a particular liability in six months' time, then you could simply buy a bond with the same face value that matures at that time. Assuming the absence of default risk, you have now neutralized your position as regards that liability. You have both a projected inflow and a projected outflow due to occur in the same amount at the same time.

For various reasons, though, many financial players choose duration matching. Here, instead of buying a bond with the same maturity date, you buy one with the same duration. The reason for this is a little complicated, but you can hope to gain a slight cash-flow advantage, which arises as a result of the duration having been calculated on a discounted basis. However, as with everything in finance, there is an associated trade-off. Should interest rates rise in the meantime, before payment of the liability becomes due, the price of your bond will fall, and as you are relying on being able to sell this to meet your liability, then you may actually suffer a shortfall rather than the planned surplus. This does not happen with cash-flow matching, of course, because you are relying only on the redemption payment, which remains the same regardless of what happens to interest rates.

Please note that this is a deliberately simplistic example. Most institutions will aim not to match individual liabilities against assets, but rather *all* their liabilities against *all* their assets. This may be because they have so many individual liabilities that the former approach would not be practical, or because some of their liabilities are so long term that it is not possible to find matching bonds. A pension fund would fall into both these categories. However, there will always be something called the duration gap, since the duration of their liabilities will classically be greater than the duration of their bond portfolio. Again, we will return to this in a later chapter.

It is thus vitally important to have some measure of how sensitive a bond may be to changes in interest rates. There are some very complicated ways of working this out, but Macaulay duration is a very good litmus test. In general, if interest rates change by 1%, then the duration of the bond is an indicator of how far its value (price) will move in percentage terms in the other direction. Thus, in the case of our bond that we modelled as having a duration of 5.31 years, should interest rates go up by 1% then the price of the bond should fall by 5.31%, while if interest rates fall by 1% then the price of the bond would rise by 5.31%.

Unfortunately finance folk seem incapable of speaking without constant recourse to the Greek alphabet. The Macaulay duration is often referred to as the Lambda (λ) of a bond. This should not be confused with the dollar duration, which shows the likely change in money rather than percentage terms and is called the Delta (Δ). Incidentally, for those of you who know your Greek alphabet, there seems no good reason why mathematicians should use lowercase for the former yet uppercase for the latter, except perhaps that uppercase Lambda is sufficiently similar to Delta as to cause potential confusion.

Finding bond durations using Excel

The Macaulay duration of a bond may be calculated using an Excel function, which is:

=DURATION (settlement,maturity,coupon,yield,frequency,basis)

Both the settlement date (the date when the bond is assumed to be bought) and the maturity date (redemption date) must be entered in Date format.

Coupon (interest) and yield are entered as percentages.

Frequency is the number of interest payments per year – normally a number between 1 and 4.

Basis is an optional input, and refers to the number of days in a year. This may seem a strange input to require, but certain types of financial analysis work on the basis that there are fewer than 365! To illustrate this, if you leave it out (which does no harm at all), it will assume that a year consists of 12 months each of 30 days, and thus that a year has only 360 days.

Summary

- The redemption yield measures the compound return on a bond that will be earned over the remaining period until its maturity (redemption). It therefore takes account of all remaining cash-flows, including the redemption (repayment) of the bond at its face value on maturity.
- The redemption yield (also known as the yield to maturity or YTM) can most easily be measured by means of a simple IRR calculation, treating the current price of the bond as a negative cash-flow at the beginning of the sequence. The traditional formula calls for a trial and error calculation to find a present value matching the current price by iteration.
- The price of a bond is assumed to be the same as its Net Present Value. The NPV is the present value of the interest payments added to the present value of the redemption payment. The discount factor used is the required yield.
- Assuming that the rate of interest paid by the bond remains fixed during its lifetime, then there is a fixed and inverse relationship between the price of the bond and its yield. The pricing of the bond can only be affected by taking a different yield as the discount factor. The yield of a bond, whether current or YTM, can only be changed by a movement in the price.
- The discount rate/required yield may be affected by market sentiment as to bonds (or certain types of bonds) generally, or by a change in the rating (perceived risk of default) of an individual issuer.
- In addition, should interest rates go up, then the required yield will also need to go up in order to maintain the same excess return (return over the risk free rate), thus leading to a lower price, and vice versa. There is thus an inverse relationship between interest rates and bond prices; as one goes up, the other goes down.
- Many financial institutions hold bonds not as investments, but as a means of matching liabilities, whether singly or overall. It is possible to measure the duration of a bond, the tipping point at which the present values of the remaining cash-flows to either side of the point are exactly equal to each other. The duration is a measure of the sensitivity of the price of a bond to changes in interest rates.

13
Equities

As we saw in the last chapter, prime government bonds have traditionally been seen as a good way of deploying cash in such a way that it may match your liabilities, and will hopefully also protect you against the effects of inflation. As we have noted already, this hope may be unfounded, and certainly will be whenever an investor is also a taxpayer.

The one thing that they cannot be relied upon to do, however, is to produce what we might call a proper investment return. Since this is not a standard financial term, let us be very careful to define what we mean. Investors typically think about their target return in one of four ways:

1. As some absolute number, such as 8.5%.

2. By reference to some recognized benchmark, such as a quoted equities index, for example 'MSCI World plus 1.5%'.

3. By reference to the rate of inflation, for example 'inflation plus 2%', or '2% in real terms'.

4. By reference to the risk free rate, for example '3.5% excess return' or 'short-term gilts plus 3.5%'.

Now prime bonds may sometimes deliver a better return than option 2, most obviously when stock market returns are negative. There will thus be a great deal of uncertainty as to whether, in any one year, your equity portfolio outperforms bonds; it will depend not just on bond prices and yields, but also on whether the stock market is going up or down at the time. This uncertainty of outcome that arises as a result of holding equities rather than bonds is often called 'equity risk', especially by pension funds and those who advise them. Remember, incidentally, that finance is here using its own view of risk as volatility, so equity risk will be calculated by looking at the Standard Deviation of the difference between the equity return and the bond return in each period (usually years).

It seems clear, however, that prime bonds cannot normally be expected to deliver anything like the other types of investment return referred to above. They could only intermittently and occasionally deliver option 1, and that would have to be at a time of high interest rates and thus presumably also high inflation (since the former is normally used to try to cure the latter). Much research shows that over a long period they will at best only slightly outperform inflation, and then only if you are a non-taxpayer. As for option 4, they *are* the risk free return and thus by definition cannot be expected to outperform it.

So, if someone is looking to actually grow the value of their capital over time, as opposed to preserving it (which is the best you can hope for with prime bonds, and not even that if you pay tax), then clearly they have to look elsewhere. We have already seen one option they might explore: to accept more risk within their bond portfolio in the hope of moving their efficient portfolio to a more high risk/high reward profile. The only other option that has been pursued to any significant extent in the past (though this is changing and will change further, as we will see in a later chapter) is to invest in equities, by which we mean collectively the shares or stock of publicly quoted companies or corporations.

Characteristics of equities: income

We have already seen that bonds and equities differ in both legal and accounting terms. Bonds are debt whereas equities are (you guessed it, didn't you?) equity. So bonds are treated as liabilities while equities are treated as capital, and thus they belong in different places on the balance sheet.

They are also different in investment terms, both as to income and capital values or payments. Remember that bonds, being debt instruments, pay a fixed rate of interest expressed as a percentage of their face value, and repay (redeem) that face value on maturity, which is itself a fixed date. Equities are different.

Let's look at the income side of things first. For the purposes of learning about finance we will assume that the issuer of a bond *must* pay the interest due to the bond-holder every year, though in practice there are some special types of bonds that have slightly more flexible arrangements. This is not the case with equities. The directors *choose* whether to pay a dividend in respect of any one year; they are not obliged to, and in general there is little shareholders can do to challenge their decision. Thus while you may hold equities in the expectation of receiving a dividend, there is no guarantee that this will actually happen.

Nor is there any certainty as to the amount. If a bond with a face value of $100 pays 5% interest, then the amount of the interest payment every year will be $5, irrespective of whether the current price of the bond is $200 or $50. In the case of dividends, the directors decide how much to pay in respect of every share; again, they have complete discretion on this. The only exception to this are preference shares or preferred stock, which do usually carry a fixed rate of dividend, but in practice most investors treat these in much the same way as they do bonds. There is only one essential difference, and it affects the business rather than the investor: interest payments on bonds are paid before tax and may be deducted as a legitimate expense when calculating the business's tax liability, whereas dividends, even on preference shares, are payable after tax. As we saw earlier, when viewed purely from the viewpoint of tax efficiency, it is much more desirable for a business to raise debt finance rather than equity (remember the Theory of the Efficient Firm).

So, with equities there is a right to receive a dividend only if the directors decide to grant one, and even then there is no certainty as to how much it will be. As a matter of practice, however, most public companies, particularly in the UK, once having established a customary rate of dividend, will strive to maintain it if they possibly can. Cutting the dividend can be a key indicator of problems within the business and will frequently also cause a drop in the share price, thus both making the company more vulnerable to a take-over and leading to general shareholder dissatisfaction.

We have already seen in an earlier chapter how to calculate the dividend yield for any share (stock):

$$\frac{\text{dividend paid}}{\text{share price}}$$

If you want to track the dividend policy of a company, you can do it by using the dividend payout ratio. This operates in two ways, one at the level of one individual share, and the other at the level of the company as a whole (though both should give the same result!):

$$\frac{\text{dividend paid}}{\text{earnings per share}} \text{ or } \frac{\text{dividends}}{\text{net income}}$$

Note that 'net income' is here being used in the sense of earnings after tax, or what is sometimes referred to as earnings available for distribution (a dividend is a distribution to shareholders). The inverse of the dividend payout ratio is called the **retention ratio:**

$$\frac{\text{net income} - \text{dividends}}{\text{net income}}$$

Whichever one of these you choose to use, they are valuable analysis tools. Is a company maintaining the dividend yield, but only at the expense of paying out more and more of the company's profits? If so, how will it fund any necessary capital expenditure in coming years, and what areas might it be starving of cash – new product development, perhaps? On the other hand, if a business has a large cash pile but is distributing a relatively small amount of earnings every year, then might it not do better to increase the dividend yield, or even to offer to buy back some of its shares from the shareholders?

Characteristics of equities: capital

Bonds are generally issued for a fixed term, during which they are traded on a public exchange. Thus you have a choice of buying on the primary market (when they are issued) or the secondary (where you buy an existing bond that has already used up some of its lifetime from another investor). When it comes to realizing some capital, you also have a choice. You can hold the bond to maturity and receive its face value by way of redemption, or you can sell it on the secondary market for its current market price.

Equities are different. There is a primary market, and where a company is coming to the market for the first time then investors will indeed have an opportunity to buy brand-new shares. As is explained more fully in another chapter, this process is variously called a **flotation**, an **offering**, or an **IPO** (initial public offering). The latter term, though at one time largely unknown outside North America, is becoming almost universal.

However, when a company that is already quoted wishes to issue more shares, then generally the existing shareholders (stockholders) will enjoy pre-emption rights (the right to purchase new shares ahead of outsiders), so here opportunities may be more limited. In practice, new shares are usually offered at a discount to the market price to encourage shareholders to take up their rights (hence the term **rights issue**, which is what an issue of new shares is generally called in the UK). We will examine these processes in more detail in a subsequent chapter.

Unlike bonds, however, shares are not issued for a fixed period, and are usually not redeemable. This means that the option of holding the instrument to maturity is not available. Thus the only exit option is to sell on the secondary market. It is the major stock exchanges of the world that provide this market. In practice, the overwhelming majority of share purchases, and all share sales, take place here.

Measurement of equity returns

There is one big difference that we face straight away when it comes to making the transition from bonds to equities. In considering just about any aspect of bonds apart from the running yield and the current yield, we were dealing with discounting. Put another way (since discounting and compounding are the mirror images of each other), we were dealing with compound rather than with periodic returns. With equities, this does not happen.

It is unclear why this should be the case. Certainly there seems little intellectual justification for it; as we have already seen, any measure of returns that ignores the time value of money is inherently unrealistic. The two most likely reasons seem to be that:

1. Finance seems always to be looking to frame universal rules that will fit all similar situations, and therefore cannot handle the problem of when an individual investor might choose to sell a share in the secondary market, compared to the certainty of when any given bond will mature.

2. When it comes to equities, finance's obsession with 'risk' really goes into over-drive and, as we have already seen, its narrow and artificial view of 'risk as historic volatility' can only be measured by reference to periodic returns. You cannot have both 'risk' and compound returns. Rather than accepting that this throws into question the validity of its view of risk, finance prefers to close its eyes to compound returns.

It is worth explaining this up front, as it is a source of much misunderstanding when it comes to discussing risk. We have already discussed risk in general terms earlier in the book, but now we need to do so more specifically with reference to equities.

As stated earlier in the book, when we are dealing with the periodic returns of more than one period, then we will always be looking at some kind of annualized returns. You might care to glance back at the chapter on returns to remind yourself of the various issues and methodology. We are also back in 'whether realized or not' territory, because if one of your shares goes down in value then you will be deemed to have made a loss on it even if you have not actually sold it, and even if you might have no intention of selling it for several years.

With equities, however, we face a number of specific issues, which are, alas, often overlooked. Most important is the question of how we should treat dividends. Let's think about equities as a whole to start with, equities as a generic group, either globally or in regard to a particular stock exchange.

Equity indices

Every major stock market has a number of different indices, which measure either all or some group of the individual company shares that are traded upon it. In London, for example, the FTSE All Share index embraces the whole market, while the FTSE 100 is limited, as its name suggests, to only the 100 largest companies.

The problem with the traditional indices is that they measure only changes in market price. Thus they capture the effect of buying and selling shares, whether at a profit or a loss, but they ignore dividends. This is frequently overlooked by journalists writing articles about stock market performance, and perhaps comparing the returns of equities to the returns of other asset types, such as real estate (property). This is wrong, and becomes progressively more wrong with every year that is added to the period under review. Equities, like real estate, produce annual income, so how can it be valid to discuss their returns without taking this income (cash-flow) into account, particularly if you are comparing them with another income-producing asset type where it *is* taken into account?

So, at the very least, you would have to find out what the dividend yield had been across whichever index you were using, and add this to the annual return of each year. Incidentally, this sounds easy but isn't, since stock markets for some obscure reason choose to make their index figures publicly available, yet not the dividend yield numbers. This is surely the financial equivalent of being asked to evaluate Laurel and Hardy as a comedy duo, but only after every frame showing Stan Laurel has first been cut out of all their films. It remains unclear why stock markets believe that hiding essential returns data should make investors more eager to invest in equities, rather than less.

This composite approach is certainly better than ignoring dividends altogether, but let's stop and think for a moment about whether there might not be an even better way of doing things. Adding the dividend yield is certainly a valid simulation of our notional investor sitting on their share portfolio and receiving the dividend stream while they do so, but what are they actually likely to do with those dividends when they receive them? Well, some may undoubtedly go out and spend them. Holding shares for income generation is one perfectly valid investment tactic.

There are others, however, who might on the contrary simply reinvest those dividends in more equities. This might be automatic, for example in the case of a family trust fund, or a deliberate tactic on the part of some investors. If so, history suggests that it would be a particularly astute one. Ongoing research by the London Business School on a wide spectrum of financial assets and markets since 1900 strongly suggests that it is this very factor – reinvestment of dividends – that has been the strongest driver of equity returns over the course of more than a century.

For this reason, most markets now provide alternative performance figures for their various indices based on a 'Total Return' basis, that is to say including assumed reinvestment of dividends. However, these Total Return indices themselves do not seem to be made public in the same way as their traditional cousins. As with dividend yields, it seems that Total Return investing is a secret that stock markets wish to keep to themselves. Interestingly, it also seems to be very difficult to find Exchange Traded Funds that can provide this investment approach. Again, there seems no good intellectual rationale for this.

Measuring the performance of equities – both individually and collectively

The traditional approach

Index performance only: based on price changes.
Pros: Index publicly available.
Cons: Not really a valid return measure as it completely ignores dividends.

The dividend yield approach

Adds the dividend yield of each year to the index gain or loss for that year.
Pros: A much better return approximation, since it takes account of dividends.
Cons: (1) Yield information not publicly available. (2) Must be self-calculated by investors and analysts.

The Total Return approach

Assumes that each year's dividend is reinvested in the relevant share or index.
Pros: The most realistic approach of all – recognizes the importance of reinvestment of dividends as a return driver.
Cons: Total Return indices generally not publicly available.

Equity risk

We have already encountered one measure, the Sharpe Ratio, which can be used to measure the risk-adjusted return of any individual asset or asset class, and this can obviously be used to calculate the attractiveness of any individual share, portfolio, stock market sector, stock market index or any stock market as a whole. However, there are two particular aspects of equity risk that we need to consider here, and both relate to the idea of holding shares not individually, but within a portfolio comprised of shares in some number of companies. Two questions need to be answered.

1. Is there some way in which we can measure the risk of holding (or not holding) any one specific share as part of a portfolio?

2. How do we make sure that any such portfolio is properly diversified?

Measuring the specific risk of a share

It is here that we make the acquaintance of the **Capital Asset Pricing Model** (CAPM), but before we look at how this works let us be very clear about exactly what we are discussing. CAPM is based on a distinction between market risk (or **systemic risk**) and **specific risk**. Specific risk is the risk of any one share. A share in BP, for example, will carry its own specific risk. However, that risk will also be a small part of the risk of the stock market as a whole. CAPM calculates this: the specific risk of one share relative to the risk of the market as a whole.

Suppose that we make an allocation to UK quoted equities, and choose to get that exposure by buying the FTSE 100 index. We might do this either by copying (replicating) the index, creating a portfolio of our own that exactly matches it, or buying units in an **index tracker** fund. In either case, the risk of our share portfolio will be exactly the same as the risk of the index. If we call the index 'the market' for our purposes, then we have market risk, but no specific risk. If, however, we decided not to match the index exactly but to overweight one share because we found it particularly attractive, or to leave one out altogether for some reason, then we have added some specific risk. CAPM is designed to help us understand the implications of these sorts of decisions.

Remember that risk is seen as the volatility of historic periodic returns. The starting point for using CAPM is to set out first the historic periodic returns of the market as a whole, and then the historic periodic returns of the individual share we wish to consider. Remember also the concept of excess return. In thinking about equity returns we need to consider to what extent they exceed or (from time to time) fall short of the risk free return, both as regards individual shares and the market as a whole. After all, if we did not believe that equity returns would outperform the risk free return in the long term, then it would be illogical to hold equities in the first place.

- So Rm – Rf, where Rm is the market return and Rf is the risk free return, gives us the excess return of the market, also known as the **market risk premium**.

- So also Ra – Rf, where Ra is the return of an individual asset such as a share, gives us the excess return of that individual asset, also known as the **individual risk premium**.

- The specific risk of an individual share is the extent to which the excess return of the individual asset (which is the same thing as the individual risk premium) is likely to be different from the excess return of the market (which is the same thing as the market risk premium). This extent is known as its beta, denoted by the appropriate Greek letter, β.

- Thus a share with a beta value of one will behave exactly as the market does. With a beta of less than one it will go up and down by less than the market. With a beta of more than one it will go up and down by more than the market.

The way in which beta can be measured is set out in the box.

The fact that CAPM appears to treat risk and return as being the same thing is a source of great confusion and puzzlement for those who come to it from a non-financial background. In fact, it is more correct to say that it treats the risk premium as being the same as the average excess return. The writer can sympathize with such puzzlement, and can do no better than to pass on the advice he himself was given when querying this during a finance lecture many years ago: 'Just learn it this way for the exams, OK?'

The Capital Asset Pricing Model (CAPM)

Individual risk premium = Ra – Rf

Market risk premium = Rm – Rf

Where Ra is the return of an individual asset,

Rm is the return of the market portfolio of which the asset forms part, and Rf is the risk-free return.

Notes:

1. The selection of an appropriate 'market portfolio' may inevitably introduce a subjective element. For example, BP forms part of the FTSE 100, the FTSE 250 and the FTSE All Share indices, but different results will be obtained depending upon which is selected.

The specific risk of an asset is measured as:

$$\beta \, (Rm – Rf)$$

Where:

$$\beta = \frac{covar \, (Ra, \, Rm)}{var \, Rm}$$

Remembering that the variance of a sample is the square of the Standard Deviation, usually denoted as σ^2.

The covariance function in Excel is '=covar(range1,range2)'

The variance function has already been explained.

You will see that beta can be measured very easily in Excel by applying the covariance function to both sets of returns, and then dividing this number by the variance of the market return. So, once you have your two sets of returns neatly laid out, then all you need to do is to check that you are dividing the top of the formula by the bottom, rather than vice versa, which can lead to some rather strange results. Covariance is a complicated concept, which fortunately it is not necessary to understand for our purposes. Briefly, it is a measure of how two series of figures move together.

Three points are particularly important here. The first is that the selection of the appropriate 'market portfolio' can make a big difference to the final outcome. The second is that beta is applied only to the *excess* market return. The third is that CAPM was designed to measure the specific risk of one asset (a share, though this is not explicitly stated) relative to the market within which it sits *and for no other purpose*. All these points are frequently lost on investors, in particular the last. The writer has come across CAPM being used for a range of improper purposes, including comparing one asset class against another, and as part of the valuation of private businesses.

Why is the idea of specific risk important?

Traditionally, whole equity investment strategies could be created around the concept of CAPM beta. In times of strong expected economic growth, a portfolio could be based around stocks with high beta values (**cyclical stocks**), on the assumption that if the market went up, then these shares would go up by even more. In less certain times, stocks with low beta values (**defensive stocks**) would be chosen so that if, as feared, the market went down, then the chosen portfolio would fare less badly.

As we will see in the next chapter, the idea of specific (or non-market) risk has become central to the whole passive/active debate, which has come to be very much at the heart of investment thinking. As we will see even sooner, it is also used to measure the effective diversification of a share portfolio. It is therefore essential at least to understand what it is that CAPM represents. Hopefully, since the mechanics can safely be left to Excel once a simple spreadsheet has been constructed, the calculation can also be easily mastered.

Measuring effective diversification

It was Sharpe, again, who most famously investigated this problem and came up with a solution. The mathematics is set out separately in the box, and works by looking at the relative value of each share within your portfolio, and the relative non-market risk of each share.

Relative value is expressed as some percentage of one. In other words, if you had only four shares in your portfolio and each was of equal value, then the relative value of each one would be 0.25, with the four together adding up to one. Relative market risk is a rather trickier notion, but in practice many people simply adopt CAPM beta. All professional analysts will have tables showing the current beta of each share. If not, this can be calculated as above.

Effective diversification

Sharpe's formula for finding the specific (non-market) risk of any portfolio is:

$$NMR = \frac{1}{\sqrt{D}}$$

Where NMR is the non-market risk of the portfolio, and

D is the effective diversification of the portfolio.

D is calculated by:

$$D = \frac{1}{\Sigma(V \times R)^2}$$

Where V is the relative value of each share, and

R is the relative non-market risk of each share. In practice, CAPM beta is usually adopted.

Methodology

In respect of each individual share, take its relative value as a percentage of one, multiply it by its CAPM beta, and square the result. Write down this figure for each share, and then add all these figures up. The total will give you D.

Divide 1 by the square root of D to find the NMR of your portfolio, expressed as one Standard Deviation.

Worked example

TABLE 13.1

	Value	Relative value (V)	CAPM Beta (R)	(V × R)²
Share 1	50	.3067	1.4	.1844
Share 2	35	.2147	1.2	.0664
Share 3	40	.2454	0.8	.0385
Share 4	38	.2331	1.1	.0657
				$\Sigma(V \times R)^2 = 0.355$

$$D = \frac{1}{0.355} = 2.8169$$

$$\text{and } NMR = \frac{1}{\sqrt{2.8169}} = \frac{1}{1.678} = 0.5959 = 59.59\%$$

The good news is that effective diversification can usually be achieved by holding quite a small number of shares, certainly fewer than most investors seem to have in their equity portfolios. The classic answer is 'less than 30' (<30) and probably somewhere around 25. If you measure the risk of the portfolio as a whole by the Standard Deviation of its historic returns, then it becomes very difficult to reduce that Standard Deviation by adding more shares beyond this number.

Summary

- In contrast with bonds, which seem to be held by many investors in the hope or expectation of preserving the value of their capital, particularly as regards inflation, equities are held with the aim of generating some significant added value, even after inflation. The terms 'equity risk' or 'equity risk premium' are sometimes used to describe this extra return that equities are expected to make relative to bonds, and thus also the corresponding extra risk.
- Whereas most bonds generate a fixed amount of income every year, a share (stock) does not. Indeed, it is in the discretion of the directors whether to pay a dividend at all and, if so, at what rate. In practice, though, in the case of public companies (corporations), once a history of paying dividends at a particular rate (the dividend policy) has been established, directors are most reluctant to tamper with it.
- We can track this dividend policy by measuring the payout ratio each year by:

$$\frac{\text{dividend paid}}{\text{earnings per share}} \quad \text{or} \quad \frac{\text{dividends}}{\text{net income}}$$

- Since equities, unlike bonds, are not redeemed by the business, the only way in which an investor can generate a capital gain is by selling their shares (stock) in the secondary market, which in the case of public companies is represented by all those investors who are buying and selling shares on a daily basis.
- There is much confusion about the way in which equity returns can, or should, be calculated.
- First, one can look simply at the movement of the individual share price or, in the case of a whole sector or market, the movement of the relevant index. However, this is misleading for two reasons: (1) it ignores dividend income; and (2) any capital gain or loss that it represents is purely theoretical unless an individual investor has actually sold at the relevant price. Otherwise it is a notional, contingent or 'paper' gain or loss.
- Even where dividend income is taken into account, a decision has to be taken whether (1) to add the dividend yield to the capital gain or loss, or (2) to assume that not only will the dividend income be received, but also reinvested. The latter is commonly known as 'Total Return', and alternative versions of some leading stock market indices are now published on this basis.
- The risk of holding a share as an investment may be split into two separate components: (1) systemic risk, being the extent to which the price of a share will move up or down simply because the whole market is moving up or down; and (2) specific risk, being the extent to which the share price moves independently of the market as a whole, which we can assume to be the result of factors that are unique to that particular company.

- We can measure the specific risk of a share by using the Capital Asset Pricing Model, which will return a value for its beta. Beta represents the tendency of the share, based on historic data, to move by more or less than the market as a whole, with one being neutral, or the beta of the market. Thus a share with a beta of one will move exactly in line with the market. A share with a beta of greater than one will tend to move in the same direction, but to a greater extent. A share with a beta of less than one will tend to move in the same direction, but to a lesser extent.
- Research into the question of how many individual shares you need to hold within a portfolio in order to diversify away specific risk suggests an answer of less than 30.

14
Alpha and beta: active and passive investment

No sooner have we learnt that **beta** represents the extent to which the return of a specific share may differ from that of the market as a whole, than we have to think of it in a very different way, namely the return of the market as a whole, with the return of a specific asset or group of assets chosen from within the market being **alpha**. There are many instances of finance playing fast and loose with the meaning of words ('risk' being the most obvious example), but this really is one of the most exasperating. Why on earth should the same Greek letter be chosen to represent both the return of a market and the extent to which something may differ from it? It is not as though there are not enough Greek letters to choose from. Unfortunately the choice of terminology is beyond our control, but let us for the record note why finance seems to see no inconsistency here, and then make quite sure that we understand what is being talked about.

Remember that a share that behaves exactly the same as the market will have a CAPM beta of one. So will the market itself. After all, if you compare the market with itself, rather than with one of its constituents, then each of the things you are comparing will be exactly the same, and so any beta calculation will return one as the answer. So, says the world of finance, since the beta of any market is one, let us adopt this as an expression of that market return. Once again, if readers should find themselves puzzled and confused by this, the writer can only offer his sympathy.

Let us be clear, then, what the world of finance is talking about when it uses the words alpha and beta in juxtaposition. Alpha means the return of any individual asset or group of assets selected from a particular market, while beta means the return of that market as a whole. For this reason, it is recommended that when talking about the other sort of beta, the sort we met in the last chapter, we describe this specifically as 'CAPM beta'.

Let us illustrate this by way of an example, using a situation that we touched upon briefly in the last chapter. Suppose that we decide to make an allocation to US quoted equities, concentrating on the 100 largest companies. Right at the outset, we have a choice to make. Do we want a beta return or an alpha return? We can phrase this same choice in a different way. Do we want to buy the S&P 100 index, or do we want to choose individual stocks from within the index, believing that we have some sort of special expertise that will enable us to select those that are likely to outperform the market as a whole? The first approach is known as **buying the market**, while the second is often called **stock-picking**.

Another way in which these different approaches are described is to call buying the market **passive investment**, since you just buy the index, sit back and do nothing, while stock-picking is called **active investment**, since you are taking decisions on individual stocks and then acting on those decisions. A debate has been raging for many years, and continues to rage, over which is the more sensible approach. We will come back to the arguments in favour of one approach or the other later in this chapter, but let us first be quite clear about exactly what is meant in the world of finance by alpha and beta. Let's take beta first.

What is beta?

Beta is the blended, overall return of a particular asset type, which may be divided further by market, sector, or some such other categorization, such as size. It is thus very important always to define your terms precisely, and to be completely certain that the others to whom you are talking, or who have conducted research or analysis on which you will rely, are using the same terms in the same way.

For example, if you were looking at quoted equities you might take some measure of global returns, such as MSCI World. Or, if you only wanted US exposure, you might limit yourself to US stocks. Yet you would still face further choices: would you want the whole market (and which one: New York? NASDAQ?) or just some part of it? As we have already seen, there is a wide choice of indices available. It is even possible that you might wish to choose a particular sector, such as banks. In all of these cases some generally accepted measures of beta return are available, but clearly they will be different. Getting the right measure becomes even more vital if you are going to use one as a benchmark against which your performance will be judged. If, for example, you intend to target the US banking sector then it would clearly be invalid to invest in MSCI World, or to use it as a comparator for performance purposes.

So, we know that beta is the return of a particular asset type, or some definable and generally recognized sub-class of it. The next problem we face is whether there is some way of measuring that return, a measure that is both publicly available and generally accepted. What other characteristics might we require from a beta return measure? The most important by far is that it should truly be representative, and it is here that most argument takes place as to whether a true beta return does or does not exist in respect of any particular type of investment.

The examples we have already mentioned are drawn from areas where there can be no possible dispute. If you want to invest in US quoted equities then there is an index available that will match your particular preferences. Yet even here, great care must be exercised. You will find that there are many investors out there who have never taken the trouble to study the methodology of their chosen index, and should they do so they might actually find, to their surprise, that it does not match their needs after all. For example, some are capital weighted, whereas others are weighted only partially or not at all. The Dow Jones indices include companies that are quoted on NASDAQ, but the favour is not returned; the NASDAQ indices do not include any stocks quoted on the New York Stock Exchange (NYSE). The NASDAQ index includes corporations whose stocks are quoted in the US but that are headquartered abroad, whereas other indices do not. Some indices exclude financial stocks, such as banks, and so on.

The question here, though, is not whether the chosen beta measure is representative, but representative *of what*. So long as you match your chosen measure to your investment preferences, there can be no real objection to its validity. Let us turn by way of contrast to some other asset types where there may be no good measure available, or at least considerable doubt as to whether one exists.

Suppose you want to invest in US real estate (property). You could certainly argue for the existence of some sort of beta return. You could, for example, gather data on the gain or loss made on every property transaction, and every rental payment made nationwide. Whatever result that gave you would undoubtedly be the beta return of US real estate. Yet there is no index that does this. There have been at various times some competing return measures, but these have a relatively short history in terms of past returns, and none claim to cover the whole market. In fairness, this weakness is recognized and is being addressed; in particular IPD, who have for some time been compiling a comprehensive index of UK commercial property, has now extended its activities to cover the US market. Yet currently you cannot 'buy the market' if you wish to invest in US real estate; you cannot even find out what the return of that market has been.

This is a most surprising omission, since US real estate is undoubtedly one of the world's most active investment areas, yet it is so. We may perhaps extract a general principle from this. To misquote Jane Austen, it is a truth universally acknowledged that an asset type that is in demand from investors must be in need of an index. Without an index then, even if a beta return does notionally exist, it is not possible to determine what it might be.

Let us take another example: hedge funds. There are a number of different hedge fund indices, covering not just hedge funds as a whole, but also individual hedge fund strategies. So far, so good. However, the first problem is that there are a number of different index providers, and that their offerings bear surprisingly little similarity to each other when you look at their output figures. So, which index provider you choose could make a big difference to what you end up with as a possible beta return candidate. A further problem here is that not all of them define the different strategies in the same way, and some have changed these definitions as they go along, making true historic comparisons all but impossible.

The biggest problem of all, though, is what is called **survivorship bias**. Briefly, this means that as funds do badly, or even fail altogether, they stop submitting their figures to the index provider, which makes them ineligible for further inclusion in the index. Thus, the argument goes, the published figures will always flatter the actual industry performance because the real laggards are being excluded. To be fair, this is a problem in other areas as well, most notably with US venture capital funds, but it is generally recognized that it is with hedge funds that it is most acute for practical purposes.

Hedge funds also serve to illustrate a further problem with using an index as a measure of beta return: is it **investable**? A clumsy word, but a highly relevant one. Let us assume for the sake of argument that, survivorship bias notwithstanding, a particular hedge fund index does properly represent global hedge fund performance. It can only do this by including the results of several thousand individual funds. Thus, the only way in which one could replicate this would be by going out and becoming an investor in each one of those several thousand funds. This would clearly be impossible even for one of the world's largest investors; nor is there any investment vehicle that claims to be able to do this, so the 'tracker fund' option is not available either.[1] So, the index may or may not be a good representation of a beta return, but whatever the case it is one that is inaccessible to investors; it is not 'investable'.

Incidentally, in recognition of this problem, index providers offer 'investable' indices alongside their mainstream products. These attempt to resolve the issue by including only a restricted number of funds. However, these can still include several hundred, as opposed to several thousand funds in some cases, and are thus hardly an ideal practical solution. Even if they were, you have now sacrificed 'representative' on the altar of 'investable'.

Real estate and hedge funds are both examples of asset types where theoretically some level of beta return must exist, but where there have so far been huge practical problems in trying to measure it, whether at all, or in ways that are both representative and investable. There are also areas of investment where there is much debate as to whether any true beta return actually exists in the first place. Good candidates here are private equity and infrastructure. In both cases, before you could even begin to calculate a beta return, you would have to define very carefully exactly what you were going to include or exclude. For example, with private equity would you look only at the very large buyout funds? Would you include venture capital, which some would argue is a completely different asset type? This is a debate that lies beyond the scope of this book, but be aware that the received wisdom, at least for the time being, is that it is in areas such as hedge funds, real estate, private equity and infrastructure that most investors believe they have little choice but to seek alpha returns instead.

What is alpha?

It seems a glib response to say that alpha is any return that is not beta, but actually this is a pretty good definition. It is also a good description of the principles underlying its calculation. If you want to analyse the performance of an active manager, you would look at the target market from which their portfolio was drawn and calculate how much that market as a whole would have returned to an investor. That is the beta return. You would then take the actual return that the manager had made on their chosen portfolio and compare the two. The difference is alpha.

The word 'difference' is an important one. Many investors seem to assume automatically that alpha must always be higher than beta, perhaps on the assumption that they will usually be accepting more risk (a higher Standard Deviation for the chosen portfolio compared to the market as a whole). This is incorrect. Alpha is only guaranteed to be different from beta, not necessarily higher. In fact, as we will see shortly, at least one famous sceptic claims that logically the return of alpha-seeking managers will usually be *lower* than beta.

Alpha return may be produced in ways other than picking individual stocks. For example, it can be produced by choosing an individual sector, such as banks, rather than the market as a whole. Importantly, it can also be produced by choosing not to invest at all by going liquid, holding cash and earning interest upon it. In analysing manager returns, therefore, investors will usually be looking to isolate and calculate four different types of return:

1. the return made as a result of the market as a whole going up or down (beta);

2. the return made as a result of choosing a particular sector or sectors;

3. the return made by picking individual stocks;

4. the return made on cash holdings.

The last three collectively are alpha. A good way to distinguish between alpha and beta returns is that beta managers have no discretion at all as to which investment they choose. They *must* track the performance of a particular market, index or asset type. This is their only objective, and they will be assessed as to how well they perform based on the **tracking error** between their actual return and the one they are trying to match. For example, they cannot choose to hold cash, as an active manager can, nor can they choose to overweight or underweight certain stocks. Any return element that comes as a result of a conscious investment *choice*, on the other hand (even if the choice is *not* to invest), is alpha.

Alpha can, however, come about as a result of at least three things: market timing, skill in choosing individual stocks or sectors, and luck. The proportion of alpha made up by the cash return can to a certain extent be taken as a proxy for the manager's skill in choosing when to be invested and when to be liquid. The others are notoriously difficult to assess!

The arguments in favour of active investment

Active managers will argue that their personal skills, whether individually or collectively as part of a team, give them a sufficient edge that they can consistently outperform the market. If we can see (as a result of our superior analysis) that a particular stock is likely to outperform, they will say, then we have the power to overweight it in our portfolio, whereas a passive manager has no choice. Even if they strongly suspects that it may outperform, they are not allowed to hold more (or less) than its relative market weighting. The same argument also runs for stocks that the active manager believes will underperform.

Where does this superior judgement come from? The main possibilities usually touted are:

- in-depth specialist analysis of individual sectors or industries;
- superior levels of knowledge about individual businesses;
- ability to take account of 'macro' considerations such as economic factors;
- quantitative analysis independent of business fundamentals.

All of these are valid in theory, but have serious limitations, at least in modern market conditions. Every large investment manager will have a specialist analyst covering a particular sector. However, given ever-tightening regulatory controls on insider dealing, it is now effectively impossible for any one of them to have information that is not available to their competitors. Of course, they may be able to interpret that information more effectively than their competitors. Yet, even if they can, what guarantee is there that this skill will not be recognized by a competing manager and the star analyst hired away? A glance at any financial newspaper will reveal that this is exactly what happens on a regular basis.

As to any manager who claims to have a higher level of knowledge about any company than is available to the market as a whole, see the comments as to insider dealing above. In years gone by, for example, an individual analyst could sometimes get an exclusive interview with a company's CEO, but such meetings have been banned for some time now.

The 'macro' argument appears a strong one at first glance. After all, Global Macro was for many years the best-performing hedge fund strategy. The flaw is that these funds are able to invest in a wide range of financial instruments in order to ride their particular hunches, most of which will be sophisticated derivative instruments that relate to things like currency, interest rates and credit. The ability of an active manager within one relatively narrow area to take such bets is very limited indeed. Their most potent weapon is probably the ability to 'go liquid' but even this is effectively limited, since most investors will be assessing their performance on a quarterly basis and usually take a dim view of managers who hold cash, saying 'We could do that ourselves without paying you a management fee'. (Which is true, but unfair. The question is not *could* they, but *would* they.)

The **quantitative** argument is also appealing. 'Quant' managers say that rather than analysing a business using the sort of methods we looked at earlier, it is possible to identify certain mathematical connections or relationships, and invest accordingly. For example, they may believe that a relationship exists between companies that have high working capital efficiency and strong stock market performance, irrespective of the more conventional considerations such as earnings growth. Quant approaches may also be applied to market timing, following moving averages to try to guess whether a market has temporarily bottomed or topped out. Non-quant approaches are known as **fundamental**, to distinguish them, and traditionally managers were pigeon-holed into one category or the other, though in practice today most use elements of each discipline. Pure quant managers are now most often found in areas such as currency, commodities and hedge funds, and will refer to their particular quant model as their **black box**.

The arguments in favour of passive investment

It was Sharpe (who surely must have won his Nobel Prize for Economics several times over) who put the argument against active managers most cogently. Assume that investing on the stock market is a zero sum game, he said. In other words, if one investor makes a gain on an investment then there must somewhere be another investor who makes a corresponding loss on that investment, since an investor can buy a stock only by another investor selling it. Very well. Put all the active equity managers in the world in a large room and allow them to trade with each other all day. If we believe in statistics and normal distribution then at the end of the day roughly half of them will have made a gain and roughly half will have made a loss.

Now send away the half who have made a loss and invite back for tomorrow those who have been successful. By the end of the second day, half of the managers who were successful the previous day will now have made a loss. Send them away and invite back the day's success stories. Continue to perform this exercise every day.

You do not have to be a mathematical genius like Sharpe to realize that after just four days of this exercise only about 6% of the managers will remain. There you are, says Sharpe, that is how low the probability is of any active manager outperforming the market for four periods consecutively, be it days, weeks, quarters or even years. In fact, he goes on, it will be even less than that. You see, active managers charge much higher fees than passive managers. So, they not only have to outperform the market, but to outperform the market *plus their fee differential*.

Again, this argument is a compelling one. While not openly disagreeing with it (the basic principle is impeccable), there are a few things that one could quibble with. First, Sharpe arguably falls victim to the tyranny that the bell jar of normal distribution exercises over the thinking of finance academics.

You see, there is actually one chance in 40 that one of the managers might not just outperform on day one, but outperform so spectacularly that they could quite comfortably ride out a number of negative periods thereafter but still have a positive result overall. So, Sharpe's view perhaps ignores the possible degree of outperformance, as opposed to the incidence of outperformance.

Second, is it necessarily the case that investment, even in something as mainstream as quoted equities, is still necessarily a zero sum game? Some 'long only' hedge fund managers, who are essentially offering the same service as an active equity manager, may use leverage by way of debt, and sometimes a lot of debt, and thus it will not be the case that their returns must find their mirror image somewhere with another investor. Their notional unleveraged return, yes, but not their actual leveraged return.

Normal distribution

Assuming normal distribution and a large enough sample, 95% of observations will fall within two (1.96) Standard Deviations on either side of the mean (average).

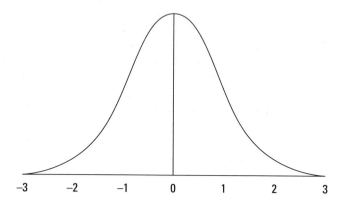

For a larger confidence interval, more than two Standard Deviations have to be used. For example, for a 99% confidence interval, three Standard Deviations are required. This is generally reckoned to be too large a spread to be meaningful for practical investment purposes. There is thus a tail of about 2.5% on both the right and the left sides of the distribution, which the world of finance assumes may safely be ignored as being too unlikely to occur. Yet 2.5% represents odds of only 40-1, while the chance of *either* a left-hand tail or right-hand tail occurring is 5%, or only 20-1.

Similarly, many managers will today make use of derivative instruments either alongside their actual equity investments or even instead of them. The counterparties to these instruments will not be other equity managers, but the investment banks and other institutions that are prepared to 'write' (issue and sell) these instruments.

Perhaps it would be a mistake to make too much of these objections. After all, you could argue that they do not stop quoted equity investment from being a zero sum game, but simply make it much more difficult to discern exactly what is going on in terms of ultimate market gains and losses. Yet it is important to be fully aware of all the issues, since the passive/active debate is one that divides the world of investment, with one or other approach sometimes gaining a temporary fashionable ascendancy, but neither ever being able to totally vanquish the other. Like it or not, if you ever find yourself with responsibility for an investment programme you *will* have to make a choice.

You will be saved from having to do so in only a small handful of situations, at least if you are an institutional investor with access to expert advice and sophisticated investment vehicles. This will be the case either where there is no proper beta return at all, or no measure of it that is both representative and investable. As we have noted, this is most likely to occur in areas such as private equity, hedge funds, real estate and infrastructure, but even here the situation is becoming less cut and dried with every year that passes.

Summary

- In the case of 'beta' we come across a situation in which finance appears to use the same word in different senses. In fact, from a strictly mathematical point of view, this is not the case, but it will appear to be so to those with a conceptual rather than a quantitative mind-set.
- As we have already seen, CAPM uses beta as a measure of the specific risk of any one share (stock) relative to the systemic risk of the market as a whole. Once we move beyond CAPM and look at the world of investment as a whole, however, we find the word 'beta' being used to represent the expected return (and hence risk) of a particular market or asset type. The return of individual assets (such as shares) selected from within the market or asset type is called 'alpha'.
- This distinction gives rise to two alternative investment philosophies. A passive investor is content to accept the beta return, so long as it is possible to access this. This approach is often known as index investing, since it can be performed either by tracking or replicating the particular index in question. An active investor will seek the alpha return by selecting particular individual assets. For this reason, this approach is often known as stock-picking.
- In looking to access a beta return, an investor should ask various questions, most importantly: (1) is the chosen measure representative? and (2) is it investable?
- Alpha return can be generated in a number of different ways, some of which are broadly qualitative and subjective, and others of which are broadly quantitative ('quant') and objective. It is essential to question any manager very closely as to exactly how they claim to be able to generate alpha, and to test their assertions by careful analysis.
- Sharpe, the famous Nobel Prize-winning finance academic, argued that it is impossible as a matter of simple arithmetic for an active manager consistently to outperform a passive manager on a cost-adjusted basis. While the argument is compelling, it is possible to quibble with a few of his assumptions.

Notes

1 Though there are some now that claim to replicate hedge fund returns either by using other means to match their investment techniques, or to create some sort of beta by investing in some number of hedge funds, often on a managed account basis.

15
Derivatives (1): futures and options

Derivative instruments (of which the most commonly encountered are futures, options and swaps) are not financial instruments in the sense that bonds and shares (stocks) are. A bond or a share is an actual financial asset, and in the old days of paper certificates, such a certificate was evidence of your rights of ownership of that asset. A derivative instrument grants you not ownership of an asset, but rights in respect of it, most usually a right either to buy or to sell it on a specific date in the future at a specific price. This may all sound very technical, but don't worry. It will seem much easier after we have considered a few practical examples.

Suppose that you are a coffee grower in South America. The dynamics of your business are very simple. Once a year (during the dry season) you harvest your coffee beans and sell them on the open market to dealers who in turn sell them on to food producers and chains of coffee shops around the world. We can probably safely assume that the total demand for coffee beans is pretty constant from one year to another. The major issue to take into account in fixing the market price, therefore, is likely to be the level of supply: how many coffee beans are likely to be available for sale?

This could in turn be influenced by a number of factors. The weather could be either hostile or helpful; sudden and prolonged rainfall at the wrong time, for example, can lead to beans rotting before they can be harvested. Disease or pests could strike some or all of a coffee-producing area. Terrorism, political unrest or even civil war could prevent farmers bringing their beans to market. Finally, the volume of coffee beans already being stored around the world must be taken into account. Sometimes these threats combine; when Hurricane Katrina struck New Orleans, it not only closed the major coffee importing port in the United States, but also destroyed a large quantity of the coffee that was already being held there.

Consequently the price of coffee can and does fluctuate from year to year, and even from day to day. Imagine, for example, that you are a coffee dealer and today you know about Hurricane Katrina whereas yesterday you did not. All of which can be very good news for traders and speculators (provided they make the right decisions), but very bad news for producers and their industrial customers. If you are a coffee farmer you want to be sure that your harvest will pay not only your operating costs for the year, but also buy you the seeds, fertilizers and insecticides you need in order to produce next year's crop. If you are a chain of coffee shops or an instant coffee manufacturer, you need to know what costs you should factor into your pricing calculations for the coming year. In short, you need certainty, yet you are operating in a very uncertain and unpredictable market environment.

Fortunately there is a way that you can achieve that certainty, yet as with all things in finance, it comes at a cost. You are reducing your risk, however you might define that in this situation, and thus you must be prepared also to reduce your return. Reducing risk, or uncertainty, always comes at a price.

Futures

If you are a coffee farmer, what you might seek to do is to sell your crop to a dealer in advance. You would estimate what sort of quantity your harvest was likely to produce, and agree to deliver this quantity on a certain date in return for a certain price. You have just entered into a futures contract, sometimes just called a **future**.[1] Let us examine the various elements of this.

First, and most importantly, it is a contract and, just like any other contract, it is legally enforceable. So, you can be forced to deliver the agreed quantity should you try to refuse, and you can force your buyer to pay the agreed amount should they try to refuse. There is a mutual obligation; both parties are bound to perform their side of the bargain.

Second, it is a contract for the delivery of a particular asset, or a particular quantity of a particular asset, on a certain future date at a certain price. Incidentally, the first example of such an arrangement is usually said to be that of Thales, the first recorded Western philosopher, who successfully bought up processing capacity in advance of an olive harvest. Everyone thought that he must be very clever if he could predict in advance that there was going to be a bumper crop. In fact he was even cleverer than they thought; what he had actually worked out was that market participants crave certainty, and will be prepared to pay for it.

If you are the supplier, you have now entered into a **short position**, which means that you have effectively sold something that you do not currently own. Your risk is therefore twofold. First, should your own crop fail you will be forced to buy somebody else's in order to be able to fulfil your obligation of delivery to your buyer. Second, by the time you come to deliver your crop, the market price may have moved against you so that you could have obtained a better price elsewhere. The first is a function of this being a contractual obligation into which you have entered. The second is effectively the price you paid in order to buy your certainty, for if the price has moved against your buyer rather than against you then they are still obliged to take delivery, and thus you have got what you contracted for: certainty of outcome.

If you are the buyer, you have entered into a **long position**, which means that you have an obligation to buy something that you do not currently own. You therefore have only one risk: that by the time delivery takes place the market price (**spot price**) has fallen below the price that you have agreed to pay (**strike price**), and so you effectively make a loss. Tough. You have got exactly what you contracted for: certainty of outcome.

However, can you see that the person who grants (writes) the contract – in this case the seller – has taken on much more risk than the buyer? The worst case scenario for the buyer is that they may have to take delivery and pay for something that has now become completely worthless. While it seems almost impossible to believe that this could happen in practice, let us assume for the sake of argument that it could occur. Thus, the maximum loss that the buyer can incur is the difference between the strike price and zero.

A long future

If you have entered into a long position under a futures contract, you have agreed to buy something at a specific price (the strike price) on a specific date (the delivery date) in the future. Here your worst case scenario is that the asset has become worthless by the time you buy it; in other words, the market price has fallen to zero. Thus your downside is limited (though it may be significant) because the market price cannot fall below zero.

Your upside is that the market price is above the strike price on the delivery date. Since there is theoretically no limit on how high the market price could climb, your upside is infinite, or unlimited.

FIGURE 15.1

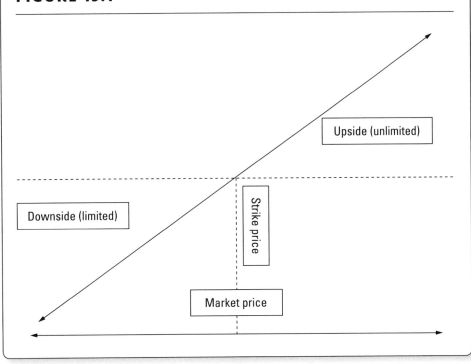

The worst case scenario for the seller is that their own crop fails and they are forced to buy in the quantity they need from elsewhere. So, the maximum loss they could incur is the difference between the strike price (which the buyer is obliged to pay them) and the market price (which is what they will have to pay to someone else for the coffee they require to discharge their own obligation of delivery). For the purposes of financial theory we assume this to be open-ended and potentially infinite.

A short future

A party who writes a futures contract enters into a short position, since they are accepting an obligation to deliver something that they do not currently own. Thus, before the delivery date they must either produce it (for example by harvesting coffee or pumping oil) or buy it in order to be able to deliver it to the other party as agreed.

Their upside is if the market price on the delivery date is lower than the strike price, since now they could, if they wish, simply buy the thing in the market and deliver it to the other party. Since the market price cannot fall below zero, the amount of their upside is limited (even though it could in some circumstances be a very large amount).

Their downside is if they are forced to buy in the market in order to honour their delivery obligations, and the market price on the delivery date is higher than the strike price. Since there is theoretically no limit to how high the market price could rise, so there is no limit to their potential downside (loss).

FIGURE 15.2

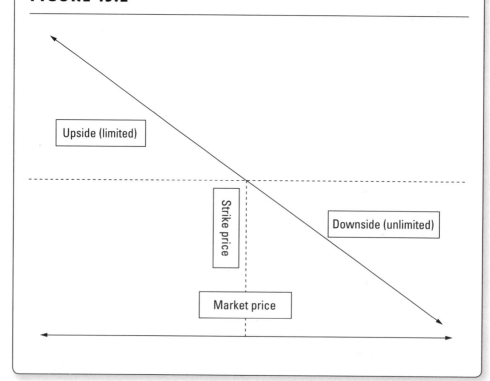

So, writing a futures contract is potentially the riskiest financial transaction into which it is possible to enter, and definitely not for the faint-hearted. In fact, precisely because of this risk, many investors find the use of futures contracts unacceptable and they are little used in the world of investment today, as opposed to the sort of commodity production/delivery situation we considered above.

In the world of investment, a contract for the future delivery of a stock or bond gives rise, as we have seen, to the potential for an unlimited loss for one of the parties. It is very difficult in the modern environment (particularly since the financial crisis) to account properly for this sort of contingent loss, or to integrate it into the regulatory regimes that now govern the likes of banks and insurance companies, let alone pension funds. The degree of uncertainty over the range of possible outcomes is simply too broad to be acceptable.

For this reason, futures have largely been superseded for most practical purposes by options, though writing a call option can give rise to exactly the same degree of risk. However, just before we leave futures contracts, you may have been intrigued by the reference to a forward contract in the endnote. What is the difference between the two?

Remember that we were talking about a contract that was entered into directly between two parties, and was for a quantity of coffee beans that they agreed between them. There are two main differences between a forward and a futures contract. First, futures are for standard quantities of something, quantities that are fixed by market rules and practice, such as 20 tons of pork bellies. Second, rather than being entered into directly between two parties, futures contracts are issued through (and can often subsequently be traded on) a recognized exchange; in the case of pork bellies, for example, this is likely to be the Chicago Mercantile Exchange. There is an important distinction between these two situations, which we will examine in more detail in the next chapter.

For now, however, let us turn our attention to options.

Options

There is one, and only one, really important difference to grasp between futures and options, and once you have done so then you will understand exactly what options are and how they operate. When you enter into a futures contract, you enter into an obligation. You must perform your stated obligation (either to buy or sell as appropriate at the agreed price) on the stated day. When you buy an option, you buy a right, not an obligation. In other words, you may enforce performance of the contract, or you may not. You have a choice, hence the word 'option'.

So, when would you enforce the option (choose to exercise your right either to buy or sell as appropriate) and when would you not? Well, clearly you would enforce the option when you stand to make money by doing so, rather than when you stand to lose money by doing so. In the first situation, the option is said to be **in the money**. In the second situation, where you would actually lose money by exercising it, it is said to be **out of the money**. This can be made clear by looking at some examples, but first let us explore the terminology of options a little more. There are two types of options, **put options** (known as putts) and **call options** (known as calls).

Put options

A put option gives you the right (but not the obligation) to *sell* a particular thing on a particular date at a particular price. There are various ways in which you might choose to remember this, depending on whether images or letters work best for you as a memory trigger. If the former, you could think about a butcher putting meat on the counter in order to sell it. If the latter, you could think about 's' for 'sell' falling between 'p' and 't' in the alphabet.

Let us suppose that you buy a put option that gives you the right to sell 1,000 shares in the Coca-Cola Corporation at $100 a share, and that the option costs you $10 a share ($10,000) to buy.

Example 1

On the expiry date the market price of Coca-Cola shares is exactly $100. Since your option has zero value, there is no point exercising it. In order to sell 1,000 shares you would have to go out into the market and buy them first at $100, only to sell them on immediately for the same price. In practice, your dealing costs would ensure that you would actually make a small loss overall.

Result: you have lost $10,000, the cost of your option.

Example 2

On the expiry date the market price of Coca-Cola Corporation is $105. Your option has expired out of the money, so there is no point in exercising it. In order to sell 1,000 shares at $100 you would first have to buy them in the market for $105, which would be irrational.

Result: you have lost $10,000, the cost of your option.

Example 3

On the expiry date, the market price of Coca-Cola Corporation has fallen to $95. Your option has expired in the money, so you exercise it, buying 1,000 shares at $95 (the market price) before selling them on under your option at $100 (the strike price).

Result: you have lost $5,000, the difference between the profit you have made on the shares ($5,000) and the cost of the option ($10,000).

Example 4

On the expiry date, the market price of Coca-Cola Corporation is $85. Your option has expired in the money, so you exercise it, buying the shares in the market at $85 and selling them on at the strike price of $100.

Result: you have made a gain of $5,000, the difference between your profit on the shares ($15,000) and the cost of the option ($10,000).

FIGURE 15.3 Holding a put option

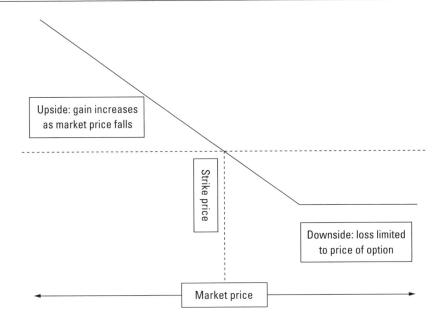

Upside: gain increases
as market price falls

Strike price

Downside: loss limited
to price of option

Market price

If you take a look at Figure 15.3 you will see this expressed graphically. Note that, unlike with futures contracts, your downside will always be limited to the cost of the option, a relatively small amount compared with what would happen if you were *forced* to sell at $100 and the price had risen in the meantime, perhaps to $200 (in which case you would make a loss of $100,000).

Call options

A call option gives you the right (but not the obligation) to *buy* a particular thing on a particular date at a particular price. You might remember this either by thinking of a customer calling at a butcher's shop in order to buy some meat, or because 'b' for 'buy' falls between 'c' and 'a' in the alphabet.

This time, let us suppose that you buy a call option that gives you the right to buy 1,000 shares in the Coca-Cola Corporation at $100 a share, and that the option costs you $10 a share ($10,000) to buy.

Example 1

On the expiry date the market price of Coca-Cola shares is exactly $100. Since your option has zero value, there is no point exercising it. If you were to exercise it then you would take delivery of 1,000 shares for which you would have to pay $100 each. All you could do with them would be to sell them straight back onto the market for the same price, and in practice your dealing costs would ensure that you would actually make a small loss overall anyway.

Result: you have lost $10,000, the price you paid for the option in the first place.

Example 2

On the expiry date, the market price of Coca-Cola Corporation is $95. Your option has expired out of the money, so you do not exercise it, since you would have to buy the shares at $100 (the strike price) only to sell them again at $95 (the market price).

Result: you have lost $10 a share, or $10,000 in total, the price you paid for the option in the first place.

Example 3

On the expiry date, the market price of Coca-Cola Corporation is $105. Your option has expired in the money so you exercise it, because you can buy the shares at $100 (the strike price) and sell them at $105 (the market price), thus making a profit per share of $5. However, the option has cost you $10 a share, so you still make a loss overall.

Result: you have lost $5 a share, or $5,000 in total, representing the difference between your profit on the shares ($5,000) and the cost of the option ($10,000).

Example 4

On the expiry date the market price of Coca-Cola Corporation is $115. Your option has expired in the money and you exercise it, buying the shares at the strike price of $100 and selling them at the market price of $115.

Result: you have made a profit of $5,000, representing the profit you have made on the shares ($15,000) less the cost of the option ($10,000).

FIGURE 15.4 Holding a call option

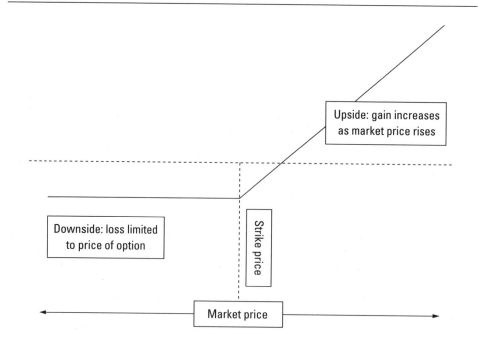

Upside: gain increases as market price rises

Downside: loss limited to price of option

Strike price

Market price

If you take a look at Figure 15.4 you will see this expressed graphically. Note that, unlike with futures contracts, your downside will always be limited to the cost of the option, a relatively small amount compared with what would happen if you were *forced* to buy at $100 and the price had fallen in the meantime, perhaps even to zero if Coca-Cola had gone into liquidation during the life of the option (in which case you would make a loss of $100,000 plus the cost of the future).

Long and short positions

Now that options have largely taken over from futures, at least in bond and equity markets worldwide, it is common to talk about someone who has bought a call option as having a long position, or being long, and someone who has bought a put option as having a short position, or being short. While now broadly accepted as having these meanings, this is not strictly accurate, and a little history may help to understand how this came about.

In the days before electronic trading and settlement, trading on most stock exchanges used to take place during account periods, typically two weeks in duration. During each account period, brokers (retailers) would buy and sell stocks face to face with jobbers (wholesalers) and at the end of the day contract notes would be issued recording all the trades entered into that day. However, settlement was only required at the end of each account period. This meant that during the account you could effectively buy shares that you did not have the money to pay for, or sell shares that you did not own, intending to sell or buy as appropriate in the market before the end of the account so as to be able to honour your settlement obligations at the end of the period, and obviously hoping to make a profit in the process. This was known as account trading, and though frowned upon by most stockbrokers (since they were personally liable under stock exchange rules to honour their clients' trades) it was actually done quite a lot, not least by stockbrokers themselves 'dealing PA' (for their own personal account).

This was where the expressions originated. If you had bought shares that you did not have the money to pay for in full, you were 'long', or had 'gone long'. If you had sold shares that you did not own, you were 'short' or had 'gone short'. In the former case you were effectively gambling on the market price going up before the end of the account (so you could sell the shares back onto the market at a profit). In the latter case you were effectively gambling on the market price going down before the end of the account (so you could buy the shares you needed to deliver for settlement at a lower price than the one you had already agreed with your buyer).

So, today buying a put option is often called 'going short' while buying a call option is called 'going long' but, as you will now understand, there is really quite a difference between options and account dealing. Most importantly, when you buy an option your downside is limited, while with account dealing you were in the same position as if you had written (granted or sold) an option, in which case your potential downside is open-ended (in the case of a call) or very significant (in the case of a put). That is why they are sold for what can seem like quite a heavy price – risk is expensive!

Incidentally, pure short selling, in the form of selling shares that you do not own, has been widely banned. It can, however, still take place by making use of stock lending. An investor will charge a fee for lending shares to a short-seller for a few days, the short-seller being under an obligation to return them as well as to pay the lending costs.

Leverage

The examples we used above of put and call options over Coca-Cola shares illustrate an important principle. Options can be used as a way of leveraging or gearing an investment position.

When we encountered gearing before it took the form of debt. If we wanted to acquire a leveraged position over Coca-Cola shares we could, for example, buy 1,000 shares but pay only 10% of the price for them out of our own pocket and borrow the remaining 90%. Thus we would have a position that we had purchased as to 10% with equity and as to 90% with debt. This may seem a somewhat unwise course to adopt, but in the heady days before the summer of 2007 there were many hedge funds that were running positions that were dramatically more highly leveraged than this.

If you think about it, an option could be said to have much the same effect. Suppose that instead of buying 1,000 shares at $100, and thus paying out $100,000, we could instead buy a call option over them for $10,000. Have we not achieved much the same effect as if we had borrowed the remaining $90,000 as in the previous example? Well, yes and no, and having read this far in the book, it will not surprise you to learn that what we encounter here is another classic example of a trade-off between risk and return.

Outcome 1

The price of Coca-Cola shares goes up to $105. As we have already seen, this would result in the option holder actually making a loss of $5,000 on the deal, as they will have to set off their gain of $5,000 on the shares against the cost of the option ($10,000). The owner of the position leveraged with debt, however, can pay off the loan and make a gain of $5,000 (a gross return of 50% on the capital invested) less whatever loan interest they have had to pay in the meantime. So, in this situation the borrower would be much happier with the outcome than would the option holder.

Outcome 2

The price of Coca-Cola shares goes down to $95. Here the option is out of the money, so the option holder does not exercise it. They lose the $10,000 they paid for the option in the first place. The borrower can sell the shares (indeed, they will probably be forced to by the terms of their loan agreement), pay back the loan and take a loss of $5,000 plus interest costs. So, again, the borrower is better off.

There is actually another important point here as well, and one that is often over-looked. Suppose that the borrower does *not* have to sell the shares to meet the requirements of their loan agreement (they might, for example, choose to inject more equity into the position instead, paying off some of the loan). They are still left with the shares, which must be worth something (their current market price), and will, the borrower hopes, be worth more in the future. So, they can hang on to them and see what happens.

The option holder, on the other hand, is left with nothing, their option having expired. If they want to **roll** their position (continue with the same holding, as the borrower has done), they must go out and buy a new option. If this one too expires out of the money then they will need to buy yet another, and so on. This steady draining away of one's capital in the purchase of a whole series of options, all of which expire out of the money, presumably because you find yourself in a **bear** (falling) **market**, is now commonly referred to as **negative roll yield**.

Outcome 3

The Coca-Cola share price collapses to $30. This is a disaster for the borrower, who not only loses all their $10,000 equity but also has to find another $60,000 to pay back the balance of the loan, losing $70,000 in total. Here the option holder is much better off, since their downside is always limited to the cost of the option ($10,000). Hence the trade-off. The option holder has limited their downside, but at the expense of having also diminished their possible upside. The borrower has geared up their potential upside (they only need the share price to increase by 10% to make a 100% capital gain), but their downside will be equally magnified; here a 70% drop in the share price means that the borrower will lose seven times their starting capital.

So, yes, it is true that an option creates some leverage compared to simply buying the shares themselves with your own capital and sitting on them, but not in the same way as buying them partly with debt. A borrower welcomes significant price change, though they usually seem to believe that it will only occur in one direction, and seeks to magnify its effect. An option holder is prepared to give up some part of their potential upside in order to protect themselves from the possibility of significant downside (in this example, as we will see in the next chapter, there are various other ways of using options).

Capital at risk

The flip side to having high levels of debt or other leverage is that you are only using small amounts of equity. It could therefore be argued that you have reduced the amount of capital that you have at risk. This is true, strictly speaking, although as we have just seen, that advantage is largely illusory in the case of borrowing unless you are certain of being both able and willing to sell your position when your equity value is wiped out (and in rapidly falling and/or illiquid markets, that may not always be possible). Similarly, in the case of options it would be wrong to ignore the possible effect of negative roll yield. As we will see in the next chapter, however, there are situations where options may be used to reduce risk both very properly and very effectively.

In this chapter we have been introduced to the basic principles of how futures and options operate. In order to achieve this, it has been necessary to adopt a deliberately simplistic approach for illustrative purposes, and to gloss over certain more complex aspects of derivatives.[2] Nor have we yet even made the acquaintance of swaps. Don't worry, we will be taking the discussion to a higher level in the next chapter, but before embarking upon it you might care to glance through this one again, particularly at the graphics, just to make sure that you have the basic theory well and truly mastered.

Summary

- Derivative instruments confer not ownership of an asset, but (usually) the ability to buy or sell the asset at a specific date (the **strike date** or expiry date) in the future, at a specific price (the strike price).
- A future confers an obligation to buy or sell an asset. It must be exercised regardless of how disadvantageous this may be for either party, and the potential downside can in some circumstances be unlimited.
- A put option carries the right to sell an asset, while a call option carries the right to buy an asset. Here the investor who has bought the option has a choice about whether to exercise it or not.
- If an investor can make money by exercising the option when it expires it is said to expire in the money, and the investor will exercise their right to sell or buy as appropriate. If exercising the option would result in the investor making a loss then it is said to expire out of the money and the investor will have lost the money they paid to purchase the option in the first place. Thus, their potential downside will always be limited to the cost of the option.
- Holding a put option is often referred to as being long, or having a long position. Holding a call option is often referred to as being short, or having a short position. While these descriptions are widely used, readers should be aware that they are not strictly speaking historically accurate.
- The use of options is often seen as a way of leveraging an investment position. While this is true, a distinction should be drawn with the use of debt. In the former case both upside and downside can be limited, while in the latter the effect of gearing on returns can be explosive (and potentially disastrous).
- It is also argued that the use of options limits the amount of capital that an investor has at risk. This is true, but ignores the possible effect of negative roll yield. Negative roll yield occurs in a steadily falling market, where successive options expire out of the money, with a new one having to be purchased each time in order to keep the position open (roll it).

Notes

1   Strictly speaking, this is a forward contract, not a futures contract, but this example is intended for illustrative purposes only, to explain the general principle.

2   For example, derivatives usually have a 'spread' rather than a particular price.

16
Derivatives (2): swaps, futures, options and how to use them

I n this chapter we will be meeting swaps, the third main type of derivative contract. However, before we do so, we need to look at some further features of options.

OTC and exchange traded options

There is an important distinction between derivative instruments that are entered into directly between two contracting partners, such as the forward contract for coffee beans with which we opened the last chapter, and those that are bought on a recognized exchange, such as CME, which we have already met, or Eurex. The former are called **OTC** instruments, with OTC standing for over the counter. The latter are **exchange traded**. So, what are the differences?

The first and most important one is that with OTC instruments there exists something that we call **counterparty risk**. What you have is a contract that, just like any other contract, relies on the parties for their performance of it. It is possible that when the time comes for performance, one of the parties is no longer financially able to fulfil the contract; in the worst case scenario they may even have become insolvent. This is counterparty risk and, if you remember, we met it when discussing bonds in an earlier chapter. It is the same thing as default risk. With an exchange traded contract, by contrast, that counterparty risk is transferred to the exchange through which it was bought and sold, for the exchange guarantees the performance of all instruments traded through it. This guarantee is backed by deposits taken from the issuers of all instruments, and the risk may therefore now be regarded as negligible.

The second difference is that exchange traded contracts are for standardized quantities (and usually also expire on standardized dates). We touched on this in the last chapter, as it is one of the differences between a forward contract and a futures contract. For example, on the New York Mercantile Exchange the standard size of a coffee futures contract is for coffee beans of 37,500 pounds in weight. That is one of the reasons why the contract we described could not be classified as a futures contract (the other was that it was not exchange traded). It was still worth learning about forward contracts, however. For example, Starbucks is rumoured to buy all its coffee through annual forward contracts entered into directly with individual suppliers (and thus OTC).

The third and most important difference is that many exchange traded options are just that – tradable. This is of course facilitated by their being standardized. The principle is straightforward; if you have an option that is already in the money, or that the market believes is likely shortly to be in the money, then it has some sort of value, and logically there should be somebody out there who will be willing to buy it from you. Thus selling the option in the market becomes an alternative to exercising it. There is a further important distinction here, however, between American and **European options**.

American and European options

So far in our story we have been assuming that an option can only be exercised on its expiry date, and at its initially stated strike price. In fact neither of these assumptions is necessarily correct, but it was a worthwhile deception to practise upon you, since it greatly simplified explaining what options were all about.

In order to understand whether an option can be exercised at any time during its life, or only on expiry, we need to know whether it is American or European. In order to know whether it can be exercised only at its initially agreed strike price or not, we need to know whether it is **vanilla** or **exotic**. Having made you aware of this latter point, however, it will now be ignored for the rest of the book as it introduces an unnecessary level of complication. We will assume that all the options we consider are plain vanilla, or in other words can be exercised only at their agreed strike price.

It *is* important, though, to know whether an option is American or European, and what the difference is between them. Briefly, a European option can only be exercised on expiry. An **American option** can be exercised at any time before the expiry date, or in other words at any time during its life.

Most traded options are American and there is a fairly obvious reason for this. An investor can only properly know the value of a European option at the end of its life. It may be significantly in the money only a few days before expiry but then, as a result of movements in the market price of the underlying asset, expire out of the money after all. Thus anyone who buys one during its life is accepting a high degree of uncertainty. With an American option this is clearly not the case, since the purchaser could exercise it immediately after buying it.

Ironically, however, finance has (as we will see) a recognized tool for calculating the value of a European option, but not of an American one.[1] We will consider that in a moment. First, let us consider the question: why should the holder of an option sell it rather than wait to exercise it later?

Part of the answer is that of course you are buying certainty. Yes, if you wait you might make more money, but equally you might make less. There is a price that any individual investor will be prepared to pay for that certainty of outcome. The other part of the answer is our old friend the time value of money. There is a price that you will be prepared to pay for being able to have your cash today rather than in a few months' time. In practice, it is the differing perceptions of these two factors held by individual investors at the same time that accounts for the pricing of traded options.

However, as a French official once reputedly said to Madeleine Albright when she was US Secretary of State: 'Ah yes, it may work in practice, but does it work in *theory*?' The ordered mind of a Eurocrat obviously abhors the possibility of not being able to regulate a real-life situation by academic rules just as much as the ordered mind of a Nobel Economics Laureate. For it was in recognition of having invented the Black-Scholes Model that Myron Scholes was awarded the Nobel Prize. (Fischer Black had unfortunately died by the time the Royal Swedish Society of Sciences got around to awarding the prize 24 years after their original paper was published, and the prize cannot be awarded posthumously.)

The Black-Scholes Model

The best piece of advice that could possibly be given to anybody about the Black-Scholes Model is to avoid it like the plague unless positively forced to do otherwise. The only excuse that can be accepted for actually considering it is that you are commanded to do so for the purposes of sitting a finance exam.

It isn't even as if it has any practical value in real-life investing. For example, in its original version it assumes that stocks do not pay dividends, that it is possible to borrow money at a risk free rate, that the volatility of the stock price will remain constant, that there are no restrictions on short selling, and that there are no transaction costs. It may or may not be thought relevant to this discussion that the hedge fund that Myron Scholes co-founded with John Merriwether, Long Term Capital Management, went spectacularly bust, leading to a massive bail-out orchestrated by the Federal Reserve, which feared major damage to the global financial system.

So, for any readers who do not need to know about the Black-Scholes model for the purposes of an exam, it is a model that purports to measure the value of an option. Now please stop reading and skip to the next section where it says 'It's OK to open your eyes again now'. To the rest of you, the writer expresses his profound sympathies and will do the best he can.

Black-Scholes explained

First let's ignore the maths for a while and consider what the model actually does. As we already know, it attempts to put a price on an option. It does this by considering the range of market prices that might apply on the expiry date (for the mathematicians out there, it assumes that this could range between plus infinity and minus infinity). If you can calculate the probability of each of these possible outcomes, plus the gain or loss that would ensue relative to the strike price in each case, then you can calculate the expected value of the option.

Expected value example

Suppose that on expiry there were only five possible outcomes, rather than thousands.

TABLE 16.1

Outcome	A Probability	B Gain / (loss)	C A × B
#1	20%	$10	$2
#2	10%	($20)	($2)
#3	25%	$20	$5
#4	20%	$15	$3
#5	20%	($5)	($1)
			Σ(A × B) = $7

So in this case, our expected value would be $7. Remember that the Σ symbol simply means 'the total of' all the specified values.

Let's assume we are modelling the value of a call option. The model works by applying this basic idea of expected value, and looking at two specific aspects of the situation: (1) the expected value of the stock that you would receive if you exercised the option; and (2) the value of the cash that you are going to need to exercise the option with.

Aspect (1) clearly only has any relevance if the market price of the stock is above the strike price on expiry of the option. So, we need a mathematical notation that represents the market price if it is above the strike price, but is zero if the market price is equal to or less than the strike price. This notation is N(d1)S, with S here standing for Stock (price) or market price, and N(d1) for whatever number you would have to multiply this by.

Point (2) only has relevance if the market price is above the strike price. But there is a further complication here, since the cash will be paid not today, but in the future. Thus we have to take into account the time value of money, and the model does this, somewhat confusingly, by using the notation e^{-rf} to represent a discount rate equal to the risk free rate.

So here we have N(d2)K e^{-rf}, where K represents the strike price and N(d2) represents the probability that the market price will be above the strike price. Remember, e^{-rf} simply means 'discounted at the risk free rate'. In situations where only a matter of days remain until expiry, this step could theoretically be omitted without making any great difference to the final outcome.

The basic model

Think about what value you will receive if you exercise a call option. This will be represented by the market value of the stock that you receive, less the cash that you pay (the strike price). Black-Scholes represents this as:

$$N(d1)M - N(d2)S \, e^{-rf}$$

We know M, the market price, we know S, the strike price, and we know (or can calculate) e^{-rf} if we know, or assume, a risk free rate. So, the only missing pieces of the puzzle are N(d1) and N(d2). In order to calculate these we need to know both the mean and the Standard Deviation of the historic price of the underlying stock. Usually an annualized mean and Standard Deviation are used.

N represents the cumulative distribution function. This can be calculated for any value provided that you know both the mean and the Standard Deviation (σ). This can be done either by means of look-up tables or by using the Excel function =NORMDIST.

Using Excel to find the cumulative distribution function

The cumulative distribution function represents the probability of a particular value occurring within any distribution delineated by a given mean (average) and Standard Deviation. The Excel function requires four inputs: the particular number, the mean, the Standard Deviation, and the 'cumulative'. In this case, enter 'true' as the cumulative. If you enter 'false' then Excel will calculate the probability mass function, which is something different.

So, what you need is:

=NORMDIST(number, mean, Standard Deviation, true)

Now all you need to do is to calculate d1 and d2. This is easier than it looks: all you have to do is substitute values for symbols, thus:

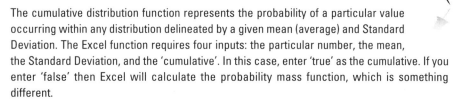

$$d1 = \frac{log\left(\frac{M}{S}\right) + \left(r + \frac{\sigma^2}{2}\right)T}{\sigma\sqrt{T}}$$

Where log is the normal logarithm (in this case of $\frac{M}{S}$),
   M is the market price,
   S is the strike price,
   r is the risk free rate,
   σ is the Standard Deviation of the market price,
   and T is the time to expiry measured as a percentage of one year.
   d2 is easier as it can be simplified as:
   $d2 = d1 - \sigma\sqrt{T}$

It's OK to open your eyes again now

Just before we leave options, one final word of apology and explanation is required. In the course of this description of options, they have been represented throughout as being bought for a particular sum of money. This was convenient in explaining the way in which they worked in financial terms. It is correct that the 'price' of an option represents the maximum downside that the option-holder can suffer. However, in practice many of them are actually priced by means of a bid/offer spread mechanism. This disclosure is made purely for the purposes of completeness. It will not in any way affect your understanding of how options actually work.

Swaps

Swaps are the third member of the derivatives family, and are widely used by many different types of investor. The name may be slightly misleading, in that it suggest the idea of two parties simply exchanging (swapping) two assets. In fact this is the broad idea, and often the intended effect, but actually they are a little more complex than that. Swaps may be better thought of as exchanging the *benefit* of one or more assets, rather than handing over the assets themselves. Hopefully this will become clearer if we look at some specific examples.

Example 1

A pension fund may be required to increase its benefit payments in line with inflation. It would like to try to match this sensitivity to inflation with its assets, for example by buying inflation lined (index-linked) bonds. These pay not a fixed rate of interest, such as those we have been considering so far, but a rate that goes up and down from one year to another based on some underlying index of inflation, such as the Retail Price Index.

Often it may not be possible for the pension fund to buy these bonds as it would wish to, for practical reasons; for example, the number of index-linked bonds available in the market at any one time is normally very small compared to fixed rate bonds. So there may simply not be enough to go round, particularly if there is a general view in the market that inflation is likely to rise, in which case it would be odd for anybody holding index-linked bonds to wish to sell them.

It may, however, be possible to structure a swap arrangement whereby for at least a few years the holder of the index-linked bond will pass on to the other party whatever income they actually receive from the index-linked bond in exchange for the certain income that the other party would receive on a similar fixed rate bond. Of course, this will come at a price; it will be for the other party to decide whether paying that price is worthwhile when measured against any possible benefit.

Equally, this could work in reverse where the holder of an index-linked bond is not sure that inflation will be above the fixed rate bond yield over the next few years, but thinks it may well pick up thereafter. They may be understandably nervous of selling the index-linked bond to replace it with a fixed rate one, since they may fear it will prove impossible to buy it back at a reasonable price in a few years' time. So instead they might offer a swap to someone like the pension fund we have just mentioned. What we have just described is both sides of an interest swap or **interest rate swap**, with a fixed rate being exchanged for a variable rate. This specific example of it may also be called (particularly in the pension fund industry) an inflation risk swap. (If you hear a pension fund say they have 'swapped out their inflation risk', it will be this to which they are referring.)

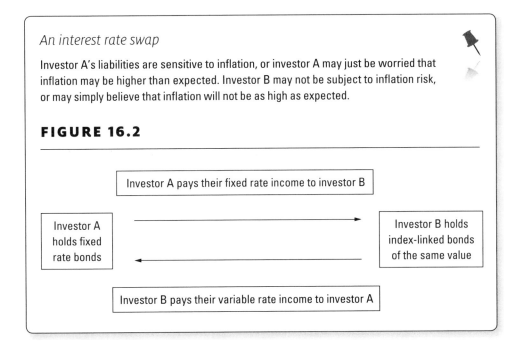

An interest rate swap

Investor A's liabilities are sensitive to inflation, or investor A may just be worried that inflation may be higher than expected. Investor B may not be subject to inflation risk, or may simply believe that inflation will not be as high as expected.

FIGURE 16.2

Investor A pays their fixed rate income to investor B

Investor A holds fixed rate bonds

Investor B holds index-linked bonds of the same value

Investor B pays their variable rate income to investor A

Example 2

An investor is holding a long-term asset, perhaps an infrastructure project, which will provide predictable income in US dollars starting in about five years' time and going on for another 20 years or so. This matches the investor's liability profile (they might be a pension fund and thus have fairly predictable payments that they will need to make to retirees in years 5 to 25). However, those liabilities are denominated in euros.

If we were talking about months rather than years, then our investor could make use of currency futures contracts, but these are generally for fairly short periods; certainly nothing like 25 years. So here the investor could look to enter into a **currency swap** whereby they agree with a counterparty to swap dollars for euros at a specified rate on specified dates in the future.

This is a simple example. Currency swaps can in fact be much more complex animals, involving swapping interest streams in different currencies (and thus the underlying interest rates) as well as, or instead of, a principal sum.

Example 3

An investor would like to have exposure to the beta return of the UK corporate property (real estate) market. However, let us assume there is no investment fund available that claims to offer this; indeed, it would be difficult to imagine how it could, since it would need to hold a large enough component of total British property assets as to be truly representative of the market as a whole. That would be one whole large amount of property!

A Total Return Swap

Investor A wishes to invest in UK real estate but wants to avoid the added risk of an alpha-seeking manager. They would be content to accept the beta return of the market as a whole measured by the IPD index, but this is not accessible through any available investment vehicle. So, they enter into a Total Return Swap with Bank B, under which A pays a fixed amount every year, assessed as LIBOR plus 2%. There is then a balancing payment at the end of the year according to whether the IPD index has outperformed or underperformed this fixed amount.

FIGURE 16.3

Situation 1: the IPD index outperforms the fixed amount.

Result: investor A pays out LIBOR +2% and receives some greater sum in return, making a profit.

Situation 2: the IPD index underperforms the fixed amount (but is above zero).

Result: investor A pays out LIBOR +2% and receives some lesser sum in return, making a loss.

Situation 3: the IPD index return is less than zero.

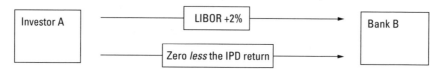

Result: investor A pays out LIBOR +2% *plus* the amount by which the IPD return was less than zero, making a loss.

There is a way round this, however. The beta of the market can be measured (by the IPD index), even if it cannot be replicated. Thus, providing our investor can find a willing counterparty, usually a bank, they can agree to pay them a fixed rate every year (usually expressed as LIBOR plus a certain margin). Should the IPD index rise in any one year by more than the fixed amount being paid, the bank will pay the difference to the investor. If it rises by less (or falls), the investor will pay the difference to the bank. This is called a **Total Return Swap**.

Note that the investor is not placed quite in the position of holding a portfolio of properties that would perfectly track the market. Instead they are in the position of having borrowed to purchase such a portfolio, with the fixed amount they have to pay every year representing notional interest on a hypothetical loan. This is a common feature of total return swaps. Admittedly it is not ideal, but then in this situation it is difficult to think of any other practical solution. In this particular situation it should also be noted that the IPD index represents not just the capital gains made on property transactions, but also rental income, so it could be argued that notionally all one is doing is using the (actual) rental income component of the index to service the (notional) loan interest.

This is a necessarily simplistic review of swaps. It is only necessary to understand what they are and how they work, not every technical intricacy of every swap instrument available.

There are for example **credit default swaps**, where you can effectively sell the amount you expect to receive when a loan is repaid in the future for a fixed sum now. As the name implies, what is being bought and sold here is the default risk; the risk that the borrower may be unable to repay the lender when the loan period expires. A number of observers believe that an over-proliferation of these CDS instruments was one of the factors leading to the banking crisis of 2007.

There are also **rental swaps**, under which you can swap a fixed rate or price for the right to receive the rental income from a particular property or portfolio of properties. An **equity swap** is where you exchange a fixed rate or amount for the return on a particular stock, portfolio of stocks, or stock exchange index; and so on.

It should also be mentioned that it is possible in some cases to buy an option to enter into a swap on pre-defined terms. Inevitably, this is known as a **swaption**.

Technical considerations

All of the examples we have considered have certain things in common. First, most of them exist because other ways of achieving that particular objective are either non-existent (as with the IPD example) or raise serious practical problems. Second, in many cases a fixed return or amount is being swapped for a variable one; thus often what is being bought or sold is effectively certainty of outcome, and, as always in finance, certainty comes at a price.

Third, many swaps are tailor-made for particular investors in particular situations. This is good, in the sense that there is market flexibility to meet investors' needs. Less good (and perhaps less well recognized) is that because of this most swaps are OTC instruments, and thus come subject to our old friend, counterparty risk. Often (particularly in the case of interest rate swaps) there may be a bank in the middle, acting as counterparty to both sides, but many times there will not, so that your counterparty might be a property company or an oil company. Even where there is a bank involved, this fact is no longer as reassuring as it once was, and in any event it comes at a price, since the bank will usually be charging a spread between the two swap positions and thus making money from both sides.

As with futures and options, swaps are derivative instruments; derivative in the sense that they derive from some underlying asset or instrument. Actually, 'vicarious' would probably be a better description, meaning 'representing at second hand' but then, as we have already seen, finance is not over-concerned with precise use of language.

Another description you will hear is **synthetic**, and you will hear a lot more of this term in years to come, as many people believe that so far as investing in general is concerned, the future will be synthetic. This, of course, just means something that is made artificially, and would cover, for example, the IPD total return swap that we considered earlier. There are investors who are now starting to ask why they should not seek all their real estate exposure in this way, rather than going out and buying individual properties; it is in this sense that the future of investing may become increasingly synthetic. 'Synthetic exposure' is already becoming a buzz-phrase, and is already being used by many **Exchange Traded Funds** (ETFs).

Hedging

We have seen how derivatives are used in many cases to sell uncertainty and buy certainty, paying a price in the process. If you think about it, what we are really talking about here is risk, since finance seems to assume that risk and uncertainty of outcome are the same thing (or at least that risk is a measure of the range of possible uncertainty). As we have seen, there is always a relationship between risk and return. Thus, if we want to get rid of some risk from our investment position, then we have to be prepared to accept a lower return; we are buying relative certainty, and the lower return is the price we pay. Conversely, there are people out there who are happy to be on the other side of the derivative position, either because they want a higher return and are happy to accept more risk in the process, or because their type of risk may be different, and the two can be exchanged for each other (as in the case of a currency swap).

We call this process, whereby we seek to get rid of risk from our portfolio, accepting a lower return in exchange, **de-risking**. This tends to be quite a general term, however, and usually means nothing more than seeking to lower the volatility, as measured by one Standard Deviation, across our whole portfolio, for example by selling shares with a high CAPM beta and buying shares with a low CAPM beta. Things become a little tricky, however, when we seek to do this across different asset types, as we will see shortly.

More specifically, an investor may seek to **hedge** their position. We saw a classic example of this in a business context when looking at our coffee bean farmer. He was prepared to accept a certain price for his crop now rather than wait for an uncertain price in the future, even though it was quite likely that the future price would in fact be higher. He was prepared to trade that chance of a higher price at harvest time for the certainty of a lower price today.

As well as in the field of commodities, hedging in business often operates in the field of currency. For example, if an Asian airline knows that it will have to pay for aviation fuel throughout the year in US dollars, it may enter into a series of swaps or futures to lock in certain exchange rates now, thus facilitating its budgeting exercise.

Hedging also happens in investment, and shares the same characteristics: an underlying asset or liability, and the desire to buy certainty while acknowledging that this comes at a price. For example, if you are an equity manager and have an annual performance target of 10%, you may find yourself at the end of November already having made enough gain during the year to hit your target. It may now be very tempting simply to sell your entire position, thus locking in your bonus or performance fee, go on holiday for a month, and then come back in January and start again.

But what happens if you follow this approach, only to read in a two day-old FT while lying on a beach in Thailand that the market has gone up another 5%? Bitterly you realize that you have made a huge mistake in closing out your position. Instead of the Porsche Boxster that you are planning to buy on your return, you could in fact have bought five Porsche 911s with enough money left over to put your dear old mum into that awfully nice home for the terminally bewildered.

So, as Mr Bennet tells his daughter in *Pride and Prejudice*, an awful dilemma confronts you. In her case, if she refuses to marry Mr Collins her mother will never speak to her again, while if she agrees to marry him her father will never speak to her again. In the case of our investment manager, do they trade the certainty of a Porsche Boxster for the three possible outcomes of: (1) five Porsche 911s; or (2) nothing; or (3) something in between?

Being a wily investor, of course, you will seek to have the best of both worlds. You will not sell your position, but you will buy a put option at the current market price to expire at the end of December. If the market goes down then you calculate that the profit you make on the option should compensate you for the loss in value of your share portfolio. If the market goes up then you will still be able to take the benefit of this, though you will give up a little of it as you will lose the price that you paid for the option. You have eliminated the 'zero' outcome and turned your dilemma into a choice between: (1) four Porsche 911s; (2) one Porsche Boxster; or (3) something in between. Well, clever old you. You obviously don't pull down that huge salary for nothing.

This is an example of a classic hedge, using an equity market put option, but any of the many derivative instruments that we mentioned, even if briefly, can be used for hedging. They can also be used in combination with each other. For example, one of the best known hedges is a **straddle**, which involves buying both a put and a call with the same strike price and expiry date, the strike price being the current market price (so both options are **at the money**). At first sight this may seem nonsensical, but if you think about it you will realize that in this case what the investor is clearly worried about is a big movement in either direction. They are prepared to give up some money if the market stays broadly the same, but should it go up or down by a large amount then whatever they make on the relevant option will more than compensate them for the cost of the other, which expires out of the money, and/or a possible loss on an underlying equity portfolio.

The essential requirement of hedging remains the same, however. There must be some underlying asset (as in the case of the share portfolio), or liability (as in the case of the airline) that is in some way being protected by seeking to take away some or all of the uncertainty of outcome. In investment terms, one is looking to limit one's downside, at the cost of also limiting one's upside. One is narrowing the range of possible outcomes.

There are many investors active in the derivatives markets, however, who do not have any underlying asset or liability to protect, most notably and confusingly hedge funds ('confusingly' because hedging is actually the one thing they do not do). Why, then, should these people be buying and selling derivative positions? The answer is simple: it's called either investment, speculation or gambling, depending on your point of view.

Perhaps gambling literally, in fact, since retail investors can perfectly reproduce the effect of buying puts and calls by **spread betting**, which is legal in some countries, such as the UK, but not in others. Here when you 'buy' or 'sell' a particular thing at a particular price you are actually placing a bet that it will go up or down, and your payout or loss will be directly proportionate to the amount by which it has gone up or down. You will notice at once that this is like having entered into a futures contract; in many cases your liability will be unlimited. For this reason, customers are required to enter pre-agreed limits on each bet, based on the amount of cash they have in their account, at which point the bet will automatically expire.

Thus, to argue that derivatives are a 'good thing' or a 'bad thing', as some have sought to do, is pointless. It all depends for what purpose they are being used, and in what circumstances. For an airline to hedge its fuel payments liabilities is surely sensible. For a hedge fund to finance a derivatives position with 1% of equity and 99% of debt, or for banks to issue CDS instruments that have a far greater value than that of the underlying corporate loan, is perhaps less so.

Summary

- Some derivative instruments are issued over the counter (OTC), which means that they are private contractual arrangements. This will always carry counterparty risk: the risk that a party due to make a payment may prove unwilling or unable to do so. Others are issued through recognized exchanges, in which case the counterparty risk is that of the exchange, and therefore relatively minimal. These latter instruments usually have standardized quantities and expiry dates.
- A European style option can only be exercised on expiry, whereas an American style option can be exercised at any time during its life. Most tradable options are American.
- Options that can only be exercised at their strike price are known as vanilla or plain vanilla bonds. Other variants, where the strike price can be altered, are known as exotic.
- The Black-Scholes model is used to calculate the value, and thus the price, of an option.
- Swaps are the third type of derivative instrument. Here, assets or liabilities are exchanged between the parties at agreed dates and on agreed terms. Often income streams are exchanged, either for another income stream (in which case one may be a fixed rate and the other variable) or for a fixed sum payable either now or in the future.

- With a Total Return Swap, fixed payments based on a bank borrowing rate are exchanged for the return of a particular asset or, more usually, market or asset class as a whole. Many Exchange Traded Funds make use of total return swaps.
- Derivative instruments can also be known as synthetics. Synthetic exposure to an asset or asset class means gaining access to the return of an asset or asset class without actually holding it (which is in any event impossible in some cases).
- Derivative instruments are widely used by investors to hedge. Hedging involves an underlying asset or liability and looks to protect it in some way, by seeking to limit the range of possible outcomes. Investors will typically be looking to limit their downside, at the expense of also giving up some of their upside.
- Despite their name, hedge funds do not hedge. On the contrary, they look to take derivative positions without any underlying asset that they are looking to protect. Buying and selling derivatives in this way may be seen by some as speculation, or gambling.
- A pure gambling option exists, in countries where it is permitted, in the form of spread betting, where customers bet on a particular price or rate moving up or down.

Notes

1   Again, this is broadly true, but not strictly. First, there are some very complex mathematical models out there that attempt to calculate the value of an American option. Second, in practice many investors seem simply to value an American option as if it were a European one, ignoring the difference between them.

17
Capital markets and M&A transactions: events in the corporate life-cycle

W e saw in an earlier chapter that a company (corporation) is regarded by the law as a person. Just like a natural person, it can be 'born' through the formation process. It can also get married, by way of a merger with another corporation, or have children, by way of establishing **subsidiaries**. Sadly, a company can also 'die', most commonly if it becomes unable to pay its debts. In other words, there is definitely such a thing as a corporate life-cycle, and it is time now for us to examine a few of the events that can occur along the way.

We need to take a look at four different situations, though some of them defy being squeezed into neat little compartments. They are:

1. Merger and acquisition ('M&A')
2. Flotation (IPO)
3. Capital raising
4. Insolvency

Merger and acquisition

Let us get some terminology out of the way here, since it can be confusing, and indeed in some cases is used in a deliberately misleading way by the PR people. A merger, strictly speaking, is when two companies become one, either by swapping the shares of one for the shares of the other, or by setting up a new holding company and swapping its shares for the shares of both the existing companies, which thus become its subsidiaries (children). This strongly implies that a merger is both (1) freely negotiated and agreed, and (2) takes place between two companies of roughly equivalent size. It is important to understand, however, that while many corporate transactions are described as 'a merger' for diplomatic reasons, very few actually come anywhere near fulfilling these two criteria.

FIGURE 17.1 A merger: example 1

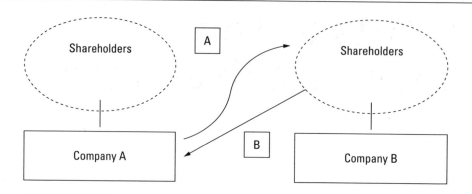

Company A issues new shares to the shareholders of Company B. In exchange, they transfer their shares in Company B to Company A.

Result: both sets of shareholders now jointly own Company A. Company B becomes a wholly-owned subsidiary of Company A.

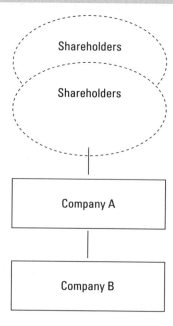

FIGURE 17.2 A merger: example 2

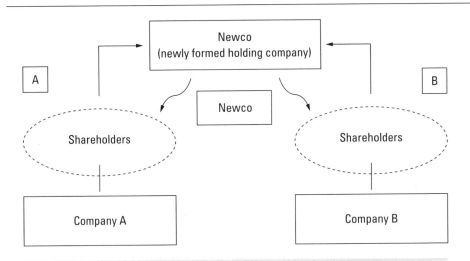

The shareholders of both companies exchange their shares for shares in Newco.

Result: both sets of shareholders now jointly own Newco, which in turn owns both Company A and Company B as subsidiaries.

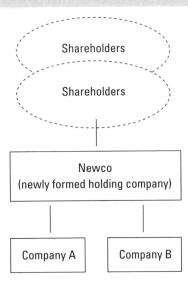

Having understood this, let us therefore talk about acquisitions, since this is in reality what most situations are. Rather than gaining a marriage partner, you are effectively adopting a fairly grown-up child.

In practice today the acquisition process will tend to be driven by the potential vendor (seller) of the business, rather than a single interested buyer, as used to be the case. This is because in recent years boards of directors have rightly become very concerned not only with delivering full value to their shareholders, but with being seen to do so. So even where an approach may be received from a potential purchaser, the vendor will still usually appoint an advisor (typically an investment bank for a large business, or what is known as a corporate finance boutique for a smaller one). This advisor will then conduct some sort of controlled auction process, including the purchaser who has made the approach but in semi-open competition with others who may wish to bid.

The way this works is that the advisor will prepare a full report on the business to be sold. This is officially called the sales memorandum, but unofficially is known simply as 'the book'. They will invite a first round of bids based largely upon what is in the book, but also upon some preliminary due diligence based on documents that are made available for inspection under controlled conditions in a data room. Once a physical room at the advisor's offices, these days, unsurprisingly, data rooms tend to be virtual data stores that are made available online subject to security protocols.

On the basis of the indicative offers made at the first cut-off date, the advisor will select a very small number of preferred bidders to go forward to the final round of the auction process. At this stage, access to the business's management will usually be allowed for due diligence purposes, but again under strictly controlled conditions.

Due diligence

Due diligence is largely the same regardless of what form of corporate transaction is being contemplated, and differs only in the identity of the party conducting it. In the case of a controlled auction, for example, the advisor will already have performed their own due diligence on the company in order to be able to prepare the sales memorandum. Thus, purchaser due diligence will be performed either (1) to check that the advisor has not overlooked anything, or (2) to dive much more deeply into specific issues that are either particularly important to the purchaser from a business point of view, or that may have emerged, or changed, since the advisor started work.

Legal due diligence will focus not just on the company's own legal status with regard to things like shareholders' rights and whether it is up to date with all its statutory meetings and filings, but also all legal agreements that it may have entered into with third parties such as suppliers and customers (do these contain change of control provisions, for example?). A purchaser will also be concerned to see the service contracts and share option agreements of all the key management. In addition, intellectual property ('IP') legal matters are now such a key feature of legal due diligence that they can properly be thought of as their own separate area.

IP will include trademarks and trade names (which can be an important part of protecting the value of a brand), copyright and patents. Trademarks are visual images, although some attempts (as yet untested in the courts) have been made to use them to protect literary characters (such as Sherlock Holmes) after the copyright period has expired. Copyright attaches to written material, including computer software, as well as to films, created images and audio material. Patents protect scientific inventions, including new drugs. The legal status of these can be key. Imagine, for example, how much MacDonald's would be worth if anyone in the world could set up burger restaurants using their name, logo and products.

Financial due diligence will not just focus on the company's accounting position, but will range across the whole financial spectrum. It will cover things such as contingent liabilities, foreign exchange policy, debt and equity structures, and taxation.

There is a further form of due diligence that has become essential, which may be called different things by different people, but will fall broadly into what might be called the field of ethics. It will cover things like environmental issues, labour policy (particularly as regards manufacturing businesses operating in third world countries), sourcing, and internal practices and procedures. In the US and Europe, this is now commonly referred to as SRI (socially responsible investing). While, as the name suggests, this refers strictly speaking to investments rather than outright acquisitions, the purchaser, be it a company itself or perhaps an investment fund, will have its own SRI requirements to think about, and will not want to take on a subsidiary that may breach these. Further, their shareholders or investors will in turn have their own SRI requirements, and thus will be monitoring the activities of the purchaser to ensure compliance. Thus, SRI sign-off is now an increasingly essential part of any acquisition process.

Contractual matters

Where the transaction is following anything like the form outlined above, then the purchaser will ask the vendor to enter into various contractual commitments known as representations and warranties ('reps and warranties'). These can be thought of as legally binding promises. They are statements of fact (for example, that all material matters have been disclosed) which, if they prove to be untrue, can give rise to an action for damages. Obviously the extent to which a vendor will be prepared to give these, or to which the purchaser will be prepared to go ahead without them, will be different in every case; a combination of bargaining power, price, the nature and location of the business to be bought, and the purchaser's confidence in the completeness of its own due diligence process.

Acquisitions of public companies (corporations)

Sometimes the target company will be publicly quoted, for example on the New York or London Stock Exchange. In this case the transaction will typically be called a take-over, and will differ from the acquisition of a private company in several important respects.

First, the shareholders of a private company always have a choice as to whether they sell the company or not. In the case of a public company, however, this is rarely the case. First, the board of the target company might believe the offer to represent good value for shareholders and recommend acceptance. This is known as a **recommended offer** or an agreed take-over. Even without a recommendation, however, the purchaser might issue an offer to the shareholders of the target, forcing them to choose whether or not to accept that offer within a specified time. Unless and until a recommendation is forthcoming, this is known as a **hostile take-over**. In either case, if a sufficient number of shareholders accept the offer, there are rules that allow the purchaser to force the remainder also to transfer their shares on the same terms. Thus there is always the danger that, even if you do not personally wish to sell your shares, you may be forced to do so.

Second, detailed due diligence of the sort described above will rarely be possible in the case of a public company, particularly in the case of a hostile bid, since obviously the co-operation of the target company's management will not be forthcoming. This is, however, partially balanced by the fact that, being a public company, a great deal of relevant information will already be publicly available by way of filings and announcements.

Third, take-overs of public companies are heavily regulated. There are rules that may affect the price that must be offered, the ability of a purchaser to withdraw an offer once it is made, and their ability to bid again within a certain time should their initial efforts prove unsuccessful.

Flotation (IPO)

The process of a company making the transition from private to public status and having its shares **quoted** (or listed)[1] on a stock exchange is known as a **flotation**, although, as with so many things in finance, the US expression **IPO** (Initial Public Offering) has become widespread and is likely to be used universally in future. In each case the basic legal process will be the same, but there are differences in the way in which a company may come to market. Caution should be exercised here, since different terminology is used in different countries, and the legal processes can differ too, so the following should be thought of as describing the practical routes to market, rather than detailing the precise minutiae.

It is quite possible for a company simply to have an **introduction**, whereby its existing shares become publicly quoted but no new shares are issued, and thus no new capital is raised. In this scenario, if you were looking to invest in the company you would be dependent on some of the existing shareholders wanting to sell some of their shares, which does in fact commonly happen, particularly in the case of a company that has been backed by venture capital (early stage private equity) funds. However, pure introductions are rare, for one very good practical reason. The expense of becoming publicly quoted is considerable, not least because of the fees of the lawyers, accountants and investment bankers concerned, and thus the company will normally wish to raise some new capital if only to help pay these costs.

The company could decide to look at a **placement**. In this scenario the company's brokers and/or investment bankers will approach specific individual investors and persuade them each to contract to take a certain number of shares, thus together contributing all the new capital that the company is seeking.[2] A placement may also encompass some existing shares, perhaps held by some of the company's original founders or private investors.

Finally there is the **offering** or public offering that gives an IPO its name. Here the new shares are offered to the public at a particular price by means of a prospectus (offering memorandum), which, rather like the sales memorandum we have already met, gives detailed information about the company, but this time with heavy legal sanctions in the case of any inaccuracy. It is now open to anyone at all to subscribe for shares, using the form supplied with the prospectus. This last route is the most heavily regulated of all since, understandably, stock exchanges are extremely wary about what might be quite complex investment instruments being sold directly to the public.

In any cases involving capital raising (on which more below), the issue of new shares may be **underwritten**. Indeed, in some cases, such as where new shares are being issued to fund a cash offer to acquire another company, this may be required. Underwriting can be thought of as a sort of guarantee or insurance policy; in respect of any shares that are not taken up by investors, the underwriters are committed to taking these themselves. Naturally, there is a fee for this, and this can add considerably to the cost of an issue, particularly in times of market uncertainty.

Capital raising: issue of new bonds or shares (stock)

We have just seen how a company, the shares of which are becoming publicly quoted for the first time, can raise new capital as part of the flotation process. Similar processes are available to companies that are already public.

As we already know, there are only two ways in which a company can raise finance: either with debt or with equity. We have already seen how a company can either borrow money by way of a bank loan, or issue bonds. We have also seen how, in the case of a bond issue, the market might go about pricing these. What of equity, though?

Essentially this follows exactly the sort of procedure we have just reviewed as part of the flotation process. The only difference, of course, is that the company's existing shares are already publicly quoted. Rather than a private company becoming public and issuing some new shares in the process, here we have a public company issuing some new shares specifically for the purpose of raising additional finance.

So far as pricing is concerned, the offer price for the new shares will normally be set slightly below the existing market price, since clearly it is in the interests both of the company and of anybody who is underwriting the new issue that investors should be motivated to take it up. However, this is a very delicate art. On the one hand, the difference needs to be as large as possible to act as a motivation, particularly if the company has been under-performing and now needs to recapitalize itself. On the other hand, issuing shares at less than the prevailing market price is capital dilutive, and thus the difference needs to be as little as possible. Times of market instability add a further complication, since an issue will normally need to be priced at the very least several days in advance so that the underwriting arrangements can be finalized.

In many jurisdictions, the shareholders (stockholders) in a public company will have what are known as **pre-emption rights**. As the name suggests, these represent the right to be offered new shares in the company first (at least up to a specified number) before they are then offered to outsiders. For this reason, a new equity issue is often known, particularly in the UK, as a **rights issue**.

There will usually be a time lag between the date for acceptance and the date when the new shares begin trading on the stock market. This enables a shareholder, should they wish, to accept in respect of their entitlement to new shares, but then sell the rights to them on to another investor. These are called **nil paids** and will theoretically be priced on the basis of the offer price and the likely market price of the shares that they represent on the first day of trading.

There is one remaining situation in which new shares may be issued. This is where the directors wish to declare a dividend for the year, but do not feel that the business can actually afford the cash with which to pay it. In these circumstances they may decide to issue new shares to shareholders instead of cash – for example, perhaps one new share for every 30 that they already own. This is known as a **scrip dividend** or a **scrip issue**. Again, the shareholder can sell into the market the right to receive the new shares if they wish to. In the UK this carries a slight tax advantage since the money they receive for selling the rights will be treated as a capital gain, whereas the value of the new shares received would otherwise be taxed as income.

Insolvency (bankruptcy)

It is time now, sadly, to consider the various ways in which a company (corporation) can die. Strictly speaking, there are four ways in which death can occur, and the heading of this section is somewhat misleading in that it covers only three of the four. First, the company can decide to commit suicide. Second, it can be executed. Third, it can be placed on life support until someone summons up the courage to turn off the machines. Finally, it can be mugged, usually so violently that death occurs shortly afterwards.

Let us dispose first of the assisted suicide option. It is quite possible to have what is usually known as a **voluntary winding-up**, or a **shareholders' liquidation**. Here the shareholders and the directors agree that the company has no continued reason for existence, and so they vote to dissolve it.[3] In order to do this, however, it will be necessary for the directors, advised by the auditors, to sign a declaration of solvency certifying that in the event of a winding-up the business will be able to discharge all its debts, and thus that nobody will be left being owed money. Largely for this reason, voluntary liquidations are very rare. Unfortunately, the most common reason for a company ceasing to exist is that it has become insolvent. So, let us now consider the three insolvency options.

As with so much else in this book, please be aware that these situations are referred to by different names in different countries, and will be subject to different rules. Some countries even have no real legal corporate insolvency regime at all. So please treat the following as a general outline of what usually occurs, rather than as specific guidance.

Liquidation

Liquidation, of the involuntary kind, represents execution. The state, in the shape of the judiciary, passes a death sentence. One or more of the creditors petitions the court showing that a debt is outstanding and that the company has been put on notice to pay it but has failed to do so. Unless the directors are able to show that there is some good reason for this (for example that the debt is disputed) the court orders the company to be put into liquidation. It will appoint a liquidator, whose task is to gather in and sell the company's assets, applying whatever is left of the proceeds after the expenses of the liquidation itself to the company's creditors in a pre-ordained order of priorities, which normally begins with unpaid taxes.

Incidentally, if you happen to be owed money by a company then this is usually the easiest way of recovering it. An unscrupulous creditor can ignore letters for as long as they like, and will often have ways of dragging out any legal proceedings that you institute, but directors dare not ignore a statutory notice, for if they do not settle the debt within the time specified you can issue a winding-up petition.

The US version of liquidation is known as Chapter 7 (of the Bankruptcy Code – see below).

Administration

Many countries now have a procedure under which the directors of a company can apply to the courts for protection from their creditors. This is sometimes referred to as a re-organization, and in the US is often referred to as Chapter 9, although this is a little misleading as businesses usually file for protection under Chapter 11 (of the Bankruptcy Code). Chapter 9 is reserved for public bodies, and was perhaps most famously used by Orange County. Filings under Chapter 11 have included the motor groups Chrysler and General Motors (both in 2009), and the airlines United (2002) and Delta (2005). The generic name for this type of arrangement is **administration**.

The key feature of administration is that the existing creditors of the business may not take any action to enforce repayment of their debts. Even more controversially, in some systems (for example under Chapter 11 in the United States) the business can actually negotiate new borrowings or trade credit, and grant those new creditors priority over the existing ones. In some cases, with the approval of the court, it can also choose whether or not to be bound by existing legal contracts. United, for example, took advantage of this not only by cancelling various contracts with third parties, but also by defaulting on their pension plan liabilities.

The arrangements for administration can differ markedly. For example, in the US the directors generally stay in control of the business (as a 'debtor in possession'), whereas in the UK the court will appoint an independent insolvency practitioner as administrator.

Underlying the whole process is the idea that this is a business that, while temporarily insolvent, is potentially profitable in the future, and thus can be saved if an effective rescue plan can be drawn up and implemented. It is on this basis that the court will be prepared to grant protection from a hostile creditor.

Needless to say, creditors hate administration-type arrangements, arguing that they are being prevented from exercising their basic legal right to repayment of a debt. This is a classic example of public policy triumphing over legal principle. Governments clearly have an interest in keeping a firm in business if they possibly can, not least because they hope to save the jobs of a significant number of the employees. However, it is not possible to grant an undeserved advantage to one group (allowing employees to continue working for a bankrupt business) without creating a compensating underserved disadvantage to another (preventing creditors from exercising their legal rights).

Adding to creditors' woes, administration can last for a long time. United Airlines, for example, went into administration in December 2002 and did not emerge from it until February 2006.

Receivership

A receiver is appointed by a single creditor, where their financing instrument (whether a loan agreement, a registered charge, or both) confers the right to appoint one. This used to be commonplace in the UK, as it was widely regarded as the best way for an individual creditor, usually a bank, to ensure repayment of the debt owed to them by the business. The receiver's only objective was to generate enough money from a sale of the business or its assets to repay that one creditor, though they did owe certain legal duties to other creditors as well. Unfortunately, the fact that **receivership** was public knowledge, with the dread words 'in receivership' having to appear on all business correspondence, was almost always enough to kill the company, since no third party, particularly a supplier, would now be prepared to extend credit.

With the shift in legislative opinion towards administration, however, the exercise of receivership option has become much more difficult to enforce. Indeed, in the UK the power to appoint a receiver in financing instruments has now been banned. However, there are certain jurisdictions that have preserved a more creditor-friendly attitude, and banks will often seek to make use of these in international financing structures. Another option is to seek to arrive at the same result by different means, for example by creating a stand-alone financing vehicle that will own certain key rights (perhaps the right to receive the cash-flows of a project) and over which either shareholder or board control can be exercised in certain specified circumstances.

Summary

- A company (corporation) is recognized by law as a person, in the sense that it has its own legal identity, distinct from its directors or shareholders (stockholders). Just as it can be born, through the formation process, and have children, through creating subsidiaries, so it can get married, and die. Like any natural person, it can also seek to raise money when it needs it.
- A corporate marriage is called a merger, the two companies agreeing to merge their business operations. In reality, true mergers are rare. For example, there can only be one CEO of the resulting company, and where one of the merger partners is larger and/or more valuable than the other it will generally be in a position to dictate terms. This is especially so when the 'merger' results from a hostile bid, an unsolicited approach to the target's shareholders. Thus, although the word 'merger' is much beloved by press offices and PR agencies, most mergers are in fact take-overs in one form or another.

- Where the target is a private company then the acquisition process will today almost always take the form of a controlled auction process controlled by an advisor (usually an investment bank) working for the vendor (seller), even if this is prompted by a specific approach from an interested purchaser. This is to protect the position of the board of directors, enabling them to show that they have taken all reasonable steps to maximize shareholder value.
- A private company (corporation) may change its status by joining a stock exchange, which means that its shares will now be publicly tradable. This also enables it to issue new shares and offer these directly to the public, should it so wish, though existing shareholders (stockholders) will usually enjoy at least some pre-emption rights giving them the chance of first refusal.
- Issues of new shares will usually be underwritten, an underwriter guaranteeing, in return for a fee, to take up at the official offer price any remaining shares. This can be a legal or regulatory requirement, for example when the proceeds of the issue are to be used to buy another company.
- Companies can die in a number of ways. If a declaration of solvency can be made then they are allowed to commit suicide by voting for their own dissolution. In the overwhelming majority of cases, however, death will result from insolvency (bankruptcy).
- A creditor may petition the court to place a company into liquidation. Once the court grants the order the company may no longer trade, and its assets will be sold to generate money to pay its creditors in a specified order of priority.
- However, these days administration is common, allowing a business the chance to re-structure itself by following an agreed recovery plan, and return itself to profitability. While the precise rules differ, most jurisdictions these days give a business considerable latitude in accomplishing this.
- Receivership, the right of a single creditor conferred by a financing instrument to appoint a receiver to sell the company's assets so as to discharge their individual debt, is no longer available in the UK, but can still be found in some other jurisdictions. It may also be possible to arrange a similar outcome by different means provided you retain the services of sufficiently expensive lawyers.

Notes

1   Not strictly speaking the same thing, but we will ignore that for the purposes of this book.

2   Again, this is a complex area (particularly under US securities laws and regulations) that is being deliberately simplified.

3   The exact process is a little different, and significantly more complicated than this.

18
Asset allocation

We have thus far considered both corporate finance, in the sense of how a business raises money and accounts for it, and investment, the ways in which we can consider and analyse particular instruments that are bought and sold. However, in the investment chapters we have largely considered how to view individual assets as compared to the market or asset type that they represent; how to look at particular shares within an overall share portfolio, for example.

In closing, we will take a brief look at how we should approach asset types not within themselves, but relative to each other. Since we have reached the end of our journey, we may also be allowed to reflect briefly on some of the limitations of traditional finance theory should we seek to apply it strictly to real-life investment situations.

A tale of two continents...?

Should you ever actually have anything to do with the world of finance in practice, you will find that the attitudes of investors in North America, particularly university endowments which are traditionally the most forward-thinking, are very different to those exhibited elsewhere, particularly in Europe. European pension funds are generally seen as being the opposite end of the spectrum to those US endowments, ie the least sophisticated investors of all.

Should you, for example, be reading this book because you have just been appointed a trustee of your employer's occupational pension scheme, you will find that the fund's investments are almost entirely comprised of bonds and equities, echoing the sort of finance theory that we have been examining thus far. Were you, however, to take a look on the internet at the latest annual report from a US endowment, such as Yale or Harvard, you would find a very much wider choice of asset types, including such things as real estate (property), hedge funds, private equity, energy and even forestry.

This is not a book about asset allocation, and it lies beyond its scope to examine these different types of investments and look at their pros and cons.[1] However, it is important that you should understand the reasons, both practical and theoretical, why these differences occur. In particular, we need to understand the impact of regulation, and the way in which many investors view bonds.

Regulation

Regulation is the curse of our times. Not because regulation is not needed (it is – try thinking about how a factory might operate without health and safety regulations), but because it is almost universally badly conceived and badly implemented. Think about a five-year-old girl getting hold of her mother's make-up and you have a very good image for how regulators go about their work. Instead of skilfully dabbing a few spots of blusher and eye shadow in exactly the right places for maximum effect, imagine huge amounts of make-up smeared all over the face, with a vivid gash of lipstick continuing the mouth out to the ears.

There is a reason for this. Regulators and still more so those who employ them (politicians) never actually understand what it is they are trying to control. Instead of trying to work out the precise mischief of which they complain and then coming up with exactly the right remedy for it, they frequently take aim at completely the wrong target or, even worse, adopt a blunderbuss approach because they are not even sure where the various targets are, but want to be sure of hitting *something*, no matter what it might be.

It is for this reason that businesses and investors tend to hate regulations – because they are almost always bad regulations, which add time, cost and effort to the burdens of a business without bringing any corresponding benefit. Politicians and regulators, however, *love* regulation. Politicians because it gives them a change to go on television and talk gravely of the great achievement that they have just been part of, and regulators because each new piece of regulation requires the employment of many more regulators in order to police it, perhaps even the ultimate goal of all – the opening of a whole new department, or the setting up of a whole new public body.

This problem is particularly acute in the UK. During the period of New Labour government (the Blair and Brown administrations), for example, the number of new civil servants mushroomed dramatically.[2] Clearly, though sadly, this trend towards clumsy and ever-proliferating regulation is now irreversible. In the world of finance (or rather, investment, since now that we are nearing the end of the book there is probably no harm in letting you know that there is almost certainly a difference), this dead hand on the regulatory tiller manifests itself in restricting the ability of investors such as pension funds either to assess their situation properly, or to fulfil their objectives properly.

In many countries, for example, pension funds are required to model their future liabilities and discount them back to a Net Present Value. Having eagerly devoured the earlier chapters on the time value of money, you will instantly ask: using which assumptions, and what discount rate? Neither question can be answered sensibly. The assumptions, particularly as regards life expectancy (longevity), are typically unrealistic. The discount rate is prescribed as being the bond rate. This latter point is of course particularly difficult to understand, unless it comes with a basic underlying assumption that a pension fund will always hold all of its money in bonds. Against this Net Present Value (which, let us remind ourselves, is an artificial, discounted figure, of which the only thing we can be sure is that it does *not* show the true value of those liabilities, whatever that might be), pension funds are then required in many countries to set the value of their assets, on a mark to market basis (a real figure, which will fluctuate from day to day and which takes no account of the time value of money).

Quite apart from the inherent illogicality of this approach, trying to compare apples with oranges, it shows no understanding of how a pension fund actually operates. A pension fund does not need to pay all its future liabilities today, but only as they fall due at different times in the future. It therefore needs to be able to plan how best to meet these liabilities at the time, not how to juggle two meaningless accounting entries in the meantime. What final salary (**Defined Benefit**) pension plans actually have (or rather *had*, since many have now closed down) represented a long-term investment problem, not a short-term solvency problem. By prescribing the right medicine for the wrong disease, regulators succeeded only in making the real illness much worse.

It is for this reason that many pension funds outside North America hold their money largely, or even solely, in bonds. In some cases they are specifically required to do so, and where this occurs they are usually also restricted to holding the bonds of their own government, thus providing a ready buyer of those bonds whatever the scale of a sovereign debt crisis. In other cases, with the sledge-hammer of the mark to market regulations hanging over their heads, they feel they have little choice. The most regrettable thing is that this approach is often presented as following sound finance theory, whereas in fact exactly the opposite is the case.

The truth about bonds

If you remember, we looked earlier at one of the most useful characteristics of bonds, which is that they can be set off against specific short-term liabilities with the same duration. This is good, sensible financial practice. Trying to set off a portfolio of bonds against non-specific long-term liabilities is not.

For one thing, because of the way the bond market works it will be impossible ever to match the respective durations. The duration of the liabilities, even if one believes and accepts the assumptions being made, will always be much longer than that of the bonds. This gives rise to pension funds believing that they are subject to something that they call 'interest rate risk' (which is actually just the man-made 'risk' of trying to match two unmatchable accounting figures), which can in turn result in them tying up a large amount of their remaining available assets in trying to hedge against this.

The other fairly obvious point to make (but not so obvious that it is apparent to pension trustees, consultants or regulators) is that even if you ignore all the other objections, you can only pursue this course of action if your current assets at least match your discounted liabilities. If there is already a deficit then it can never make sense, unless you are banking (gambling?) on some new inflows of capital from somewhere to make good the difference.

Even then, it can only possibly make any sense at all if you believe that holding capital tied up in bonds will preserve its value in real terms; remember, most pension liabilities are linked to inflation. Again, it is an implicit assumption of most regulators that this must be the case. Yet the facts do not bear this out. If you had bought UK Government bonds in 1973, for example, you would have had to wait until 1985 to recover the real value of your starting capital – 12 years later, *and this assumes that you do not pay any tax*. Granted, pension funds typically do not pay tax, but other investors do.

Finally, how can there be any guarantee of capital preservation when a mark to market regime itself makes it impossible? If bond yields are pulled upwards, whether by inflation, interest rates or both, then, as we have seen, this can only happen by bond prices being driven correspondingly lower. Thus the bonds that you held yesterday will no longer be worth the same today and you must write them down, suffering a loss. In fact if you look at bond prices over almost any period you will see that within themselves (as against being compared with other asset types such as equities) they are actually pretty volatile, thus making a mockery of the suggestion that they are 'risk free'.

You may have noticed that nowhere in this book do we talk about 'investing in bonds'. As noted in an earlier chapter, there is a simple reason for this. If we define an investment as something that we hope will significantly increase the value of our capital in real terms, then a bond can never qualify as an investment. If you are a non-taxpayer then it is possible that bonds may keep pace with inflation, although even this will be dependent upon when you buy and sell. If you are a taxpayer then they can never even do this.

Bear in mind too, that the money you have tied up in bonds is money that could otherwise be deployed in things that *do* have a chance of increasing the value of your capital. So, you are incurring what we call an **opportunity cost**. Any time you have bonds in your portfolio it is like driving a car with the hand-brake on. Bonds are superb for short-term liquidity and liability matching purposes, but the trick is to keep that liquidity reserve or liability matching section of your portfolio as small as possible, since your long-term objective is to make a significant investment return in real terms, and bonds can never do this for you.

Diversification

It seems only common sense to seek diversification within a portfolio. Most people would instinctively agree that it would be better to hold some number of company shares (stocks) rather than only one within an equity portfolio, and in an earlier chapter we looked at how we might go about measuring the appropriate number (which turned out to be surprisingly small – less than 30).

Yet when it comes to diversification *between* different asset types, as opposed to *within* one single asset type (such as asking how many individual stocks you should hold in an equity portfolio), common sense seems to fly out of the window. Investors who would not dream of holding an equity portfolio composed of shares in one single company are quite content to have an overall portfolio that has only one asset type (equities) as an investment.

Remember, most investment portfolios outside North America are composed either entirely of bonds, or of bonds and equities, and we have already concluded that bonds do not qualify as an 'investment'. Even if you disagree with this, you are still looking at a maximum of only two different investment types. Why is this?

We have already looked at the pernicious influence of regulation. Some investors effectively do not have a choice; it is as though their hands have been handcuffed behind their backs and they are powerless to resist. But others *do* have a choice and yet choose to do nothing about it. Why?

Traditional diversification tools

We have looked already at the ways in which we might go about fine-tuning the individual stocks to hold within an equity portfolio. We can measure the Standard Deviation (risk) of a whole portfolio and see how this changes as we add or subtract stocks. We can use CAPM to choose between high and low beta stocks depending on how aggressive or defensive we wish our stock selection to be. Finally, there is the Sharpe Ratio, which gives us another dial on the dashboard, this time showing the annualized return of an asset on a risk-adjusted basis.

These are all very valuable tools, and it is most important that we should understand how to use them. Just as important, however, but all too often ignored by finance courses, is that we should understand *what* they are calculating, and *why*. This is particularly important here since these traditional tools, very useful though they are when used in the right way for the right purposes, are often misused, particularly when people start applying them to situations for which they were never intended.

Central to this discussion, incidentally, is an elephant in the room. That elephant, whose presence everyone secretly acknowledges but is not prepared publicly to admit, is the nature of risk. We now understand what finance means by this term, and how to calculate it. As we noted in the first chapter, however, this meaning is at odds with the normal, everyday meaning of the word, and a reconsideration of the true nature of risk is long over-due. Certainly many now suspect that, whatever it may be, it is something infinitely more complex and less quantifiable than the traditional view. Such a discussion lies beyond the scope of this book,[3] so let us note it and move on.

There is of course another assumption that underlies these tools whose validity is equally suspect, though again accepted without question by the world of finance. This is that actual historic returns provide a good guide to likely returns in the future. Again, though, let us simply note this point and move on. The function of this book is to teach finance theory, not question it.

Even if we accept that the volatility of historic returns *is* a good measure of the risk of an investment, however, we hit a snag as soon as we start trying to apply any risk measure across different asset classes. As we have seen, we measure volatility across the historic returns of different periods, be they years, quarters, months or even days.

This is fine where they are a valid measure of return for the purposes for which we are employing them; it is impossible to measure VaR (Value at Risk), for example, without daily performance data. Yet, and this is something that many investors do not even realize, there are some asset types where for various reasons periodic returns are *not* a valid measure of performance. Chief among these would be what some people are starting to call 'private' or 'private market' assets, notably private equity and some kinds of both real estate (property) and infrastructure investment vehicles. For these we really need to use measures of compound return such as an IRR, which we considered earlier.

So, even if you accept that volatility of historic periodic returns is normally a good measure of risk, you must accept that your view of risk cannot embrace these private asset types. Finance World, being a police state, does not react well to those who do not conform. Compound return-based asset types have historically been loaded onto cattle wagons and shipped off to concentration camps, with investors being forbidden by their consultants even to talk about, much less consider investing in them, because 'we can't fit them into our risk model'.

The other approach of a police state is to pretend that actually they do conform, and that any apparent dissent is the invention of trouble-making foreign journalists. Under this option, compound return-based assets are given periodic return and volatility numbers anyway, with these frequently being altered, and made-up figures substituted, where they begin to lead to embarrassing conclusions. Both approaches are unfortunate and unnecessary, because actually finance theory is equal to the task, or at least could be if given the chance.

For a start, you could simply re-state the returns of every asset type as compound returns, in which case direct comparisons could easily be made. It is in fact ironic that the likes of pension consultants do not do this, since such an approach actually boosts the returns of their beloved bonds and equities (which produce regular income) when compared with the likes of private equity, commodities, energy and gold (which do not). Such a suggestion is alas too radical, however, to have any chance of it being adopted, at least any time soon.

Those who advocate diversification between asset types do have a second arrow in their quiver, though. It is called **correlation**.

Correlation

Sadly, most investors outside North America ignore correlation completely, and even those who do not often misunderstand it, usually by confusing it with volatility. The difference can most easily be explained (and hopefully remembered) by pointing out that volatility is concerned with just one thing, whereas correlation is concerned with two. Volatility measures the extent to which the returns of one particular investment, or sector or market, go up and down over time. It matters not what you are measuring, or for how long. The crucial factor that distinguishes it from correlation is that it measures one thing, and one thing only.

Correlation, by contrast, measures the extent to which two things behave in the same way at the same time. If you have a portfolio consisting of two shares, for example, and one of them goes up consistently, what happens to the other one? Does it go up too, does it go down instead, or does it behave completely independently?

Let us consider three quite extreme possibilities by way of illustration. You will see them set out in Figure 18.1.

Assume that in each case share number 1 goes up consistently. In our first example, share number 2 also goes up consistently. In fact, it behaves in exactly the same way as share number 1. If one goes up 10%, then the other also goes up 10%, and so on. If you were to plot these on a chart you would of course see only one line, which both shares would follow, one overlaid on the other. We call this perfect correlation, or +1 correlation, or 100% correlation: different descriptions of the same thing.

Consider now what would happen if share 2 always behaved in exactly the opposite way to share 1. Now if share 1 goes up 10%, share 2 goes *down* 10%, and so on. Now if you plot the two shares on the chart and assume that share 1 will go up consistently, then clearly share 2 must go down consistently. We call this perfect negative correlation, or -1 correlation, or -100% correlation.

In our final example, the behaviour of share 2 relative to share 1 is entirely random; there appears to be no pattern at all to their relative performance. In this case, if share 1 was to go up consistently then share 2 would head around all over the place, sometimes up and sometimes down, but its general trend line would be flat, as shown in Figure 18.1. We call this zero correlation.

FIGURE 18.1 Correlation (trend line of share 2 assuming share 1 goes up continuously)

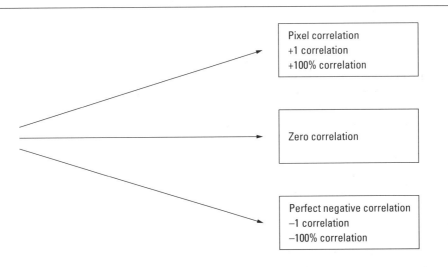

So, why is this important? Because those who use the tools of traditional finance and assume that they must define their portfolio (and indeed their whole investment thinking) in terms of return and volatility completely miss out on this important third dimension, which can magically transform the whole situation.

Consider CAPM for a moment. Remember that CAPM beta purports to measure the extent to which any individual share will move relative to the stock market as a whole, but *in the same direction*. Why does it assume this? Because it is a reasonable assumption to make based on actual observation. In the absence of company-specific events occurring, then most shares listed on a stock exchange will tend to move in the same direction most of the time.

This is called stock market beta, the return of the stock market, and if you think about it, its existence is self-evident. Let us assume that you look at a particular stock market index, say the S&P 100. What is this? Why, simply a composite of all the 100 companies that it comprises. As the market prices of those 100 companies go up and down, the index will be recalculated and will go up and down too. It is simply the aggregate of all its component companies.[4] Therefore it simply is not possible for the index to go up, certainly not to go up by a lot, unless the majority of the individual shares within it are also going up.

The financial crisis showed us, as went through 2007 and 2008, that it was much more difficult to escape stock market beta than we had ever imagined. It is as if stock market beta acts as a magnet, dragging other returns towards it. For example, many investors had sought to access things like real estate and private equity through investment vehicles quoted on the stock market. Great for liquidity but, as it turned out, horrible for volatility. These vehicles started to get dragged up and down (in this case, down) with the market, thus failing totally in the purpose for which they were being held, which was to provide some diversification *away from* stock market beta.

This is where correlation comes in. Remember the efficient frontier (see Figure 11.2, page 126)? If you assume that the only parameters you need to consider are risk and return then, as we saw earlier, you can slide your portfolio up and down the efficient frontier by increasing or decreasing its overall risk. You would not seek to drop below the efficient frontier because that would be irrational (you would be accepting unrewarded risk). You would not seek to rise above the efficient frontier because that is impossible... or is it?

Yes, says traditional finance, because the efficient portfolio is the one that gives you the maximum return for any given level of risk. Therefore, by definition, you cannot do better. Can you spot the possible flaw in this argument?

Well, we come back to the difference between looking at what happens within one particular asset type, and what happens between or across different asset types. Discussion of the efficient portfolio typically focuses on a portfolio that is composed entirely of equities, or partly of equities and partly of bonds. In either case, the only risk (volatility) you are really considering is equity risk, because remember that finance looks at bond risk not as volatility of returns or pricing, but as default risk. Even if you were to look at bond volatility relative to equity volatility rather than within itself, it would be very low. So, whatever the case you are looking only or mainly at equity risk.

Now think back to the CAPM and stock market beta. As we saw, stock market beta will tend to drag most shares in the same direction most of the time. But what might happen if we were to add not more equities to our portfolio but a different asset type altogether – say real estate or commodities? If that asset type has low or even negative correlation with the stock market, then it could go up while the stock market goes down, or vice versa. In other words, our assumption that stock market beta would pull everything up or down with it would no longer hold true.

This is a crucial point. In fact, it is the one key concept that makes possible the holy grail of investing, breaking free of the presumed fixed relationship between risk and return. Sadly, it is a concept that is never even considered by most of the world's investors. This omission is difficult to explain, since finance academics have been exploring and discussing this idea for the last 40 years, so being ignorant that the possibility even exists is rather like being stuck in the finance kindergarten.

There is an interesting parallel here with the world of physics. Newton envisaged the time/space continuum as a straight line, much as the world of traditional finance does with the risk/return continuum. Einstein, however, posited that in certain circumstance it was not a straight line but a curve. It seems that in the case of finance this can be true too, and even more interestingly, the curve seems to take very much the sort of shape that Einstein put forward.

FIGURE 18.2 Extending the efficient frontier by adding uncorrelated assets

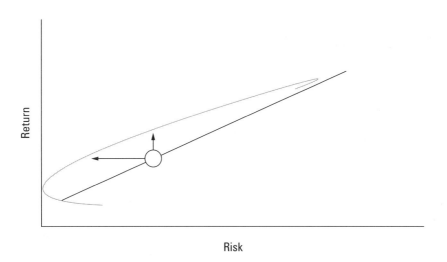

Perhaps the clue to this lack of interest lies in the word 'can'. There are no guarantees here, no certainty. If you bring some uncorrelated assets together, then you *may* be able to increase your return without also increasing your risk, or you *may* be able to decrease your risk without also decreasing your return. Often it happens but sometimes it does not, and it is certainly impossible to predict in advance whether it will occur or not. This is because all we have to work with is historic data, and in the real world future returns often very irritatingly (and most unaccountably as far as finance's killer robots are concerned) refuse to follow the pattern they have described before. Yet it *does* happen, and it is possible to model all sorts of multi-asset portfolios to prove this. By bringing together different asset types whose returns exhibit low or negative correlation with each other, it is possible to increase your return without also increasing your risk (moving the portfolio upwards on Figure 18.2), or to decrease your risk without also decreasing your return (moving it to the left).

Finance, however, sees itself as a branch of mathematics, and is not concerned with things that *may* happen, only things that *will* happen, or at least can be assumed to happen. So we come full circle back to what was explained at the beginning of this book. As Aldous Huxley said, science ignores anything that it cannot calculate. Like Deep Thought, finance is concerned only with questions that have just one right answer, an answer that can be mathematically calculated. Finance does not think it a valid method of enquiry to ask a question that you cannot be sure in advance is capable of being answered by mathematical analysis.

So it is that finance has shirked this challenge, has held back from exploring this particular undiscovered country, because to do so would force upon it a radical shift in thinking, a radical change in its method of enquiry. Finance is very good at many things, but open-mindedness, conceptual analysis, and qualitative or subjective methods of enquiry are not among them. Nor is any sort of readiness to admit that it has got things wrong. On the contrary, its instinctive reaction to anyone questioning its beliefs is to send out the killer robots to blast the universe into conformity.

The challenge: matching theory with reality

If you have been sufficiently interested by what you have encountered so far to go out and work in the world of finance, you will discover that there is not just one unexplored country, but many. Basic concepts such as risk, return and value still lie at a very basic level of discussion. Factors such as emotion, subjectivity, perception and both individual and group behaviour are still not properly understood, and indeed are resolutely ignored.

Hopefully you will find this a challenge rather than a disappointment, exciting rather than frustrating. For finance is still a very young subject, and has become stuck at a very early stage of intellectual development by the adoption of theory as dogma. Yet Catholic dogma was swept away by the Reformation, and sooner or later something similar will happen in finance.

So much is obviously wrong with the traditional approach to finance that there is no excuse for taking anything for granted just because a finance lecturer or a pension consultant says it is so. On the contrary, there is much that is yet to be discovered and explored, and your opinion is as valuable as anyone else's. So, the next time you have some pension consultants or investment managers sitting in front of you, and you find that you can now grill them meaningfully, while your colleagues gaze at you admiringly, about what they mean by risk, whether they are using arithmetic or geometric means, and why they are ignoring correlation, you may discover that, yes, finance can even be fun.

Summary

- Finance has a number of tools that assist in portfolio construction. We can, for example, measure the Standard Deviation of a portfolio as a whole. We can use CAPM to select high or low beta shares. We can use the Sharpe Ratio to measure a risk-adjusted return.
- However, with the exception of the Sharpe Ratio, these tools are designed to select assets from within a single asset class, typically individual shares within an equity portfolio, not to select a portfolio of different asset types. Even the Sharpe Ratio is not always a valid tool for this purpose given the differing return characteristics of various asset types.

- The main limitation of these tools is that they all rely upon a two-dimensional view of finance as being purely a relationship between risk (volatility) and return. In fact there is another very important dimension to consider when we start looking at mixing different asset types together, which is correlation.
- Correlation measures the extent to which two different things move in the same direction at the same time. Assets that tend to move together have high positive correlation. Assets that tend to move in opposite directions have negative correlation. Assets that seem to move at random relative to each other have zero correlation.
- There are situations in which it is possible to extend the efficient frontier by introducing lowly correlated assets into a portfolio. In other words, it is possible to construct a new portfolio that may either have higher return for the same level of risk, or lower risk for the same level of return.
- However, while this is possible, it is not guaranteed. It may happen or it may not. It is, however, possible to model many actual portfolios to prove that it can and does happen.
- Outside North America, this approach has been almost completely ignored. It is possible that the uncertainty of outcome may have something to do with this.
- The effect of correlation in **extending the efficient frontier** is but one of many areas of finance that remain to be explored. Sadly, this process is likely to be long delayed by a blinkered view of finance as being a purely mathematical field of enquiry, and by an ongoing acceptance of theory as dogma.

Notes

1 See Fraser-Sampson: *Alternative Assets: Investments for a post-crisis world*, John Wiley, London and New York 2010.

2 Office for National Statistics (ONS)

3 See Fraser-Sampson: *Multi-Asset Class Investment Strategy*, John Wiley, London and New York 2006.

4 Different indices are calculated in different ways, but all share this common characteristic.

Appendix: key formulae

Accounting equation (balance sheet)

Assets = capital + liabilities

Acid test ratio (quick ratio)

$$\frac{\text{current assets less stock}}{\text{current (short-term) liabilities}}$$

Annuity (present value)

We find the present value of an annuity by:

$$PV = \frac{A}{r}\left(1 - \frac{1}{(1+r)^n}\right)$$

Where:

PV is the present value,

A is the annual amount payable,

r is the discount rate, and

n is the number of years for which the annuity is to be paid.

Note: In some books you may see C used instead of A, and i instead of r. It is submitted that the above notation is more sensible and thus also easier to remember.

Bond duration (Macaulay duration)

$$\frac{\sum_{t=1}^{n}\frac{t \times A}{(1+r)^t} + \frac{n \times M}{(1+r)^n}}{P}$$

Where:

n is the number of (interest) cash-flows,

t is the time to maturity,

A is the amount of each (interest) cash-flow,

r is the rate (required yield),

M is the maturity/redemption/face value,

and P is the price of the bond.

Black-Scholes Model (to find the price of a European option)

$N(d1)M - N(d2)S \, e^{-rf}$

Where:

N is the cumulative distribution function,

M is the market price,

S is the strike price,

and e^{-rf} means 'discounted by the risk free rate'.

$$d1 = \frac{\log\left(\frac{M}{S}\right) + \left(r + \frac{\sigma^2}{2}\right)T}{\sigma\sqrt{T}}$$

Where log is the normal logarithm (in this case of $\frac{M}{S}$),

M is the market price,

S is the strike price,

r is the risk free rate,

σ is the Standard Deviation of the market price,

and T is the time to expiry measured as a percentage of one year.

$$d2 = d1 - \sigma\sqrt{T}$$

Bond pricing (finding the NPV of a bond)

Remember that the bond price = PV of interest payments + PV of redemption payment on maturity, and that we need to find each and then add them together, so:

$$\text{PV of interest payments} = A \times \left(\frac{1 - \left(\frac{1}{1+r}\right)^n}{r}\right)$$

Where A is the annual interest payment,

r is the discount rate, and

n is the number of years remaining until the maturity of the bond.

$$\text{PV of redemption payments} = M \times \left(\frac{1}{1+r}\right)^n$$

Where M is the amount payable on maturity.

$$\text{So bond price} = A \times \left(\frac{1 - \left(\frac{1}{1+r}\right)^n}{r}\right) + M \times \left(\frac{1}{1+r}\right)^n$$

Creditor days

$$\frac{\text{creditors}}{\text{cost of goods sold}} \times 365$$

Current ratio

$$\frac{\text{current assets}}{\text{current (short-term) liabilities}}$$

Current yield (of a bond)

$$\left(\frac{\text{interest}}{\text{market price}}\right) \times 100$$

Debtor days

$$\frac{\text{debtors}}{\text{sales}} \times 365$$

Dividend payout ratio

$$\frac{\text{dividend paid}}{\text{earnings per share}} \quad \text{or} \quad \frac{\text{dividends}}{\text{net come}}$$

NB: 'Earnings' here are earnings after tax (earnings available for distribution).

Dividend yield

$$\frac{\text{dividend}}{\text{share price}} \quad \text{or} \quad \frac{\text{total divident paid}}{\text{market capitalization}} \times 100$$

Gearing (leverage)

$$\frac{\text{debt}}{\text{debt + equity}} \times 100$$

Gross margin

$$\frac{\text{gross profit}}{\text{sales}} \times 100$$

Note: 'Gross profit' is here used in the sense of manufacturing profit, not profit before tax. See Chapter 5 for a full explanation.

Gordon Growth Model (perpetuity or annuity)

Instead of $\dfrac{C}{r}$

Where C is the periodic cash-flow and
r is the discount rate, we use:

$$\frac{C}{r - g}$$

Where g is the growth rate (and is less than r)

Individual risk premium
Ra – Rf
Where Ra is the return of an individual asset, and
Rf is the risk free rate of return.

Interest cover

$$\frac{\text{EBITDA}}{\text{loan and overdraft interest}}$$

Market risk premium
Rm – Rf
Where Rm is the return of the market, and
Rf is the risk free rate of return.

Modified current yield (of a bond)

$$\left(\frac{\text{interest}}{\text{market price}}\right) \times 100 + \left(\frac{100 - \text{market price}}{\text{years to maturity}}\right)$$

Net margin

$$\frac{\text{EBIT}}{\text{sales}} \times 100$$

Perpetuity (present value)

$$\frac{C}{r}$$

Where C is the periodic cash-flow, and
r is the discount rate.

Retention ratio

$$\frac{\text{net income} - \text{dividends}}{\text{net income}}$$

Return on capital/Return on capital employed

$$\frac{\text{EBIT}}{\text{share capital} + \text{reserves}} \times 100$$

Running yield (of a bond)

$$\frac{\text{interest}}{\text{face value}} \times 100$$

Sharpe Ratio

$$\frac{(r - rf)}{\sigma(r - rf)}$$

Where r = the annualized return,
rf = the risk free return,
(r – rf) = the excess return, and
$\sigma(r - rf)$ = the Standard Deviation of the excess return.

Stock days
Average stock ratio × 365

Stock ratio (traditional)

$$\frac{\text{Cost of goods sold}}{\text{closing stock}}$$

Stock ratio (increasingly common)

$$\frac{\text{Cost of goods sold}}{\text{average stock}}$$

Where average stock $= \dfrac{\text{opening stock} + \text{closing stock}}{2}$

Glossary of financial terms

Accounting equation	The basic equation underlying the preparation of a balance sheet, namely assets = capital + liabilities.
Active investment	Stock-picking. Selecting individual assets in which to invest, rather than being content to buy the market, perhaps by investing in an index tracker.
Administration	Insolvency (bankruptcy) regime under which a company is allowed to continue in business with a view to recovery, and is granted protection from its creditors in the meantime. In the US, typically occurs under Chapter 11 of the Bankruptcy Code.
Alpha	The opposite of beta (see below). A return that will be generated by selecting individual assets in which to invest, rather than investing in the market as a whole.
American option	An option that can be exercised at any time during its life.
Amortization	Similar to depreciation but with reference to intangible assets such as intellectual property used within a business.
Annuity	A fixed payment made once a year for a fixed number of years.
Arbitrage	An opportunity, where some error has crept into the pricing of an asset or where it is priced or valued differently in different places or situations, to exploit the difference between its market price and its true value.
Arithmetic mean	An average calculated by addition – see Average.
Asset	Something of value that is held either as an investment or for use within a business.

At the money	Used to describe any derivative instrument whose strike price (see below) is the same as the current market price.
Average (mean)	The total of a sample of values divided by their number (n).
Bad debt	A debt that the business has decided is unlikely to be paid, for example because the debtor has become insolvent. For accounting purposes, specific individual bad debts are usually tax-deductible, whereas a general provision for bad debts is not.
Balance sheet	A financial accounting statement that records the assets and liabilities of a business on a particular date.
Balanced portfolio	A portfolio chosen to target certain levels of risk and return by including investments from right across the risk/return spectrum, with the intention that their aggregate levels of risk and return will fall within the target parameters.
Balloon	A form of loan on which no repayments at all are made during its term, both the principal and accrued interest being repaid at the end.
Bear	One who invests on the assumption that market prices will fall.
Bear market	A market where prices are falling, often strongly and over a prolonged period.
Beta	(1) The extent to which any individual share is likely to go up or down by a greater or lesser extent compared to the market as a whole. Often known as CAPM beta to distinguish it from (2) the return of a market as a whole, often measured by an index.
Black box	A computer model, about which its owners are usually extremely vague and secretive, which claims to be able to generate superior investment performance by quantitative analysis.
Bull	One who invests on the assumption that prices will rise.
Bull market	A market where prices are rising, often strongly and over a prolonged period.
Buying the market	Passive investing – seeking the beta return of a market or asset type.

Call	An option or future where the investor has the right (in the case of an option) or the obligation (in the case of a future) to buy something at a specified price on a specified date in the future.
Capital allowances	Sums representing the depreciation in the accounting value of a business's assets that may be set off against the business's tax liability.
Capital Asset Pricing Model (CAPM)	A tool for comparing specific and systemic risk (see below).
Cash-flow matching	Planning to have an inflow from a specific asset (typically bonds) occur at the same time as an outflow of a similar value, the outflow being triggered by the need to pay a liability. Also known as liability matching.
Cash pile	An unexpectedly large cash balance on a business's balance sheet.
Clean price	A price for a bond or other instrument that includes accrued entitlement to interest.
Common stock	See Ordinary shares.
Company (or corporation)	A vehicle that has its own legal personality. The liability of its shareholders will be limited to the amount of capital that they subscribe.
Contango effect	See Negative roll yield.
Correlation	A measure of the tendency of two different things to move in the same direction at the same time. Things that move up and down together in a similar way are said to have positive correlation. Things that tend to move in opposite directions are said to have negative correlation.
Counterparty risk	The risk that one party to a contract may be unable or unwilling to perform their obligations under it when the time comes.
Coupon	The agreed interest payable on a bond or other debt instrument.
Credit default swap (CDS)	An agreement whereby one investor effectively guarantees, for a fee, repayment of a loan or redemption of a bond by a third party.
Creditor days	An indicator of how long a business takes to pay its debts. See the list of formulae in the Appendix.

Currency swap	A derivative instrument whereby the parties agree to exchange the qualities of one currency (usually the principal and interest of a loan of a specified amount) with another. Currency swaps can be 'principal only'. Interest only swaps are often known instead as a type of 'interest rate swap'. Currency swaps are typically OTC (see below).
Current assets	Things owned by a company that are considered in accounting terms to be capable of being turned into cash. Examples would include cash itself, stock and trade debtors.
Current liabilities	Obligations that the business must discharge within a relatively short time. One year is generally used for financial accounting purposes.
Cyclical stocks	Stocks (shares) that enjoy a high CAPM beta. Traditionally investors would target these if they felt the market was likely to rise, on the basis that these stocks would rise by even more.
Days payable	See Creditor days.
Debtor days	An indicator of how long a business takes to collect its debts. See the list of formulae in the Appendix.
Default risk	The counterparty risk on a bond or loan. The risk that the issuer/borrower may miss one or more payments, whether on redemption/repayment or during the life of the bond/loan.
Defensive stocks	Stocks (shares) that exhibit low CAPM beta. Traditionally investors would target these if they feared the market might fall, on the basis that these stocks were likely to fall by a lesser amount.
Defined Benefit (DB)	A type of pension plan, provided by an employer but to which the employee also contributes, which pays out benefits based on the employee's salary, either on retirement or averaged over some number of years. Also known as final salary.
Defined Contribution (DC)	A type of pension fund, provided by an employer, which provides not an annual pension, but a lump sum on retirement, with which the pensioner must buy an annuity. Also known as money purchase.
Depreciation	A deemed fall in the value of an asset owned by a business. The business will write this off against its turnover when calculating its profits.
De-risking	Seeking to reduce the overall volatility of a portfolio, as measured by the Standard Deviation of its annualized return.

Derivatives	Swaps, options and futures. See Synthetics.
Dirty price	A price for a bond or other instrument that takes no account of accrued entitlement to interest, and thus goes up and down on payment dates.
Discount bond	A bond that is currently trading below its par value.
Discount factor	A value arrived at by dividing the number one by a chosen discount rate. The discount factor is then applied to one or more future cash-flows in order to calculate a Net Present Value.
Discount rate	A rate chosen as the most appropriate for any discounting exercise. It is customary to use WACC where relevant.
Dividend payout ratio	A measure of how much of its earnings a company is paying out in dividends (dividend policy). See the Appendix.
Dumbbell portfolio	A portfolio chosen to target certain levels of risk and return by including only investments from each end of the risk/return spectrum (ie low risk/low return and high risk/high return) with the intention that their aggregate levels of risk and return will fall within the target parameters.
Duration (of a bond)	The duration of a bond is the tipping point in time at which the present values of the cash-flows on each side of that point are exactly the same. Duration is a measure of bond price sensitivity to interest rate changes.
Earnings statement	Another name for a profit and loss account.
EBIT	Earnings Before Interest and Tax. A measure of earnings (profit). Often stated as operating profit.
EBITDA	Earnings Before Interest, Tax, Depreciation and Amortization. A measure of cash-flow.
Efficient frontier	The line that can be constructed by showing the maximum level of return that can be achieved by any portfolio for any given level of risk; in other words the position of every possible efficient portfolio (see below).
Efficient portfolio	For any given level of risk, the portfolio that can be constructed so as to give the highest possible return, or for any given level of return, the portfolio that can be constructed to give the lowest possible level of risk. The efficient portfolio sits on the efficient frontier.

Equity kickers   See Kickers.

Equity swap   A derivative instrument whereby an investor swaps a specified
                      sum or return for the return actually generated by the
                      specified stock (share).

European option   An option that can be exercised only on expiry.

Exchange Traded   An investment vehicle traded on a stock exchange and
Fund (ETF)   offering a beta return. This was originally accomplished by
                      holding a bundle of underlying assets replicating the beta
                      measure, but these days more complex approaches, often
                      involving Total Return Swaps, are employed.

Exchange traded   Used to describe a derivative instrument that is not OTC (see
option   below). The main qualities of an exchange traded instrument
                      are: (1) that it is for a standard quantity of the underlying
                      asset; and (2) that the relevant exchange guarantees
                      settlement of the contract.

Exotic   Opposite of vanilla (see below). An option with a strike price
                      that may be altered one or more times on a pre-agreed basis.

Extending the   Adding uncorrelated assets to a portfolio so as to achieve
efficient frontier   either a higher level of return than would otherwise be
                      possible for a given level of risk, or a lower level of risk than
                      would otherwise be possible for any given level of return.

Fire sale   A forced sale. Selling assets at whatever price you have to
                      accept in order to dispose of them quickly.

Fixed assets   Things that are owned by a business but cannot easily or
                      quickly be turned into cash. Examples would include a
                      building or plant and machinery.

Fixed charge   A legal charge that is registered over all or some part of the
                      assets of a business, usually by way of security for a loan,
                      giving the charge-holder a priority right to the proceeds of a
                      sale.

Fixed income   Those instruments that produce an agreed fixed rate of
(securities)   income every year. Strictly speaking this definition would
                      include preference shares (preferred stock), but in practice
                      'fixed income' is synonymous with 'bonds'.

Floating charge	A legal charge that does not directly affect the assets of a business unless and until an act of default occurs under the relevant loan agreement. The charge will then 'crystallize' and attach to any available assets, but taking priority *after* any existing fixed charges.
Flotation	The process by which a company that is currently privately owned converts to public company status and has its shares listed on a stock exchange. See IPO.
Focused portfolio	A portfolio chosen to target certain levels of risk and return by focusing only upon investments that themselves exhibit those levels of risk and return.
Fundamental	The opposite of quant (see below). Analysis of the fundamentals of a business will focus on all the things traditionally taken into account, such as the strength of its management, the nature of its market, and its position relative to its competitors.
Future	A contract that confers the obligation to buy or sell a particular asset at a specified price (the strike price) on a specified date in the future. Should not be confused with an option (see below), which confers a right but not an obligation.
Future value	The value of a cash-flow that is due to occur in the future on the date when it is due to occur.
GAAP	Generally accepted accounting principles. Despite the name, these can vary from one country to another.
Gearing	See Leverage.
Geometric mean	An average calculated by multiplying all the data points together and then applying the root of their number (n).
Going concern	(1) An accounting concept which states that the accounts of all businesses should be prepared on the basis that there is no apparent reason why it should not be able to finance its activities for the next 12 months, unless there is clear evidence to the contrary. (2) A more general concept which recognizes that a business will be constantly having to recycle and replenish its working capital; in other words that a working capital surplus is illusory, since it cannot actually be realized without closing down the business.

Gordon Growth Model	A mathematical model that returns the value of a project, business or investment based upon its future cash-flows and an assumed constant rate of growth.
Gross margin	$\dfrac{\text{Gross profit}}{\text{sales}} \times 100$
Gross profit	(1) Profit before tax. (2) In manufacturing businesses, profit calculated after deduction of the direct costs of the manufacturing process ('cost of goods sold') but before deduction of all the business's other costs.
Hedge	Seeking to protect the value of a portfolio, asset or position by buying a derivative instrument that will reduce the impact of any possible loss. Since there will be a cost involved in acquiring the derivative, this can be seen as being content to give up some possible upside (the price of the derivative) in return for limiting one's downside.
Hostile take-over	Used to describe any offer to take control of a company that is not recommended by the board of directors of the company.
Hurdle rate	A target rate of return that must be at least equalled. In the case of an investor, this may be their cost of capital, so that if they do not match this they will make a loss. In the case of an investment manager, this may be the minimum rate of return required to trigger a performance-related payment. In either case, it may be used as a discount rate (see above).
In the money	An option that it would currently be advantageous to exercise having regard to the current market price of the underlying asset.
Income statement	Another name for a profit and loss account.
Index tracker	A fund where the manager has no discretion at all as to the selection of investments, but is required to match exactly the composition and performance of a specified index.
Individual risk premium	The extent to which the annualized return of an individual asset exceeds the annualized risk free return. (This is treated as being the same as the excess return of the individual asset.)
Interest cover	A ratio showing the number of times the company's cash-flow matches the required interest payments under the loan.
Interest rate swap	Where two investors exchange interest rates, perhaps a fixed rate for a variable rate, or rates in two different currencies.

Internal Rate of Return (IRR)	The compound return represented by a series of cash-flows over time, the first of which is negative. Strictly, the discount rate that when applied to a series of cash-flows as a discount factor produces an NPV of zero.
Introduction	The process by which a formerly private company joins a stock exchange as a public company. This can take place independently of any associated capital-raising, but this is rare.
Investable	A measure of beta return, often an index, in which one can invest effectively and practicably, either by replication of its constituents or through some sort of tracker vehicle.
IPO	Initial Public Offering. Another name for a flotation (see above).
Iteration	Performing the same calculation again and again, changing the value of the same one input each time. This is the only way of calculating an IRR.
Just in time (JIT)	A manufacturing policy under which an item does not begin the manufacturing process until an order for it has already been received.
Kickers	Rights to convert existing instruments into ordinary shares (common stock) on certain conditions being fulfilled or certain agreed periods elapsing.
Leverage	The extent to which a business or project is financed by debt relative to equity. Also known as gearing.
Liability	A debt or other financial obligation owed to a third party.
Limited partnership	A form of partnership that consists partly of limited partners (LPs), who take no part in the management of the business, and general partners (GPs), who do. GPs do not enjoy limited liability. LPs' liability is limited to the amount of capital they have committed to the partnership.
Liquidation	The process of closing down a business and selling all its assets. Where a company is solvent this can be done voluntarily, with any surplus assets being distributed to the shareholders. More usually, however, liquidation will occur when a business is insolvent (bankrupt), in which case the proceeds will be paid to its creditors according to a specified order of priority.

Liquidity	(1) The extent to which a specific investment may quickly and easily be turned into cash. (2) The extent to which a business can pay its short-term liabilities, by reference to current assets.
Long position	Traditionally, where an investor agrees to buy something they do not currently own (see also Call). Today, any situation where you have effectively bet on the price of something rising.
Long-term liabilities	In accounting terms, liabilities that should arise more than one year into the future.
Margins	See Gross margin and Net margin.
Mark to market	A requirement that you must revalue your assets, perhaps even daily, based on current market price. A central part of many regulatory regimes.
Market risk premium	The extent to which the annualized return of a market exceeds the annualized risk free return. (This is treated as being the same as the excess return of the market.)
Maturity date	The agreed date for repayment by the issuer of the face value of a bond.
Mean	See Average.
Modified current yield	A method of measuring the yield of a bond that takes some account of its redemption value. See the Appendix.
Modigliani and Miller Model ('M&M')	Shows that the capital structure of a company is irrelevant to its value. Note that this relies upon various assumptions that may be thought fanciful, for example that nobody pays taxes and that everybody can borrow money at the same rate.
Negative roll yield	The cost of rolling a position over successive time periods. Sometimes referred to as the contango effect, but this term is best avoided as contango can also (and more usually does) refer to a particular state of a futures market.
Net margin	$\dfrac{\text{EBIT}}{\text{sales}} \times 100$
Net Present Value ('NPV')	The value today of a number of cash-flows that are due to occur in the future, with the various positive and negative cash-flows being netted off against each other.
Nil paids	The right to subscribe for new shares, which have not yet been paid for.

Offering	Offering securities to be issued to the public at large. Usually anybody can apply and the bank responsible for the offering must treat all investors the same, but in accordance with whatever terms are specified in the offering document. In the case of a privatization, for example, the issuer (the government) may wish to favour small investors.
Operating profit	See EBIT.
Opportunity cost	Some value that could have been obtained by making an alternative use of a sum of money. For example, if you decide to take money off a deposit at the bank and use it to buy a house, the opportunity cost will be the amount of bank interest that you would have earned had you left your money where it was.
Option	An instrument that grants the right, but not the obligation, to buy or sell a particular asset at a specified price (the strike price) on a specified date (the strike date or exercise date).
Ordinary shares	Also known as common stock. Shares that confer full rights of voting and the right to receive a dividend should the directors elect to declare one. Ordinary shareholders/common stockholders stand right at the end of the queue for priority on liquidation, and thus are likely to lose all their capital should a business fail.
OTC	Over the counter. Name given to any investment instrument that takes the form of a private contractual arrangement (and is thus subject to counterparty risk – see above), rather than being issued through a recognized investment exchange.
Out of the money	An option that it would currently be disadvantageous to exercise given the current market price of the underlying asset.
Overdraft	A temporary loan facility extended by a bank, which can usually be withdrawn at any time without notice. Also known as overdraft protection or an overdraft facility.
Par value	Of a bond; its face value. The amount that the issuer must pay to its current holder on redemption (see below).
Passive investment	The opposite of active investment (see above). Here the investor is content to accept the market return (beta), perhaps by investing in an index tracker.
Perpetuity	An annuity that lasts for ever.

PIK bonds	Payment in kind bonds, where the issuer can elect to pay the coupon for a particular year by an issue of more bonds, rather than paying cash. There will often be a 'toggle' under which this right can be switched on or off from one year to another.
Placement	Allocating securities to be issued among a number of different investors on a private basis. Distinguished from an offering (see above).
Power	Multiplying a number by itself a specified number of times.
Pre-emption rights	A right to buy something that takes priority over other interested purchasers; a right of first refusal. Often enjoyed by the shareholders of public companies in respect of any issue of new shares.
Preference shares (preferred stock)	Instruments that are treated as shares (equity) for accounting purposes but in fact more closely resemble debt. They are entitled to a pre-agreed dividend every year regardless of whether the directors elect to pay one or not, and rank ahead of ordinary shares (common stock) in a liquidation. However, as they are legally equity, preference dividends are paid *after* tax.
Premium bond	A bond that is currently trading above its par value.
Present value	The value today of a cash-flow that is due to occur in the future.
Primary market	The market in which securities, loans, etc are first issued. Can be thought of as buying a new car direct from its manufacturer.
Prime bonds	Those bonds issued by a very small number of governments, and traditionally regarded as risk-free. Now includes the European Central Bank as an issuer.
Profit	Any positive balance that is left over after deducting the payment of a business's expenses from its turnover. Certain accounting items, such as depreciation, are also deducted.
Profit and loss account ('P&L')	A financial accounting statement that records the income received and liabilities paid during a period, and thus whether a profit or a loss was made. May also be referred to as an income statement or an earnings statement.
Put	An option or future where you have the right (in the case of an option) or the obligation (in the case of a future) to sell something at a specified price on a specified date in the future.

| Quantitative ('quant') | Quant approaches to investing treat investment data as pure mathematics and seek numerical patterns and relationships. They may, for example, compare current market price with a moving average, or look for companies that have certain common characteristics in their P&L or balance sheet. |

Quick ratio

The most severe test of the ability of a business to pay its debts in the short term. Also known as the acid test ratio.

$$\frac{\text{current assets} - \text{stocks}}{\text{current liabilites}}$$

Quoted

Where a company's shares are traded on a stock exchange, both the company and its shares (stock) are said to be quoted. Strictly speaking, 'quoted' means having a minimum number of market-makers being prepared to offer a firm price for the shares. If not, the company and its shares are simply 'listed', but this distinction seems increasingly to be ignored.

Receivership

Discontinued in many countries, the contractual right of a specific creditor to appoint an insolvency practitioner to take over the running of a business and sell off either the business itself or its assets to satisfy their debt.

Recommended offer

An offer to buy all the shares (stock) in a company, addressed to the shareholders (stockholders) of the target company, but recommended for acceptance by the board of directors of the target. Unless and until such a recommendation is forthcoming, an offer to buy all the shares in a company is known as hostile bid. In some countries a recommended offer can be known as a tender offer.

Redemption

The agreed maturity date of a bond, when its term (lifetime) comes to an end and the issuer pays the holder of the bond its par value (face value).

Redemption yield

Also known as yield to maturity (YTM). The discount rate that, when applied to all the future cash-flows of a bond, including the redemption payment, produces an NPV that is the same as the market price. More easily calculated as the IRR of all the future cash-flows, treating the bond's price today as an initial negative cash-flow.

Rental swap

Agreement by the owner of a property to exchange its rental income in return for a fixed sum or fixed series of cash-flows.

Return on capital

$$\frac{\text{EBIT}}{\text{share capital and reserves}} \times 100$$

Return on equity	See Return on capital.
Rights issue	A name often applied to the issue of new shares (stock) by a public company, so called because the existing shareholders (stockholders) frequently enjoy pre-emption rights.
Risk free return	The idea that there is a base level of return that can be earned by an investor without taking any risk is central to finance theory, and underlies many of its devices, such as the Sharpe Ratio (see below and Appendix). For US dollar investors, the US Treasury bill rate is usually adopted. For sterling investors, the UK Government short bond rate is used. Note, however, that in practice there is probably no longer any such thing as a totally risk free return, if there ever was.
Roll (a position)	Extending or renewing an option or swap. See Negative roll yield.
Running yield	(1) Used to emphasize the income nature of a return to distinguish it from a capital gain. (2) A specific measure of bond yield, based on the par value of the bond.
Sample	A selection of data chosen for analysis purposes. A sample is a sub-set of the population, which represents every possible data point that could have been chosen.
Secondary market	A market in which loans and instruments that have already been issued are bought and sold. Can be thought of as buying a second-hand car from its current owner.
Scrip (dividend or issue)	The payment of a dividend by issuing new shares rather than paying cash.
Shareholders' liquidation	See Voluntary winding-up.
Sharpe Ratio	A measure for calculating the risk-adjusted rate of return of any asset, sector, market or asset type relative to the risk free rate of return.
Short position	Traditionally, where an investor agrees to sell something that they do not currently own (also known as 'short selling'). Today, any situation where an investor has effectively bet upon the price of something falling. Also see Put above.
Short-term liabilities	See Current liabilities.
Specific risk	The risk of holding one individual asset within a portfolio of similar assets.

Spot price	The price at which a standard quantity of a specified asset (for example a barrel of Brent Crude) can be instantly bought or sold.
Spread betting	Betting that a particular price or rate will go up or down, and being rewarded pro rata to the extent of the change. Legal in some countries but not in others.
Square	The power of two. Multiplying a number by itself (once).
Square root	The number that, when multiplied by itself, gives the value to which the square root is being applied.
Squeeze the debtors	Attempt to shorten the number of days that it takes for the business's customers to settle their invoices. A device for improving working capital.
Standard Deviation	A measure of the dispersion of any data sample, found by taking the square root of the Variance. One Standard Deviation is commonly used as a measure of the volatility of the historic returns of any investment, and this is assumed to be the same thing as the risk of the investment.
Stock-picking	Active investing – seeking an alpha return.
Straddle	A put and call bought together, both at the money, having the same strike date and the same strike price, the strike price being the current market price.
Stretch the creditors	Attempt to lengthen the number of days taken before settling the invoices of suppliers. A device for improving working capital.
Strike date	The agreed date on which a put or call is to be exercised. Also known as the expiry date or the exercise date.
Strike price	The agreed price at which a put or call is to be exercised.
Subsidiary	A company that is owned by another company (its parent or holding company).
Sunk costs	Costs that have already been incurred and cannot be recovered, and thus that should be ignored when evaluating the future of the project in question.
Survivorship bias	The tendency of under-performing investment funds or managers to drop out of the population used by a returns index, either voluntarily or because they are unable to raise new capital, thus tending to flatter the reported performance figures.

Swap	In its simplest form, an instrument that allows two investors effectively to put each other in the position they would have been in had they held each other's assets. For example, the holder of a fixed rate bond may swap its income stream with that of a variable rate bond held by another investor. Can also operate in respect of financial measures such as interest and exchange rates.
Swaption	An option to enter into a swap, on pre-agreed terms.
Syndication	A process in which one institution will take the whole of a financial issue (usually debt), and then sell down ('lay off') parts of it to others.
Synthetic (instruments)	Investments that grant a right and/or confer an obligation in respect of other assets or financial measures, such as interest or exchange rates. Most common examples are futures, options and swaps. Also known as derivatives.
Systemic risk	Market risk. The volatility of the historic returns of a whole market, index or sector, as contrasted with specific risk (see above).
Theory of the Efficient Firm	States that a company (corporation) should borrow money with which to buy back shares, so long as the return on equity is higher than the cost of debt net of any tax advantage.
Total Return Swap	A contractual arrangement whereby one investor pays a fixed or interest rate-based amount to another investor in return for the cash equivalent of the return they could have earned on another asset, or on an index. Used extensively where physical ownership of the asset in question may be difficult or impossible.
Tracking error	A performance indicator for an index tracking manager, measuring the difference between their actual performance and that of the market or index they are seeking to match.
Turnover	Income received by a business. May also be referred to as 'sales' or 'revenues'.
Turns	A measure of how many times a year stock is turned over within a business.
Underwriting	A process whereby an institution or investor agrees to take up whatever securities are left unallocated as a result of a placing or offering. May in some cases be legally required, for example when the proceeds are intended to be used to acquire another company.

Unrewarded risk	Risk that is assumed by an investor unnecessarily and/or without the reasonable expectation of any compensating higher return. A classic example would be a portfolio that sits below the efficient frontier. In other words, wherever a different portfolio could be constructed that would have a lower level of risk without diminishing the level of return, unrewarded risk is present.
Value at Risk (VaR)	A way of analysing the maximum amount of money a particular portfolio or investment position might lose in a given time, usually in the course of a single day.
Vanilla (or plain vanilla)	An option that can be exercised only at the agreed strike price.
Variance	A measure of how broad the spread of any sample data is around the average (or mean). Found by squaring the distance of each observation from the mean and then taking the arithmetic mean of these values.
Voluntary winding-up	Where the shareholders agree to the company ceasing business, selling off its assets and dissolving itself. It is a pre-condition that the company must be able to pay all its creditors in the process.
War chest	A cash pile (see above) that is earmarked for use in acquiring other businesses.
Wasting asset	Any asset that loses value over time, such as a motor vehicle used in the business.
Weighted average cost of capital (WACC)	A number arrived at by taking both a business's cost of equity and cost of debt, and blending these pro rata to the amounts of equity and debt outstanding.
Working capital	(1) Generally, that capital which is tied up directly in the operation of a business, eg stocks, debtors and creditors. (2) As a specific accounting term, current assets less current (short-term) liabilities.
Working capital deficit (or deficiency)	Where the current assets of a business are not sufficient to pay its short-term liabilities, even assuming all the assets could be turned quickly into cash at their balance sheet values.
Write down	A reduction for accounting purposes in the value of an asset.
Write off	To reduce to zero for accounting purposes the value of an asset.
Write up	An increase for accounting purposes in the value of an asset.

Writing-down allowance	Another name for capital allowances, amounts that may be set off against tax in recognition of the purchase of business assets.
Yield	Income generated by, for example, a bond or a share (stock) by way of interest or dividend respectively. Can also be applied to other income-producing assets such as real estate (property).
Yield to maturity (YTM)	See Redemption yield.
Zero coupon	An instrument, typically a bond, which pays no interest and thus does not generate any interest, only a redemption value.

INDEX

(*italics* indicate a figure in the text)